KINGDOM OF RAGE

KINGDOM OF RAGE

*The Rise of Christian Extremism
and the Path Back to Peace*

Elizabeth Neumann

NEW YORK   NASHVILLE

Worthy
Hachette Book Group
1290 Avenue of the Americas, New York, NY 10104
worthypublishing.com
X.com/worthypub

First edition: April 2024

Worthy is a division of Hachette Book Group, Inc. The Worthy name and logo are registered
trademarks of Hachette Book Group, Inc.

The publisher is not responsible for websites (or their content) that are not
owned by the publisher.

The Hachette Speakers Bureau provides a wide range of authors for speaking events. To find
out more, go to hachettespeakersbureau.com or email HachetteSpeakers@hbgusa.com.

Worthy Books may be purchased in bulk for business, educational, or promotional use.
For information, please contact your local bookseller or the Hachette Book Group Special
Markets Department at special.markets@hbgusa.com.

Print book interior design by Timothy Shaner, NightandDayDesign.biz.

Library of Congress Cataloging-in-Publication Data has been applied for.

ISBNs: 9781546002055 (hardcover), 9781546002079 (ebook)

Printed in Canada

MRQ

Printing 1, 2024

This book is dedicated to the exhausted, tribeless, remnant of exiles:

You are not alone. Take heart, He has overcome the world.

And to my children, Joshua and Madelyne:

We long to restore communities of peace and flourishing for your children. Anchor your hope in Jesus. You are deeply loved.

CONTENTS

KINGDOM OF RAGE

INTRODUCTION

I didn't plan to do this. I'm a planner by nature. I have lots of goals; too many really. Flip through my journals, and they're filled with ideas and plans . . . and the frustrations that come when those plans don't come to fruition. I never dreamed of speaking out in the middle of an election, let alone writing a book.

In January 2020, I wrote down my professional goals: "transition out of [my role at DHS] gracefully" and find a job in the private sector that allowed me to be a part of a "healthy team culture," "doing meaningful work that contributes to the bettering of society."

I had started job hunting the previous summer. My husband, who had originally said yes to one or two years in Washington, DC, then reluctantly agreed to a third year so that I could make progress on policy related to domestic terrorism, was lovingly pressuring me to find an exit strategy so that I could be home more with our children (and escape the toxic culture of Trump world). Plus, DHS secretary Kirstjen Nielsen had been forced to resign in the spring of 2019, and rumors had been circulating that anyone associated with her or the previous secretary, John Kelly, were going to be forced out. Several of my colleagues had been fired already.

But my job search was put on hold when a spate of domestic terror attacks occurred in late July and early August 2019. They began in

Gilroy, California, and then struck El Paso, Texas, and Dayton, Ohio. Those events over the course of a weekend instantly answered any lingering questions about whether domestic terrorism was increasing.

That Saturday evening in 2019, hours after the El Paso attack, acting secretary Kevin McAleenan directed me to expedite the counterterrorism strategy my team was developing and directed us to conduct a two-week domestic terrorism "sprint" to identify capabilities that could be brought to bear against the problem. Thanks to some amazing people working eighteen-hour days, we were able to complete the Strategic Framework for Countering Terrorism and Targeted Violence in a few weeks.

I spent most of the fall briefing Congress and the White House's Office of Management and Budget on the plan and our budgetary needs—with a key focus on the need to build prevention capabilities. In December, Congress passed a budget that increased DHS's funding for prevention efforts immediately, and then OMB approved a budget proposal for the next fiscal year that increased it even further.

As the Christmas season approached, I was rejoicing the appropriations win and preparing to start the job hunt again when I was pulled into the acting chief of staff's office. He praised my team for the results we had delivered but then told me it was best that I move on to a different portfolio. I was being pushed out.

Over the Christmas holiday, I called my friend and colleague Chris Krebs, the director of the Cybersecurity and Infrastructure Security Agency (CISA), and he agreed to let me come over and help out the cyber mission for a few months; this would give me some extra time to job hunt. I made the request to acting secretary Chad Wolf, and he approved pending finding someone to serve in an acting capacity for me. This latter step took longer than expected.

On what was supposed to be my last day at the policy office, I completed my final transition briefing at around Friday at six p.m. and grabbed my phone as I walked back to my office to pack up the last of my things. There was a voicemail explaining I could not move to CISA on Monday. New rules had gone into effect that day, put into place by the new head of the Presidential Personnel Office, Trump's hatchet man John McEntee,[1] and all personnel actions had been halted.

After a week waiting for news, it became clear that the move to CISA wouldn't go forward unless I was willing to undergo a Presidential Personnel interview. These interviews were not to check qualifications, but to gauge the depth of loyalty to then president Trump. I had known since the first time I'd thought about it six months earlier that there was no way I would vote for Trump. I had seen firsthand how dangerous his chaos was for national security. Though it was uncomfortable, I was grateful that I was able to transition out on my own terms on April 10, instead of unceremoniously being escorted out, as so many of my former colleagues were.

By then we were in full lockdown from COVID-19. I spent much of the next two months catching up on sleep, helping my kids with virtual learning, and detoxing through journaling, praying, Bible reading, and exercise.

In late May, a friend from a church small group fifteen years before suggested we do a Bible study together. These women had walked with me for four years as I was coming back to my faith and God was doing some deep work in my heart. We had scattered all over the country by that time. Being stuck at home and unable to do our normal local fellowship, it seemed like a great time to catch up. Unfortunately for them, I was processing the three years of toxicity of my time serving in the DHS under the Trump administration. Somewhere in the process of sharing, someone said, "Elizabeth, you need to speak out about this. People need to know how broken it is."

I brushed this aside—we were moving in a month. And so many people had spoken out. No one seemed to care.

The suggestion became harder to ignore—soon my husband was suggesting it as well.

First came the president's remarks that the recent protests over George Floyd's murder were incited by antifa provocateurs. After years of ignoring the concerns of the counterterrorism community about the growing threat of domestic terrorism, Trump directed the attorney general to look into a domestic terrorism designation—but for the wrong movement. He needed a boogeyman.

Then came Lafayette Square—a beautiful park in front of the White House—cleared of peaceful protesters using tear gas and low-flying helicopters to allow a photo op with an upside-down Bible in front of the historic church that had been damaged in the protests the night before. It was an utterly egregious act, an excessive use of force not seen since the 1960s civil rights movement.

The final straw for me, though, was watching the men and women of the Department of Homeland Security be turned into a campaign tool, forced to "protect monuments"[2] and deploy the Border Patrol's special forces unit[3] in an urban environment in response to exaggerated claims of desecration and rioting in cities across America. The president used federal law enforcement not to bring about peace and safety, but to win an election.

And so it was in the summer of 2020, after dealing with my own personal grief, I opened my eyes to the pain the rest of the country was enduring and felt the conviction that I should find a way to help, somehow. Maybe I could help ease some of that pain if I told the truth of what I knew.

I said yes to an interview with ABC News on the COVID-19 pandemic. And I reached out to a few groups that were issuing statements condemning the actions in Lafayette Square and Portland. I eventually connected to the team at Defending Democracy Together, who was launching the Former Republican National Security Officials for Biden group. I signed a letter and I thought, *Okay, I've done what I need to do.*

Then the team at Defending Democracy asked me to make a video testimonial for their Republican Voters Against Trump (RVAT) campaign sharing my concerns about a second term for Trump. This was well beyond my comfort level. I said no.

My hesitations were primarily about safety—it was well known that conservatives and Christians who opposed Trump were harassed and threatened,[4] and often their families were threatened too.

But I also hesitated because I didn't know if I could do it well. Would I fail and be humiliated? (Thankfully, no.) Would speaking out paralyze my job search? (Yes, but God provided.) Would I lose friends and be ostracized from my community? (Yes, and this has been painful.) Would I be blacklisted from Republican politics? (Yes, but this became less of a concern because I left the party—or rather, I realized that they had left me.)

It took about a month of wrestling. I believed God was calling me to speak out, and therefore, I was to trust Him with the rest.

How did that turn out? Well, it's been an adventure, but He has always provided for and protected my family.

I've lost a few friends and have strained relationships with some others.

I'm politically homeless and finding community with others discovering the same.

It has been a season of grieving, lament, and lots of prayer. But it's also been a season of new relationships, and the winnowing experience deepens the ties with those that remain.

———

It has been a joy to write this book, to be given the luxury of time to read widely and deeply and talk with people who have experienced and thought about various aspects of this problem.

This moment we find ourselves in—how we got here and what we do about it—is exceedingly complex. Anyone giving you a simple answer is either lying to you or a fool. Anyone painting with broad brushstrokes—"all white evangelicals are unwittingly racist," "all religions radicalize," "all MAGA are extremists"—while they may have some anecdotes, is only interested in casting blame and is not serious about the hard work to solve the challenges of our day.

Further, such simplistic answers exacerbate the problem. Shaming or attempting to argue someone out of their ideology does not work. In fact, it is likely to push someone deeper into extremism. Disrupting radicalization or supporting disengagement from extremism requires compassion and empathy along with accountability. For us to empathize, we need to understand their grievances. We can do so without validating their solutions of hatred and violence.

The day the RVAT video was released, I felt a burden lift I didn't know I had been carrying. I was able to speak the full truth for the first time in three and a half years.

This book is a continuation of that truth and an invitation to step into the freedom that comes from the truth. It is a rallying cry for the "exhausted majority" to reengage our communities and an encouragement for those who experienced the disorienting and painful fracturing of relationships and communities. It is for ordinary people and ordinary believers who want our country and our houses of worship to be a beacon of peace, light, humility, and compassion in the world.

I wrote this book to equip you with the facts so you can better understand what is happening and why it is dangerous, how radicalization occurs and what you can do to thwart it. My hope for this book is that it will educate you, enlighten you, horrify you, and motivate you to be a part of the solution to the growing nightmare of extremism that exploits our faith to justify violence. To help you become ministers of reconciliation within the church and the broader community.

Can I tell you the good news up front? You are one of the best hopes we have in healing the country and preventing more violence. After twenty years of studying the drivers behind violent extremism, we now understand that it is largely psychosocial. Some of the biggest drivers are shame, humiliation, a lack of belonging and significance, loss of control, uncertainty, and a sense of unaddressed injustice. For millennia, humanity has grappled with these God-imprinted desires for meaning, belonging, being loved, and having value. Libraries are filled with religious and philosophical answers to these quandaries. If you are a Christian, you believe that the Bible offers answers to these, particularly through the life, death, and resurrection of Jesus. Not in a simplistic way. Christian culture, moral majorities, and coffee-cup Bible verses will not prevent further radicalization. But walking the Way of Jesus—loving and empathizing with those in pain and in the darkness—can point to where true light and hope can be found.

We can no longer afford to look past the idolatry of politics and the fear of losing power that poisons our churches and foments division, hatred, and violence. We must each be working actively every day in our relationships, our communities, and our churches to remind our fellow Christians and the world that we serve the Prince of Peace. It is not up to politicians and advocates to create this change; it is up to each and every one of us.

This book aims to encourage the faithful remnant. You are not alone. And we can walk this path toward peace together.

Part I
_____

RADICALIZED

ONE

WHAT HAPPENED?
From 9/11 to 1/6

It was shortly before 9:40 a.m. when my colleagues and I looked out of our tenth-floor window to see thick black smoke billowing up into a crystal blue sky from across the Potomac. We couldn't see what was on fire—another building blocked our view—but given the events of the morning, we assumed it was the Pentagon. Instinct took over. I can't remember who voiced it, but we needed to get out of downtown DC. Cell phones were down. I couldn't reach my roommate at the White House. Rumors were spreading about additional attacks—more planes, a bomb outside of the State Department, and whatever else our frightened imaginations could conjure.

I raced down the hallway to collect my briefcase from my office. At my desk, I stopped to call my mom from a landline; I let her know I was okay and would call when I got back to my apartment.

As I got in the elevator to go to the garage, a colleague told me one of the Twin Towers had collapsed. I can still remember the sense of the wind being knocked out of me and having to catch myself on the elevator railing as my knees started to give way. The devastation was unfathomable.

I had driven to work that day. No one wanted to take the Metro home—we weren't sure if one of the Metro lines by the Pentagon had been damaged in the attack. And given the coordinated nature of the attacks, we wondered what else might be planned. So my hatchback was packed to the brim with friends who normally took the Metro.

The entire city collectively decided to get out of DC as well. The roads were packed with emergency vehicles, cars, and people fleeing on foot—many ditched their shoes and were walking barefoot. I remember turning west on Independence Avenue—seeing the Capitol in my rearview mirror and wondering if it was the last time I would see it. Over an hour later and less than a mile traveled, we finally passed the White House. I was relieved to see it untouched. By this time, the news reports were indicating all planes had been accounted for, so our initial panic of getting out of DC was replaced by processing the magnitude of the horror of the morning's events.

It took four hours to drive ten miles home. It took several more hours to locate the roommate who had fled the White House. When we finally reunited back in our apartment, our small urban crew huddled around the TV, feeling the gut punch and crying every time we saw the replay of the towers fall and the dust-covered survivors in shock running from the wreckage. We pondered whether more attacks were coming and how we could help.

In the weeks that followed, I spent a lot of time with those friends. We went back to work, because our president solemnly asked us to. We had a calling to serve our country, and attempting to maintain our routines was our way of telling the terrorists we would not let them win. We reconvened in the evenings to process the horror—sometimes we talked, and sometimes we just sat together. As a nation, we worked through the stages of grief, and we found resolve to not let the attacks paralyze us in fear.

For many in my generation, September 11, 2001, was a turning point. I vowed to contribute in some way so our country would never again experience such an attack. That vow led to my joining the

Homeland Security Council at the White House, eventually making my way to the Domestic Counterterrorism Directorate and a career in homeland security and counterterrorism.

Nearly twenty years later, I stood in my living room in the DC suburbs watching the scenes stream in—reports of pipe bombs, gallows erected, brutal beatings, and perhaps even deaths swirled. I felt the gut punch yet again. After nearly twenty years of working to defeat terrorists and secure the homeland, it had happened: terrorists occupied the US Capitol.

But this time, they had invoked *my* faith to justify their actions.

Instead of hearing *Allahu Akbar*, we heard a strangely dressed man shouting "Thank You, heavenly Father for gracing us with this opportunity." He invoked the name of Jesus Christ to close his prayer in the well of the United States Senate amid shards of glass, papers tossed from senators' desks, echoes of gunshots, and the faint but acrid smell of tear gas and bear spray enveloping the grounds of America's most sacred civic shrine. Those uttering the prayer had stormed and ransacked the US Capitol, injuring nearly 150 police officers and contributing to the deaths of at least five officers in the days and weeks afterward.[1]

That dark, cloudy, cold January afternoon, I watched people from my community complete their rage-fueled metamorphosis into violent extremists. It was an evolution aided and abetted by a church that has lost its soul: living in fear, glorifying false notions of our country's past, idolizing earthly tools of power as the source of their salvation, and actively contributing to dehumanizing and apocalyptic narratives inciting violence.

GROWING MASS VIOLENCE

For some, the attack on the Capitol was enough to break the spell—a realization that the intoxicating rage had gone too far. But for others,

January 6 became yet another example of how Democrats, liberals, the elites, the deep state, and the media were persecuting and misrepresenting them. There was no moment of unity, such as after 9/11, across the political spectrum to condemn violence. No independent bipartisan committee to study why fellow Americans felt compelled to attack their own government. No demand for a public accounting of how multiple security layers failed to prevent or protect against the attack, even with all our post-9/11 investments in intelligence gathering, analysis, and protective measures.

Now, three years since the January 6 attack on the Capitol, the country is more polarized,[2] angrier,[3] and more violent.[4] Rhetoric painting the opposing political party as an existential threat and calling for violence against political opponents is at an all-time high, as are discussions about a coming civil war.[5] Some believe we're already in a "cold" civil war.

According to a series of polls conducted by the University of Chicago in 2021–2022, between 15 and 20 million Americans believe violence is justified to return Trump to office.[6] Other surveys, agnostic to the specifics of what happened on January 6, demonstrate a similar willingness by Americans to embrace violence.[7] For example, in an August 2023 survey, nearly a quarter of Americans, approximately 60 million people, believe "things have gotten so far off track, true American patriots may have to resort to violence in order to save our country."[8]

A May 2022 survey, framed less hypothetically, found that 3 percent of Americans believe "political violence was usually or always justified"—that equates to 8 million people.[9] The researchers then asked about seventeen specific political objectives—such as "preserving an American way of life I believe in."[10] Thirty-two percent of Americans—84 million people—thought "violence is usually or always justified to advance at least 1 of the 17 objectives."[11] That level of commitment to violence to advance your cause meets the definition of violent extremism.

Let that sink in for a moment.

If tomorrow the director of the National Counterterrorism Center announced there were 8 million ISIS or Al-Qaeda followers in the United States, how would the country respond? Having dealt with the communications side of threats and warnings for nearly twenty years, I am confident there would be collective panic.

The fight to live safely, in peace—to be able to go to work, go shopping, or send our kids to school without fear of a shooting or bombing—is no longer about Islamic extremism. (To be sure, the threat from ISIS and Al-Qaeda remains, but our security capabilities to keep attacks away from the US homeland are extensive, and their capabilities have been significantly weakened.) The threat is coming from within. And our security capabilities for detecting and disrupting threats inside the United States are weak.

NARRATIVES OF GRIEVANCE, ANXIETY, AND FEAR

How did this happen? How did Americans become our own worst enemy? How do we have more to fear from the hatred and division in our own country than we have to fear from international terrorists?

And why is the preponderance of the threat coming from "my side"?

I was once a political junkie, a die-hard Republican who bought into the rhetoric that the other side—the Democrats, the Clintons, the "libs," pick your label—were the problem, the enemy, even. Growing up in the Bible Belt taught me I needed to vote a certain way, that my opinions about economic policy and foreign policy needed to align with the Republican Party, because the Republican Party was God's team. And the other guys—well, they posed a grave threat to my team's way of life.

It took significant untangling of my faith to understand how misguided and unbiblical this thinking is. But the experience allows me a unique lens to understand (and empathize) with how we got here.

For nearly fifty years, our community has been swimming in the precursor narratives that laid the groundwork for radicalization. These narratives were the water in our fish tank. And as a fish doesn't know it's wet until it's removed from the water, our community has difficulty seeing these as anything but truth. In our community's story, we were the good guys, going up against a world that rejected God, His truth, and His values. And conservative Republican politics was the way to protect our way of life and push back against the evil from the other side.

But something shifted in these narratives around the early 2010s. They became darker, moving past an "us versus them" story played out in battles for political and cultural power to existential threats justifying hostile action against "them." This was enabled by an ever-increasing toxic soup of fear and outrage that dominated conservative infotainment. And it spread into some pulpits as pastors increasingly recognized that their congregants were primarily catechized by their favorite conservative talk show host instead of the Bible. Conservative white evangelical Christians were repeatedly told we were being marginalized and humiliated, and examples of "progressives" firing or suing Christians for practicing their religious beliefs were held up as examples of persecution. The solution—we were told—was earthly power to protect ourselves. And if we could not obtain that power through legitimate political means, then the rules could be broken. After all, we're on God's team. Protecting our "way of life" was a way of defending God.

Historians and political scientists will tell you that it is nothing new for politicians, monarchs, and religious and business leaders to use religion for power and political purposes. The role of Christianity in the United States' history has both horrid and honorable moments. Some of those horrid moments meet the definition of extremism. But during most of my lifetime, extremists were not allowed to participate in mainstream political discussions. They were kept at the fringes of society. This reality has changed in the last decade as well, with violent extremist views being expressed openly—in political fora, in our interactions at the community level, and, perhaps most distressingly, within our churches.

As is often the case in extremism, there are merits to certain arguments about the "threat" to a way of life. Our economy *is* rapidly changing, creating great uncertainty and leaving some behind. Demographically, we are on our way to being a nation of minorities. In the 2040s, whites will no longer be the majority race in the US. The percentage of Americans who identify as religious or participating in an organized religion has continued to decline rapidly over the past two decades. For the first time ever, those identifying as religious are a minority. And American culture is evolving, moving away from the dominance of traditions, values, and virtues that are associated with the country's strong ties to Protestant Christianity. We might even find empathy or compassion for those who feel as if the world is hostile to their way of life and expression of faith.

For too many in our community these uncertainties and perceived threats created vulnerability to extremist narratives. When we are vulnerable—due to either external factors like a recent crisis or internal factors like humiliation or loneliness—and we do not have sufficient protective factors in place, some of us become susceptible to extremist "solutions"—that is, hostile action against those perceived to be a threat.

It is perplexing that a group or individual can claim to be Christian (and perhaps they are) and advocate for or support violence. Outside of self-defense or "just war," harm or violence carried out against a group or individual is contradictory to the traditional teach-ings of our faith.[12] This is the role extremist ideologies play: provid-ing a justification for violence that removes any nuance and argues the end (survival) justifies the means (violence). And one of the most common narratives in conservative Christian culture recently is the need to defend our Christian way of life. Seeing traditional values and faith under siege, we are told to fear that our children and grandchil-dren will no longer be able to practice their faith. Therefore, these narratives claim, we need to defend Christianity.

But let's be clear: anyone making an argument that *Christianity* is facing an existential threat is heretical. The teachings of orthodox Christianity believe that the Kingdom of God cannot be thwarted by men. God is sovereign and all powerful, and Scripture makes it abun-dantly clear that He will bring His plans to fulfillment in His timing.

On this point, I should clarify some of my terms. I use the term *orthodoxy* or *orthodox* to describe the traditional or affirmed doctrines and biblical canon (the collection of books Christians consider scrip-ture) of the Christian faith that were established by the early church and are adhered to around the globe in different branches, denom-inations, and movements of the faith.[13] It is not intended to imply that the early church was perfect; rather these are the beliefs and interpretations which are core to faithful followers of Jesus across the millennia.

When I use the terms *Christian, disciple,* and *believer,* I am refer-ring to individuals who believe the good news of the gospel.[14] But that is not necessarily how others use those terms. In the United States, Protestant Christianity—one of the three primary branches of the Christian faith—has significant historical and cultural influence.[15] Some Americans who identify as Christian do so because they see it as a social or cultural identity. They're not using the label because they have a relationship with Jesus Christ and see him as their King or because they believe the tenets of orthodox Christianity. They say "Christian" because they were born in a time and place where that is what it meant to be an American; it is part of their heritage.

When I use the term *cultural Christianity* or *Christian community*, I'm referencing an identity group that captures both of these categories: individuals holding genuine orthodox Christian beliefs as well as individuals who view the label as a societal or cultural identity.

Within the United States, the majority of Protestant Christians identify as evangelical.[16] The National Association of Evangelicals (NAE) uses a broad definition for evangelicals: people who "take the Bible seriously and believe in Jesus Christ as Savior and Lord."[17] It is first associated with the Great Awakening, when *evangelical* became "identified with revivalists who emphasized a personal relationship with God, the joy of being born again, and the call to spread the gospel around the globe."[18]

In seeking to understand extremism in the United States, we will be looking at drivers that stem primarily from the white evangelical Christian church and politically conservative communities. There are exceptions, of course: Catholics, Greek and Russian Orthodox, mainline Protestants, as well as Black and Hispanic evangelicals who have succumbed to fear-mongering narratives that their way of life is under attack and hostile action is necessary to defend it. However, they represent a much smaller percentage of the in-group we are exploring.

So often in discussions about the extremes, we overlook the majority, who are anything but extreme. Christianity is bigger than the American church. Even within the American white evangelical church, there are numerous distinctions in doctrinal beliefs, worship style, and governance. And *most* people who identify as white conservative evangelicals are *not* extremists by the definition I use in this book.

The Barna Group published a study in 2019 that ranked cities by the percentage of people meeting their definition of post-Christian. To be considered a post-Christian individual, you must meet nine or more of the sixteen criteria indicating "a lack of Christian identity, belief and practice." Of the one hundred media markets they surveyed, most of the cities I've lived in as an adult were post-Christian. Seattle was tenth on the list with 54 percent of their population not identifying, believing, or practicing the Christian faith. DC is twenty-ninth, and Denver thirty-second.

Dallas—where I grew up—was ninetieth out of one hundred.

Perhaps that's why I missed how much our community had changed. Or maybe I was the one that changed? Ten years ago, my husband and I thought we were in the mainstream, albeit the nerdy branch (i.e., reformed), of the evangelical church. But when we moved back to Dallas in 2015, we realized we didn't fit in with American Christian culture anymore.

It did not happen all at once. A policy debate would arise, or the latest culture war issue, and we became convinced that the Bible's teachings differed from our political community's default position.

By 2020 I had concluded that neither political party was addressing our nation's challenges in a manner consistent with Scripture's teachings. It was never an option for us to simply withdraw. But it left us wondering, *Where do we then belong? Whose "team" should we join?*

The late theologian and pastor Tim Keller explains the challenge this way, "The historical Christian positions on social issues don't match up with contemporary political alignments;" yet Scripture does not allow us to "withdraw and try to be apolitical," and neither can we "assimilate and adopt one Party's whole package in order to have your place at the table."[19]

Embracing this truth does not prohibit us from belonging or siding with a political party or movement. But the party shouldn't be core to our identity or our faith. And we need to see that party or political movement with an accurate lens: They are not perfect. Neither is the other side pure evil. The unentangling of our faith from our politics helps us better understand what Jesus told us long ago: His Kingdom is not of this world (John 18:36).

The answer to "what happened?" is that too many of us forgot this truth. What started fifty-plus years ago as an alliance between white evangelical Christians and the Republican Party for political power has solidified as the core identity for a strong majority of the white evangelical Christian community.[20] With our identity tied to a political party, whenever that political power was diminished or threatened, our community feels threatened. The door was open for politicians and conservative media to create fear and anxiety about our future. Our success, maybe even our survival, is at stake. And as we will discover in the next chapter, this framing is the precursor to extremism.

TWO

THE PATH TO EXTREMISM

How Radicalization Works

Americans were compelled to become students of terrorism in the immediate aftermath of the attacks of 9/11. Such out-of-the-blue horror led to soul-searching and seeking to understand how anyone could have so much hate. Specifically, why did *they* hate *us*? And how do communities and individuals give way to the kind of hatred that makes them willing to kill for their beliefs?

There were few counterterrorism experts and even fewer scholars of terrorism on 9/11. As with any crisis, many sought to understand—some without the necessary credentials or experience. Scholars have now been studying the problem for twenty years, and as a result we possess a much clearer understanding of the process of radicalization and the psychology of extremism.

POST-9/11 SIMPLISTIC ANSWERS FOR THE CAUSE OF TERRORISM

In the years immediately following the 9/11 attacks, a still prevalent supposition asserted that people join terrorist groups because their interpretation of the Muslim faith compels them to. We now understand that while ideology plays a role in the radicalization process, it is not the underlying reason why people become extremists.

Another prominent set of hypotheses argued that it was societal inequality, lack of education, or poverty that propelled individuals and communities toward radicalization. Scholars call these forces "structural development factors."[1] This theory of terrorism has been around since the 1970s[2] and was (and in some places still is) a popular theory for politicians and policymakers.[3] The US invested billions of dollars in humanitarian aid and strengthening educational and economic opportunities in the post-9/11 years.[4] There is nothing wrong with the US and NGOs funding such efforts; they are a critical part of our diplomatic and humanitarian efforts. But multiple studies debunk the social inequality hypothesis.[5]

J.M. Berger summarizes the problem with these discredited theories by reminding us of the global scale of human suffering, "Billions of people around the world face problems in their personal lives and in their communities—injustice, oppression, discrimination, poverty, unemployment, crime, and more. But only a small fraction of people with problems take up extremism."[6]

We want the answers to be simple. It makes us feel safer, more in control, if we can explain the horror away as a problem of poverty, education, or religion. But as it turns out, what pushes groups and people toward radicalization and extremism is more complex than these simple explanations afford.

WHAT IS EXTREMISM?

Sometimes it's the simple things, like definitions, that stump you. As a policymaker and practitioner of countering extremism, I often absorbed an understanding of terms from the practical experience of what does and does not work. So, when I started looking for a standard definition of *extremism* that scholars use, I was startled to discover a lack of consensus. It turns out that we use the term a lot in the field but don't have solid agreement on what it means.

Failing to define extremism has had "huge real-world conse-quences."[7] It has led to an overemphasis on understanding ideologies or religions and an underappreciation of the structures that lead to extremism. It also leads to politicians, the media, and the public apply-ing the term injudiciously and creating stigmas that are undeserved.

Extremism is a contextual term. What is considered extreme depends on the context of the norm or standard. We can look at the arc of history and appreciate that there are ideas and beliefs that are the cherished norm today but were previously considered extreme, including many of the core tenets of classical liberalism. As the Overton window—the range of policies acceptable to the mainstream at any given time—shifts, the range of ideas and cultural norms that were once considered extreme become acceptable.[8] Thus we need a definition that goes beyond "new" or "weird" and the small size of the group adhering to those beliefs.

For our purposes, we will use the definition of J.M. Berger, an extremism researcher and expert:

> *Extremism is the belief that an in-group's success or survival can never be separated from the need for hostile action against an out-group.*[9]

The elements of this definition are important to explain. First, a bit of social psychology to explain the references to *in-group* and *out-group* in the definition. Social identity theory was developed by Henri Tajfel and John C. Turner in 1979. Its basic concept is that we define our identity in comparison to others. We categorize those with whom we have similarities as our in-group (*us*) and people who don't fit into that category are the out-group (*them*). Importantly, "the *in* in *in-group* does not denote dominance, popularity, or value judgement."[10] We can categorize based on any number of factors, for example, race; sex; religion; what country, state, or city you are from; education level;

marital status; profession; coffee or tea; favorite sports team; Protestant or Catholic; egalitarian or complementarian. In healthy, pluralistic societies, differences are accepted and even celebrated.[11]

This process of identifying our in-group is a normal, healthy human activity that our brains do "to protect and bolster self-identity."[12] You only need to travel to your nearest middle school to see this effect in action. But just as things can go wrong in those adolescent years when we search for identity, we need to be aware of the natural bias that can accompany our categorizations. Studies have repeatedly demonstrated our "tendency to view one's own group with a positive bias vis-a-vis the out-group."[13] So, left unchecked, we tend to give people "like us" the benefit of the doubt and not offer the same grace to people we categorize as different from us. This tendency is exceedingly magnified in extremist movements.[14]

Now, you might think the idea of hostility toward an out-group sounds like prejudice or racism. There is certainly an aspect of prejudice, but extremism goes further than bias. It asserts that the "out-group must *always* be *actively opposed* because its fundamental identity is intrinsically harmful to the in-group."[15]

Hostile action spans a range of nonviolent to violent activities—from verbal attacks, discrimination, and derision to hate crimes, terrorism, and genocide. Which also means that some nonviolent hostile action, in certain contexts, is not necessarily criminal and is even protected by the First Amendment. This is part of the reason why the United States government has fewer tools to counter extremism based within the US. Speech, even hate speech, is protected under the First Amendment. While incitement to violence is illegal, it is very difficult to prosecute. Some types of harassment and discrimination can be criminal but likewise extremely hard to prosecute. In fact, most often, remedies are provided through civil court.

US law enforcement focuses primarily on investigating hate crimes and terrorism. Where the government is limited, civil society plays a key role in pushing back against harassment and discrimination.

Ideology: Identity Narratives to Explain Our Crisis and Offer "Solutions"

All extremist groups and movements have some form of ideology, a collection of books, images, lectures, videos, or conversations that "describe who is part of the in-group, who is part of an out-group, and how the in-group should interact with the out-group."[16]

Narrative is hugely important in the in-group/out-group formation process if the grouping extends beyond the obvious. For example, even though I don't live there anymore, I identify as a Texan because I was raised there and spent two years as an adult there. I don't have to further explain why I'm a Texan; it's defined by my geographic location during my childhood. When we go beyond the obvious, or when people outwardly look similar and the group needs to draw a distinction— what it means to be a part of *this* group—a narrative is woven.

These identity narratives develop over time. The group may also morph and change in ways that appear contradictory. This process occurs in healthy, unbiased, non-extreme groups all of the time. Usually the out-group is simply anyone who doesn't meet the definition of the in-group.

The problem arises when a group begins constructing narratives about an out-group's opposition to them. They define the out-group's beliefs, traits, and practices, relying on information that may be unreliable, exaggerated, or based solely on an in-group member's negative experience with the out-group.[17] They perceive that the out-group poses a threat to them. Extremism sets in when the in-group "adopts hostile attitudes toward the out-group."[18] A group may be moving toward extremism when the narrative about the other group is increasingly fictitious and toxic, particularly when a group aggressively "highlight[s] negative data points and ignor[es] or rebut[s] positive data points."[19]

The extremist's ideology is the story that weaves all these factors together—a narrative that defines the legitimacy and significance of the in-group, the threat posed by the out-group, and a "solution" that justifies extraordinary measures of hostile action toward the out-group.

Scholars call this the crisis-solution construct, and it offers a "competitive system of meaning" for supporters to perceive and judge the world.[20] Categories of crisis narratives can include impurity (a corruption of the group's beliefs, practices, or traits, conspiracies; the out-group is secretly manipulating things to control the in-group), existential threat (the out-group will destroy the in-group), and apocalypse (out-groups will usher in the end of the world in the near future).[21] "Solutions" are the various types of hostile actions we discussed earlier—from harassment, discrimination, and hate speech to violence, terrorism, and genocide.[22]

THE RADICALIZATION PROCESS

How does an individual or group move from being in the mainstream of society to a place where they believe and fear that their success or survival is threatened by the out-group, so much so that hostile action is necessary? Through a process of moral change. During the radicalization process, the individual or group moves from society's set of moral norms (e.g., violence is wrong) to embracing views that accept hostile action as "morally legitimate."[23] However, radicalization does not necessitate extremist action. In other words, an individual may radicalize—adopting the view that hostile action is morally justified—but never take action. So, radicalization is a mindset that potentially sets the stage for mobilization to violence.

While radicalization does not necessarily follow a linear path, we can organize the elements of extremism to describe the general process a *group* goes through to radicalize to extremism. Berger outlines four steps: [24]

1. Define the in-group.
2. Define the out-group.
3. Define the existence of the out-group as an acute crisis for the in-group.
4. Define hostile actions (solutions) that must be applied to the out-group.

Recruitment

Once an extremist identity has been established, the group needs to recruit from what Berger calls the "eligible in-group," which is the "broader identity group from which the extremists came" and which the extremist group "claims to represent."[25]

As a movement is forming and developing its identity and narratives, the group begins to articulate strict boundary lines for their group: who can be "in," and who does not meet the group's criteria for traits, beliefs, or practices. As the extremist in-group attempts to recruit from the eligible in-group, they will meet pushback from the broader in-group. That disagreement could be over the characterization of the out-group, or that the larger group doesn't see a threat being posed by the out-group that reaches the level of a crisis, or perhaps they agree on both of those points but disagree that the solution requires hostile action.

If members of the broader in-group reject the extremist movement,[26] they are considered ineligible in-group members.

Individual Radicalization

There is consensus among researchers of different academic expertise that there is no one path, no one personality type, and no standard background of violent extremists.[27] Contrary to popular myth, most extremists are not mentally ill. Studies of terrorists (extremists who plot or conduct acts of terrorism or join terrorist groups) indicate that individuals who radicalize to the point of violent action do not have higher rates of psychosis or diagnosable personality disorders than the general population.[28] In fact, the "consensus among experts" is that the most "common characteristic of terrorists is their normality."[29] This consensus applies to terrorists who act as part of a group; some studies indicate slightly higher levels of diagnosable mental illness in lone offenders as compared to the general population.[30] However, other researchers disagree.[31]

Radicalization, by and large, happens to normal, functional people. Radicalization can happen to people we know. Radicalization can happen to us. One need look no further than Nazi Germany for a powerful reminder of how radical extremism can become normalized. People we know and love can be radicalized to extremism. Understanding and acknowledging this reality allows us to make a conscious effort to build resilience factors in our communities, strengthen our children, and encourage our friends and loved ones.

Individual radicalization could occur as part of the group's process. Or it may occur after the group or movement has a well-defined identity and crisis-solution narrative. Berger identifies nine steps an individual walks through to radicalize:[32]

1. *Identification with the eligible in-group.*
2. *Negative views toward an out-group.* These negatives views are based on the out-group's intrinsic identity rather than a short-term conflict.

3. *Perception of a crisis*, which they may or may not attribute to the out-group.
4. *Curiosity about the extremist in-group*, including research, which mostly occurs online but occasionally in person, to learn about the ideology.
5. *Consideration of the extremist in-group*. The key question asked by the individual is whether the extremist in-group offers a genuine solution to the eligible in-group crisis.
6. *Identification with the extremist in-group*. Direct contact may or may not occur; it's more about identifying yourself as an adherent of the ideology.
7. *Self-critique*. Am I doing enough for the cause?
8. *Escalation*. If the answer to the previous question is no, the individual may escalate their actions on behalf of the extremist group.
9. *After-action critique*. Further evaluating if the escalation was enough or if more needs to be done.

The radicalization process is often talked about as a funnel or a narrowing staircase.[33] The number of people who are vulnerable is much larger than the number of people who start the process, and the population size continues to decrease through each successive step in the stages of radicalization. Individuals who are at-risk or vulnerable to radicalization align with steps 1–3 above. An individual who is radicalizing is conducting steps 4 and 5. A radicalized individual is at step 6, adopting the extremist ideology. And it's within this self-critique evaluation cycle of steps 7, 8, and 9 that we become most concerned about an individual or group mobilizing to violence. Some may arrive at one step and never proceed further. But often an outside trigger such as a personal crisis, an event perceived as a threat to the in-group, or a charismatic leader challenging the group or individual to consider what more they can do can propel individuals to go further down the funnel.

WHY PEOPLE RADICALIZE: NEEDS, NARRATIVES, AND NETWORKS

Exposure to extremists or their ideology is not enough to cause someone to radicalize. The individual must be cognitively open to the ideology. We call this pre-radicalization state vulnerability. Someone can be vulnerable but, if never exposed to extremist ideology, never radicalize. Someone can also have risk factors that create vulnerability but build up "protective factors" or "resilience" that reduce the likelihood of radicalization.

There are more than one hundred risk factors that researchers believe create vulnerability to extremism. Some are stronger than others. As the authors of one study on radicalization risk factors explain, "There is likely no single driver of radicalization, rather it is the crystallization of personal and situational characteristics converging in time and space, which results in radicalization for some."[34] The most significant vulnerabilities can be classified as unmet psychosocial needs, often caused by experiences of humiliation or disrespect, psychological distress, a recent crisis, or loss of significance.[35]

These can be group or personal experiences. For instance, humiliation can be caused by an oppressive regime or social group; disenfranchisement or discrimination of a given ethnic, religious, or national group; or occupation of one's homeland by a foreign entity. Humiliation could also stem from personal circumstances, including personal failure, personal victimization, loss of a loved one at the hands of an enemy, or a social stigma within one's community.

The psychological effect of these experiences is understood to be a key factor in the radicalization process. Humans have a fundamental need to feel worthy or significant—to feel important, valued, and respected in the eyes of others. The hurt or humiliated individual thus searches for routes by which they can restore their feelings of value and worth.

Likewise, a crisis creates uncertainty, anxiety, and fear. We want answers: Why did this happen? Who can we blame? What do we do now? Uncertainty–identity theory concludes that moments with great uncertainty may lead some individuals to be drawn to extremist groups for the rigidity and structure their ideologies provide.[36] When the status quo is disrupted, the resulting grievance and uncertainty it brings can set the stage for individuals to find reassurance in the black-and-white identity, narrative, and solution extremists offer.

However, if experiencing a crisis, humiliation, trauma, or hardship was the only factor in radicalization, we'd have innumerable radicalized individuals.[37] Arguably, most humans go through crises and humiliating experiences at some point in life and leverage a variety of healthier, or at least nonviolent, means to address the need.

This is where the next two factors—narratives and networks—advance the radicalization process. Extremists address that unmet need, that moment of chaos or pain, and offer narratives with overly simplistic explanations. They offer someone to blame and "justif[y] aggression against [them] on moral grounds."[38] The narrative indoctrinates the individual into "a simplistic way of thinking that sees the world in black and white terms."[39] A group or network of extremists provides belonging and creates a permission structure for otherwise psychologically normal people to feel that violence is justified.

Accelerating Factors: The Role of Social Media in Radicalization

Every metric we use to measure the level extremism in the United States has been rising for the last decade. The University of Maryland's National Consortium for the Study of Terrorism and Response to Terrorism (START) found a dramatic shift over the period of 2005–2016 in the way in which extremists were exposed to the narratives

and networks that facilitated their radicalization process. Between
2005 and 2010, 73.37 percent of the individuals they studied indicated
that social media played no role in their radicalization and 25 percent
said it played a secondary role. Only 1.63 percent indicated that social
media played a major role in their radicalization. But from 2011 to
2016, those numbers invert: 26.78 percent say social media played no
role, while the remaining 73.22 percent say it played a primary or
secondary role, and if you isolate the data for just 2016 the rate is 90
percent. The most important finding, though, was that social media
was accelerating the radicalization process.

A separate study funded by the Department of Justice found that
radicalization before 2010 took about 63.95 months. After 2010, it had
reduced to 18.53 months—or 3.5 times faster.[40] FBI director Christopher Wray drew a similar conclusion in 2020, when he asserted that
"terrorism moves at the speed of social media" and reported that homegrown and domestic violent extremists largely self-radicalize online
and mobilize to violence sometimes in a matter of weeks or days.[41]
During my tenure at DHS, I was briefed on a case that occurred over-
seas where the "flash to bang" was less than ten days. (*Flash-to-bang*
refers to the length of time between lightning and thunder—in the
context of counterterrorism, it's the length of time between an individual's initial radicalization step and when they begin to mobilize to
violence.) The phenomenon of quick radicalization makes it extremely
difficult for law enforcement to detect and disrupt an attack.

We cannot put this genie back in the bottle. Social media is a part
of our society now. While some responsible companies make efforts
to reduce extremist content being shared on their platforms, it is a bit
like a game of Whac-a-Mole—it's nearly impossible to keep up with
new content being generated every minute. Further, there are plenty of
irresponsible companies that make no effort to prevent the spread of
extremist material on their platforms. Even if you do not seek it out,

most of us who do any sort of work or have a social life online will come across extremist content at some point. It is in the mainstream.

This means that we need to be very concerned that in the past ten years, the number of people in America who are vulnerable to radicalization has swelled to a size we haven't seen in modern times. Our community is a parched tinderbox, and sparks of grievance are carelessly thrown about by politicians and the media. Those who are vulnerable will most likely be exposed to extremist narratives and networks at some point.

And if polls are measuring accurately, a sizeable percentage of people have already radicalized. Approximately 45 percent of self-identifying Christian Republicans assert that force may be necessary to preserve the "traditional American way of life."[42] Yes, there is a big difference between someone *saying* or *believing* violence is justified and making plans to commit an act of violence. But while the percentage of people who move from radicalization to violence is small, when the potential pool of vulnerable and radicalized is in the tens of millions, the resulting number of acts of violence and loss of life is too great.

THREE

TOO CLOSE TO HOME

The Greatest Extremist Threat Comes from Our Community

efore we explore the particulars of Christian extremism in
the US, let's look more broadly at the overarching context of
today's domestic violent extremist threat. Specifically, I want
to show you why officials in both the Trump and Biden administrations asserted that certain domestic violent extremist movements pose
a greater threat to the homeland than ISIS- or Al-Qaeda-directed
attacks.[1] For those who experienced 9/11 firsthand, it may seem auda-
cious to suggest that the graver threat today comes from people inside
the United States. There are two primary reasons why this is. The first
has to do with the way terrorist tactics have evolved and the limitations
in using our counterterrorism tools on domestic groups and movements. The second is simply what the data shows us—that far-right
extremism is the most prevalent and lethal in the United States today.

DOMESTIC VIOLENT EXTREMISM IS HARDER TO DETECT AND DISRUPT

Terrorism is criminal violence against a civilian (nonmilitary) population, intended to cause fear in order to coerce, intimidate, or send a
message to a government or society to achieve a political or ideological

aim.[2] While acts of terrorism cause death, destruction, and pain to
the direct community impacted, it's the far-reaching psychological repercussions that make it appealing to extremist actors.[3] Today,
terrorism is a tactic of "relatively weak movements to have a dispropor-
tionate impact on large and powerful" groups.[4] A form of asymmet-
ric warfare—designed to take advantage of vulnerabilities of states or
large enemies.[5]

The US has a (sadly) rich history of domestic terrorism. The
previous high-water mark occurred in the 1990s with several high-
profile terrorist attacks, including the Oklahoma City bombing and
the Centennial Olympic Park bombing in Atlanta, Georgia. Domestic
violent extremist activity diminished in the years immediately after
9/11, but it never disappeared.

Meanwhile, in response to 9/11, the US government rightly
strengthened its ability to counter international terrorism.[6] Groups
such as Al-Qaeda, ISIS, and their affiliates were designated by the US
as foreign terrorist organizations, which is a legally rigorous process
that allows a whole host of military, intelligence, and law enforcement
tools to be used to detect, disrupt, and dismantle such groups.

Domestically, law enforcement and homeland security measures
focused on preventing and protecting against the preferred terrorist
plot—a complex, coordinated attack. The Al-Qaeda model of terrorism involved small cells of individuals with different roles and skill sets
who traveled to centralized locations for training and attack planning.
Preparing for an attack required significant money to support the
cell's basic living necessities and procuring materials and/or expertise
to obtain or build weapons of mass destruction. The complex nature of
the attacks often meant that certain parts of the attack plan were prac-
ticed in advance. This complexity created opportunities for the security community (or the public) to detect a plot underway.

To detect and disrupt these complex plots, the homeland security community spent significant time ensuring that precursor materials to weapons of mass destruction were difficult to obtain and that we would be alerted right away if they were stolen. We strengthened our surveillance of those financing terrorism. We created a terrorist identities database and built partnerships around the globe to ensure those terrorists couldn't travel to the United States. We taught law enforcement and critical infrastructure operators the signs and indicators of attack planning and created a robust system for suspicious activity to be reported and analyzed. We taught the public that if they *see something*, they should *say something*. Data points were collected, and analysts looked to see if connections could be made to determine where a cell is operating or where an attack might be planned. As we "hardened" targets and pushed our borders out, it made it harder for terrorists to get into the United States.

When ISIS emerged from dregs of Al-Qaeda in Iraq and declared a caliphate in 2014, they encouraged people to leave their home countries and join them. At one point, ISIS held 33 percent of Syria and 40 percent of Iraq.[7] But by the end of 2017, they had lost 95 percent of that territory.

As ISIS began experiencing battlefield and territorial losses, they changed their tactics. Instead of coming to the caliphate, it encouraged people already within Europe and the United States to fight where they were and use whatever weapon they had access to. In Europe, this manifested predominantly as vehicle ramming and knife attacks. In the US, the weapon of choice was usually a gun. The attacks at a company holiday party in San Bernardino, California, in December 2015, which killed fourteen people, and at an Orlando nightclub, which killed fifty-three people, were two of the more deadly attacks inside the US inspired by ISIS.[8]

Shortening the planning cycle and encouraging people to "commit violent jihad" where they were, without coordinating with other people, made it nearly impossible for law enforcement to detect the pre-attack indicators that might allow an attack to be stopped. Bruce Hoffman notes that compared to the hierarchal structure of foreign terrorist groups of the past, today's movements are "looser, flatter, and more linear," with leadership that is "less a direct command and control relationship" and more "inspirational and motivational."[9]

Decentralization—while new for ISIS and Al-Qaeda—has been a tactic of domestic extremist movements since the 1980s, when they called for "leaderless resistance."[10] Whether it was a rediscovery of this old guidance, seeing the success of ISIS-inspired attacks, or a natural by-product of online radicalization that removes the requirement of meeting someone in real life in order to be exposed to the ideology, domestic violent extremists' tactics of the past decade have tended toward the lone actor approach. A recent study of individuals arrested for domestic violent extremist attacks and plots found that extremists actors "without organizational affiliations were more likely to have carried out lethal attacks" and those who planned alone were "more likely to succeed."[11]

Domestic violent extremists' preferred tactics make it significantly more difficult for law enforcement to detect when someone is on the pathway to violence. This is part of why they are a more challenging and graver threat than international violent extremists. But the "domestic" nature of the extremist's ideology also creates barriers to detect and disrupt a plot.

The distinction between international and domestic terrorism, while imperfect, worked well fifty years ago, before the age of cheap international travel and the internet. Today, however, while geography still influences extremist movements, the movements aren't constrained by a border. And yet US law treats international terrorism and domestic terrorism differently.

Part of that is due to the protections and rights afforded to people located within the United States by the Constitution. But it is also because unlike international terrorism, there is no stand-alone criminal statute for domestic terrorism. The lack of legal clarity around domestic terrorism creates both legal and practical distinctions in how we can counter domestic actors planning acts of terrorism. For example, the intelligence community is authorized to collect, retain, and disseminate information about non-US persons outside of the United States if it meets an authorized intelligence objective. The National Counterterrorism Center is authorized to maintain a database of identities and other associated information about individuals known or suspected to be terrorists affiliated with a foreign terrorist organization. But there is no such collection authority or list for individuals suspected of affiliating with domestic violent extremist groups or movements, in part because there is no process for *designating* extremist groups or movements that originate within the United States.

This brings us to the second distinction. While Congress and the president have outlined the roles and responsibilities of various federal agencies in combatting international terrorism, Congress has not done so for combatting domestic terrorism. During my tenure at DHS, as it was becoming clear that domestic terrorism was on the rise, we did an examination of existing authorities. We found while existing authorities *could* be leveraged to work on domestic violent extremism, primarily at DOJ, FBI, and DHS, and a small part of NCTC, there was no clear authorizing language from Congress *directing* it.

Congress is notorious for moving slowly, but on matters of national security, bipartisanship and urgency usually have been the rule. Unfortunately, that now seems to occur only by exception. When you have different parties in power in the House and Senate, or the control shifts frequently, the ambiguity in the law leads to constant whiplash. As an executive branch official, I was simultaneously lambasted by one house of Congress for not doing enough to counter domestic extremism and by the other chamber for focusing too much on it.

It also means that among federal agencies, no one has the designated lead. Now this might sound a bit childish, but unless the president or Congress tells an agency they must share their information with another agency, it's been my experience that the bureaucracy defaults to assertions of why they are not authorized to share certain information. This should ring alarm bells. One of the primary findings of the 9/11 Commission was that we did not detect the attack planning underway because information was not shared between and among law enforcement and intelligence agencies. Post-9/11 reforms created the National Counterterrorism Center in part to address this flaw for international terrorism. Those reforms also directed all agencies to share their data with the NCTC. While presidents can direct that agencies share—President George W. Bush did this for international terrorism data through executive orders before and after laws were passed and President Joe Biden has done this for domestic terrorism—certain structural changes require amending and changing existing law.

Absent a clear mandate about the sharing of data and, more important, assigning responsibility to an agency to understand domestic violent extremist movements, the mission will remain underresourced and inconsistently executed. Bureaucratic cultures reward risk aversion. And given how politically sensitive this topic is, you can imagine how difficult it is for anyone trying to do the right thing to overcome that inertia.

I want to be clear that I am not asserting a specific legislative solution. For the sake of translating these challenges into lay terms, I have run the risk of oversimplifying complex matters of law, ethics, and political considerations. It is a complicated task to update our systems to better address domestic terrorism. Some tools we use to combat international terrorism should never be used domestically. We must be honest that our history is rich with examples of abusing authority when we fear being attacked (e.g., Japanese internment camps during World War II and McCarthyism in the 1950s) and when we fear the status quo changing and our power is waning (e.g., the FBI's tactics under J. Edgar Hoover against the civil rights movement and others). In fact, much of our national security apparatus today operates under policies developed because of the Church Committee's investigations into domestic abuses of authority.

As I said in testimony before Congress in 2020 and 2021, I think the gravity of the situation, combined with the outdated structure of our laws and bureaucracy, deserves an outside commission of experts who can wrestle with these matters and make recommendations to Congress.

These challenges make it more difficult for the security community to detect and deter domestic terrorism compared to international terrorism. But these difficulties would not pose as great a challenge if there were only a small number of extremists, or if the tactics they used were nonviolent. Instead, we see significant growth in domestic violent extremist propaganda, activities, and lethal attacks, and their coded language increasingly shows up in "mainstream" American discourse.

AN OVERVIEW OF DOMESTIC VIOLENT EXTREMISM IDEOLOGIES IN THE UNITED STATES

The government's definition of a domestic violent extremist is "an individual based and operating primarily in the United States without direction or inspiration from a foreign terrorist group or other foreign power and who seeks to further political or social goals, wholly or in part, through unlawful acts of force or violence."[12] Since 2019, the federal government has used five threat categories for domestic violent extremists:

- *Racially or ethnically motivated violent extremism* (RMVE)— including white supremacist extremism, antisemitism, Black Hebrew Israelite extremism, and Black nationalism, separatists, or identity extremism
- *Antigovernment or anti-authority violent extremism* (AGAAVE)—including the patriot movement, militia, sovereign citizens, anarchists, and antifascists (antifa)
- *Animal rights or environmental violent extremism*
- *Abortion-related violent extremism*—both anti-abortion extremism and pro-abortion extremism
- *All other domestic terrorism threats*—including potential bias related to religion, gender, or sexual orientation;[13] recent examples include
  - *Incel and misogynist extremism*
  - *Anti-LGBTQ+ extremism*
  - *Boogaloo*—an ideology that seeks to accelerate a civil war and the collapse of society

There is no shortage of critiques from scholars on these catego-ries.[14] While labels are helpful for researchers, statisticians, and polit-ical polls, they cannot possibly sketch a three-dimensional picture of an individual's unique experiences and beliefs. Many extremist groups and individuals do not neatly fit into one category. They may overlap or share common grievances, crises, and solutions. And the idea that such ideologies are solely "domestic" is misleading when in fact we are seeing increases in extremism motivated by such ideologies across the globe. They are, however, the categories that the FBI and DHS use to track attacks, plots, and deaths since 2015, and thus they are useful in helping us see recent trends. A brief description of these ideologies and the number of attacks, plots, and deaths associated with them can be found at PathBacktoPeace.org. Because of their relevance to our topic, the RMVE-related ideologies of white power and antisemitism, the AGAAVE patriot movement ideologies, and white nationalism and Christian nationalism will be covered in more depth in the next chapter.

Given the subject of this book, there are two other extremism categories to introduce that researchers and scholars use but the federal government does not, likely due to their historically low occurrence domestically within the US in recent decades.

Religious Extremism

Religious extremists are motivated by a faith-based belief system. Islam, Judaism, Christianity, Hinduism, Buddhism, and Sikhism all have groups or individuals that have co-opted religion to justify extremism.[15] Most mainstream adherents of these religions would be quick to tell you that violence is antithetical to the tenets of their faith.

Most religions, by their nature, have an element of exclusivity and superiority for their in-group. Their god or gods, religious texts, beliefs, and practices are the one true way. The fact that a religious in-group perceives their beliefs to be superior to others does not make them extreme. Most religions teach that the penalty for an out-group's "lostness" occurs after death and is handled by a god or gods or karma. It is when a religious group "imposes penalties on out-groups here in the temporal world" that it crosses the line into religious extremism.[16] For the religiously motivated terrorist "the violence is first and foremost a sacramental act or divine duty executed in direct response to some theological demand or imperative."[17] Sacred texts and clerical authorities "claiming to speak for the divine," serve as a "legitimating force justifying violence."[18]

Religiously motivated terrorism is not new. In fact, before the French Revolution, religious extremism was the primary category of terrorism carried out on a routine basis. One of the by-products of the

Age of Enlightenment and the concept of self-government through democracies and republics was a change in how humanity viewed authorities and, particularly, religion. Ideologies were developed and, for some, became a substitute for religion. Thus, in the nineteenth and twentieth centuries, religious-based extremism experienced a lengthy hiatus. The predominant forms of terrorism during this period were secular and ideologically based. This is when we see anarchist extremism enter in the late 1800s, left-wing Marxist-Leninist terrorist groups develop during the Cold War, and postcolonial ethnonationalist/separatist movements bloom in the 1960s and '70s.[19]

That changed in the 1980s, when the first religious terrorist groups formed in the aftermath of the Iranian revolution. Initially, policy-makers and security services focused their concerns about religious extremism on Islam, but by the 1990s, all major religions, as well as smaller and cultic religions, had extremist groups claiming religion as their primary motive. By 2000, nearly half of all foreign terrorist groups tracked by the State Department were religiously affiliated or motivated.[20] By 2016, the number had grown to 75 percent.[21]

This corresponds with observations about growth in religions generally during this period. Samuel Huntington noted, "in the last quarter of the twentieth century, however, the march toward secularism was reversed. An almost global resurgence of religion got underway, manifest in almost every part of the world—except western Europe. Elsewhere in countries all over the world, religious political movements gained supporters."[22] Secular ideologies born out of the Age of Enlightenment peaked in the 1960s, and by the 1980s the weakness and crises in secular ideologies are believed to be "one of the major causes of religious resurgence."[23] So perhaps it's not surprising that along with a general resurgence in religion, we also see a resurgence in religious extremism.

In the US, there are no domestic violent extremist groups that are solely categorized as religiously motivated. As we will explore in the next few chapters, though, elements of religious extremism can be found in the white power movement, militias, and a recent resurgence of nationalism—our next category.

Nationalism Extremism

Nationalism is a political ideology that goes beyond patriotic "love of country." In Paul Miller's book on Christian nationalism, he explains that nationalism is "about how we define our country, how we draw the boundary lines and say who is a part of the nation and who is not, and it is also an argument about the nature, purposes, and duties of government."[24] Nationalism asserts that a nation should be defined by a cultural identity often based on common ethnicity, language, heritage, customs, and religion. When fully embraced, nationalism believes that the government should have jurisdiction over culture. While US federal and state governments do pass certain laws that arguably establish "culture"—for example, designating holidays, naming a state bird or flower, or providing funding for the arts—our constitutional structure prevents us from being a full-fledged nationalistic country.

Nationalist sentiment and some countries' modern implementation of nationalism are not by themselves extremist. On the moderate side of the spectrum, a country may have an official state religion (e.g., the monarch of the United Kingdom is also head of the Church of England) but not mandate that its citizens be members of that religion or provide any privileges to those who are. But certain aspects of nationalism create a natural on-ramp for extremism. For example, authoritarian regimes may enforce ethnic hierarchies (e.g., India's caste system or the Nuremberg laws) and condone or encourage persecution of the out-group.[25]

Even if cultural identity isn't defined by the state, we perceive and have a sense of what our cultural identity is—what it means to be "an American." When new individuals move into our communities— or we move into theirs—we have something to contrast against, and the boundary lines can become sharper. If we're not careful, instead of celebrating differences, the contrast can start to form in-group/ out-group narratives that presume ill of the other.

Beginning in the 1870s and surging in the 1920s, the United States held strong nationalist opposition to immigrants—first Chinese, then Japanese, then Jews from Europe and Central and Southern Euro-peans; even Catholics were argued to be a threat to US sovereignty. More recently, anti-immigration forms of nationalism in the US have opposed Muslims, Hispanics, and anyone not "European." Histori-cally, major changes in demographics, including the various immi-gration waves and drops in birth rates among the majority, have led to nationalist sentiment.

The most dangerous extreme of nationalism is when it merges with arguments that a nation's religion, ethnicity, or race must be protected from being polluted by outsiders—often framed as less-than-human invaders. The intellectual roots behind today's white nationalism in the US come from Europe. In the early twentieth century, the father of French nationalism, Maurice Barrès, argued that the French people were being corrupted by immigration and it would "ruin [their] home-land."[26] Adolf Hitler's *Mein Kampf*, written in 1924, devotes a chap-ter to nation and race—examining how the Aryan race was being lost due to "race-crossing," with a particular emphasis on the dangers the Jews pose to Aryans.[27] Later in the 1970s, Frenchman Jean Raspail published the *Camp of the Saints*—a racist novel that depicts migrants from India, the Middle East, and Africa invading France and even-tually the world.[28] And it was another Frenchman, Renaud Camus, who popularized the phrase *great replacement* in 2011 to summarize the idea of "white genocide": that global elites (often a euphemism for Jews) were seeking to eliminate white people through immigration, multiculturalism, and other nefarious means.[29] This fear of losing your nation's racial "purity," cultural primacy, and geographic territory is prominent in white power ideology.

Sadly, the great replacement theory has transitioned into mainstream political discourse in recent years, often with watered-down language to make it more acceptable. For example, it is common to hear the assertion that Democrats are trying to increase immigration so that the percentage of white people in the population decreases, thereby decreasing Republicans' power.[30] Republican congressman Matt Gaetz argued on Fox News that debates about how to understand America's history are actually an "attempted cultural genocide" and that the left wants to "replace America."[31] It is a clever way to stir up fear and nationalist sentiment, framing it as a policy issue (immigration) instead of bias against certain races and nationalities.

But former president Donald Trump went further in an October 2023 interview. When asked about immigration and the southern border, he stated, "It's poisoning the blood of our country,"[32] a statement that echoes Hitler's genocidal ideology in *Mein Kampf*: "All great cultures of the past perished only because the originally creative race died off through blood-poisoning."[33]

Many people, including me, have legitimate concerns about our country's immigration laws and border security. Likewise, people's bias for the status quo means that it's quite normal for people to wish we could slow down change or to be able to return to the ways things used to be, particularly in an era of unprecedented and rapid change. Political movements exploit these concerns and experiences for their gain—often leading people to embrace a nationalist sentiment.

In the US the most prevalent forms of nationalism today are white nationalism and white Christian nationalism. Nativism and nationalism, including Christian nationalism, have featured prominently in the ideology of white power and patriot movements. And not without consequence. Great replacement theory has inspired at least four terrorist attacks in the US since 2018.[34]

RECOGNIZING FAR-RIGHT EXTREMISM AS OUR GREATEST THREAT

With these categories defined and an appreciation that such labels cannot fully capture the diverse breadth and fluidity of individuals' ideology, we can leverage data to help us understand trends. If you are interested in learning more, visit PathBacktoPeace.org to compare the number of plots/attacks and the number of deaths perpetrated by threat types, which the FBI and DHS tracked. But to really appreciate how drastic a shift we experienced in the past decade, we need a dataset covering a longer period of time.

The Center for Strategic and International Studies (CSIS), a bipartisan national security policy research organization, evaluated 1,040 attacks and plots carried out inside the US by both domestic and international terrorists between 1994 and 2021. They categorized the attacks into four violent extremist categories—ethnonationalist (also known as nationalism), religious, violent far left, and violent far right—plus an "other" category.[35] Notably, these categories are different from the terms the federal government uses, but as you can see in table 1, the government's categories are incorporated into either violent far left or violent far right. The terms *violent far left* and *violent far right* are not related to political parties or political philosophies but rather to certain fringe elements of right or left ideologies that justify, threaten, or use violence.

TABLE 1.

FAR-LEFT EXTREMISM	FAR-RIGHT EXTREMISM
RMVE: Black identity, Black separatist, Black Nationalism	RMVE: Racial or ethnic supremacy, including white power and antisemitism
AGAAVE: Anarchist extremism, antifacist extremism (antifa), antipolice or antigovernment sentiment	AGAAVE: Patriot movement, which includes tax protests, militia, sovereign citizens; antigovernment sentiment focused often on federal or state government authorities
Pro-Abortion Extremism	Anti-Abortion Extremism
Classist extremism; opposition to capitalism, imperialism, or colonialism; pro-communist or pro-socialist[36]	Violent misogyny, including incels
Environmental or animal rights extremism	Violence based on sexuality or gender

Figure 3.1 shows how the extremist categories and subcategories fall on the left-right spectrum. Note the religious category—the third line from the bottom. All the attacks CSIS coded as religious were Salafi-jihadist–inspired (while some scholars categorize anti-abortion extremist violence as Christian-inspired, CSIS places abortion-related extremist attacks in the "other" category). Given the focus we've had as a country on Salafi-jihadist terrorism (i.e., Al-Qaeda and ISIS), there have been relatively few attacks and plots. CSIS noted that the types of ethnonationalist attacks in this time period "included political divisions within Haitian and Cuban exile communities and Puerto Rican independence."[37] Attacks that could be aligned as white nationalist in nature were classified under the far-right extremist category.

Look at the top line and notice the volume of violent far-right attacks and plots in the late nineties, the previous apex of white

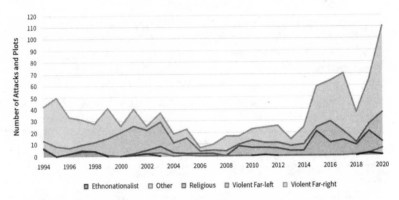

FIGURE 3.1: US TERRORIST ATTACKS AND PLOTS BY PERPETRATOR ORIENTATION, 1994–2021.

SOURCE: Data compiled by CSIS Transnational Threats Project.

supremacist and antigovernment extremist activity, and a drop off in the post-9/11 period, when we were a nation at war.

You can see an overall spike in attacks and plots beginning in 2015. Increases in the religious category correspond to ISIS and homegrown violent extremism (attacks inspired but not directed by ISIS), but the biggest increase is in violent far-right attacks. In fact, during 2015, 2017, 2019, and 2020, the number of attacks and plots from the far right exceeded the previous high-water mark of right-wing extremism—1995, the year of the Oklahoma City bombing.[38]

Discovering the Far-Right Threat

I returned to government in 2017. At the time, there were few discussions on domestic terrorism. The primary focus of the counterterrorism community was defeating ISIS.

On a weekend in August 2017 in Charlottesville, Virginia, a white power gathering euphemistically named "Unite the Right" evolved into a street brawl in which thirty-five people were injured and Heather Heyer was murdered. The scenes of khaki-clad, polo-wearing young adults marching down the street carrying tiki torches could almost be confused for a fraternity gathering before a football game but for the chants: "Jews will not replace us!" interspersed with "You will not replace us!"—the latter phrase being a reference to great replacement theory. Afterward, I asked the relatively small number of DHS analysts that occasionally worked on domestic terrorism: What does this mean? Are we seeing a reemergence of Neo-Nazis—except they look more presentable than the skinheads of the 1980s? Should we expect to see more attacks? How does this compare to the 1990s?

I didn't get answers to those questions in 2017. The federal government's data collection was weak, and our analysts had spent the previous fifteen years focused on international terrorism, leaving us with a lack of analytic subject matter expertise and significant intelligence gaps. The steep upward trajectory we can now see reflected in the data manifested in 2017 as a gut feeling that something had shifted.

In 2018, I moved from deputy chief of staff for DHS to assistant secretary for counterterrorism and threat prevention. There, I oversaw eight teams responsible for implementing security measures to address a wide swath of threats: human trafficking, terrorism, transnational criminal organizations, and hostile nation-states. My teams and I worked on many policies and programs of which I am extremely proud, but it became clear to me early on that my priority needed to be domestic violent extremism and strengthening our prevention capabilities. The attacks were beginning to add up.

In late 2018, the Tree of Life synagogue in Pittsburgh was attacked during Shabbat morning services; eleven people were killed and six were injured. "Great replacement" was a theme in the attacker's manifesto.

Only a few weeks earlier, I had been briefed on a draft study by the RAND Corporation that outlined the nuts and bolts of what we now call prevention.[39] It had been clear for years that we needed to do more

to intervene earlier in the radicalization process—well before someone
crosses a criminal threshold. But many pilot attempts had failed, and
both political parties had soured on the idea. The RAND study gave
us the evidence base to put forward a practical approach to prevention.
My team and I worked throughout 2019, lobbying the White House
and Congress to support and fund locally based prevention capabilities. We had the support of DHS secretary Kirstjen Nielsen and, later,
acting secretary Kevin McAleenan, the director of the National Counterterrorism Center, and my counterparts at DOJ and FBI. But progress in Washington is sometimes too slow.

The "great replacement" was cited in the manifesto of the attacker
that killed a staggering fifty-one people in Christchurch, New Zealand,
in March 2019. The shootings in Pittsburgh and Christchurch were
cited as the inspiration for an attack on a synagogue in Poway, California, the next month. But it wasn't until the August 2019 attack
targeting the Hispanic community at a Walmart in El Paso, Texas,
which killed twenty-two people, with yet another attacker citing the
great replacement theory, that the beltway hand-wringing finally gave
way to action. Congress increased spending on prevention dramatically. It was a good start, but since our starting number was so low, the
increase wasn't nearly enough to counter the threat.

In the years since I left government, multiple reports and public
statements by the intelligence community, FBI, and DHS have
confirmed that white supremacist extremists are the most persistent
and lethal threat.[40] Antigovernment extremist attacks increased drastically in 2020–2021, primarily from militia violent extremists and
those targeting law enforcement.

The Threat from the Far Left

Looking again at figure 3.1, we will also note the rise of far-left attacks
(the second line from the top) beginning in 2016–2017. In two separate

attacks perpetrated by lone actors in July 2016, eight police officers were killed by Black Americans motivated by racial injustice in American society. Those attacks are considered antigovernment attacks. In 2017, an individual inspired by left-wing socialist causes targeted Republican members of Congress practicing for the annual congressional baseball game; he injured five people.[41]

According to CSIS, left-wing violence nearly doubled in 2020 and 2021. In the three years prior to 2020, left-wing violence accounted for only 5–11 percent of domestic terrorist attacks and plots, but in 2020, it was 23 percent, and in 2021, it was 40 percent.[42]

However, the rise in the number of left-wing attacks and plots doesn't tell the whole story. There is a vast difference in the targets of the attacks, the preferred weaponry, and the number of fatalities when we compare right-wing and left-wing extremism. From 1994 to 2020, most left-wing attacks targeted businesses, buildings, and infrastructure, not people.[43] Most analysts agree that the threat from the extreme left is not equivalent to that of the extreme right.

Seeing the Threat Within

Over the past forty years, the gravest domestic threat has come from the far right. Multiple nonpartisan think tanks and terrorism experts have arrived at this conclusion based on the data.[44] The far right perpetrates the largest percentage of attacks and plots and is responsible for the most deaths, outside of the attacks on 9/11.[45] Even in a year with increased far-left attacks, CSIS analysis of 2021 data concluded that "violent far-right incidents were significantly more likely to be lethal, both in terms of weapon choice and number of resulting fatalities."[46]

I will confess to you it took me too long to "see" it after my initial "discovery" of it. Perhaps I was being a good government employee— we are supposed to focus on the violence, not the ideology. It was easy to assume the attackers committing violent acts were the fringe, not *really* from *my* community. It was after I left government that I had a chance to think about and process the gravity of the fact that my community and I are adjacent to the far right. Some of the grievances in terrorist manifestos are topics I've discussed with friends and fellow conservatives, framed as culture-war issues or policy matters. I'm not suggesting that sharing a grievance with an extremist makes you an extremist. But it did burden me that we need to do more on the right side of the political spectrum to make clear that our grievances are not existential crises and that violence is not the solution to our griev-ances. Many good-hearted people assume everyone believes this. But apparently not.

FOUR

EXPLOITING THE CROSS

The Unholy Alliance of Right-Wing Extremism and Christianity

America in the twenty-first century is not the first time in history that an unholy union between Christianity and extremism has wreaked havoc on the world. The horrors of the Crusades and the Inquisition are the most blatant examples of Christian religious extremism. In 1095, Pope Urban II decreed: "Whoever for devotion alone, not to gain honor or money, goes to Jerusalem to liberate the Church of God, can substitute this journey for all penance."[1] Meaning: go to war, your sins will be forgiven, and you will gain your salvation. (The idea that you can perform a work and gain salvation is heretical to an orthodox Christian understanding of salvation.)

Further twisting Scripture, soldiers who joined the fight "received a piece of cloth in the shape of a cross and sowed [*sic*] it onto their garments as a sign that they were obeying the words of Christ himself: 'If any want to become my followers, let them deny themselves and take up their cross and follow me. For those who want to save their life will lose it, and those who lose their life for my sake, and for the sake of the gospel, will save it' (Mark 8:34–35)."[2]

Historian John Dickson points out that modern readers understand that Jesus was instructing his disciples to be prepared for persecution, even unto death, as Jesus was. But medieval Christians did not have the benefit of easily accessible texts and commentary they could read themselves. The common interpretation at the time was that "able-bodied men should bear the cross of fighting against the enemies of Christ."[3] Dickson calls this "a remarkable new theology within Christianity: salvation is found in fighting the infidel."[4]

Clerics and religious texts justifying violence against "God's enemies" led to tragic results. Peter the Hermit, a monk who recruited tens of thousands of men from France and Germany to Pope Urban II's crusade, slaughtered Jewish communities along the way to Jerusalem. His justification: Jews were responsible for Jesus' death—an example of the "Deicide" conspiracy that continues in extremist group ideology today.[5]

Later, the Crusaders arrived in the Holy Lands in 1099. After a one-month siege of Jerusalem, they broke into the city. Dickson describes the scene:

> According to our records, the Crusaders whipped themselves up into such an unholy frenzy that they slaughtered men, women, and children. They threw some victims over the plaza's high walls to their deaths three storeys below. They butchered the rest with swords, daggers, fire, arrows, and spears. . . . The blood reportedly filled the great promenade between the mosque and the dome. . . . With gruesome glee and obvious exaggeration, Raymond of Aguilers, a leader of the First Crusade, wrote of this fateful day . . . : ". . . It was a just and splendid judgement of God that this place should be filled with the blood of the unbelievers, since it had suffered so long from their blasphemies."[6]

From the worst parts of the heresy trials known as the Inquisition to "Christianizing" the world through conquest, colonialism, and forced conversions, the Christian faith has been exploited for power by extremist violence throughout history.

Today's Christian extremism is motivated by more than religion. It is an outgrowth of political and cultural contexts, and its strongest anchors align with nationalism, white power, and militia extremism.

That religions are interpreted in the context of their political and cultural environment is not unique to American Christianity. In fact, many teachers of Christianity over the past two millennia have interpreted the Scriptures in the context of their "current political loyalties."[7] Yet, as we will explore in chapter 6, the codependency between nationalism and evangelicalism—particularly how American nationalism "shapes evangelical biblical interpretation"—creates the backdrop for extremism to foment.[8]

The white power and militia movements are a bit different. Though historically there were strong ties between white supremacy and some American churches and pastors—which we'll examine in the next section—white power and militia movements view Christianity as a cultural marker rather than a faith. Both movements are seeking to preserve what they believe is a core part of their culture. For the white power movement, it is a white ethnic culture. For the militia movement, it is an American culture of limited government and individual freedom. Many adherents of these movements may not even believe the tenets of the Christian faith. But they leverage the veneer of Christianity to justify their vision of society. And as studies have revealed, the perceived loss of cultural and political power by whites, men, and Christians is a threat to their vision of white ethnic culture or American culture—a threat that justifies violence.

Christian extremism is the collision of these white power and antigovernment ideologies—widely considered over the last fifty years to be fringe—with a mainstream and arguably dominant cultural force of nationalism and evangelicalism. It is this particular intermingling of worldviews that makes Christian extremism so uniquely troubling and so uniquely dangerous.

———

Finding a path back to peace requires understanding how we got to this moment. We need to pinpoint not just the symptoms (which are many) but also the cause of the illness and uproot it. And we need to understand why we did not have built-up immunity to the illness. Why our community was so vulnerable—why *we* were so vulnerable.

As with most forms of extremism, it is only a small percentage of a given group who have been radicalized. The question is why that relatively small percentage has been able to gain such a large platform to spread their messages of hate and violence and persuade others to join them.

To answer that question, we must start by acknowledging where we have failed. For too long, conservatism, Republicans, and American Christianity have tolerated extremism. We tolerated all the precursor steps: the us versus them framing, the scapegoating, and pushing out moderate in-group voices, even to the point of demonizing those who called us to follow the ways of Jesus and not politicians. Without those voices, the calls for hostile action won out—primarily of the noncriminal variety (but sometimes the criminal actions were given justification too).

We tolerated the conspiracy theories—refusing to confront the lies, gossip, and slander that ran rampant throughout our community—and thus created a cognitive opening for extremists' conspiracies to become mainstream political fodder.

We tolerated extremism by turning a blind eye to extremist groups who use Christianity and its symbols within their ideology to justify violence.

We tolerated media personalities and politicians who claimed to be Christians but trafficked in extremist language and calls for violence.

We tolerated extremism by refusing to be students of history and humbly acknowledging how often violent and atrocious acts were committed in the name of Christ. And we tolerated extremism by refusing to truly mourn these past sins.

We tolerated extremism because what we really worshipped was power, control, comfort, or significance.

We tolerated extremism because we felt like we deserved the American dream and did not want to do anything that might disrupt it.

Some did this wittingly; many more were unwitting. These last few years have shaken us awake, and we no longer have an excuse to not see it and do something about it.

For those who think toleration isn't that big a deal—after all, it's not sharing the racist meme, buying bomb materials, or pulling the trigger—Jesus' own life and teachings showed us that tolerating evil within the church is a grave risk to the church and our soul. The word *toleration* appears in His address to the seven churches in the Book of Revelation. Jesus first commends the church of Thyatira for their works of love, faith, service, and patient endurance, but then starkly warns them of their toleration of evil (Revelation 2:20).

When we tolerate evil, when we lack moral clarity, when we make excuses and traffic in "whataboutisms," we are failing in our calling to be salt and light. The good, the true, and the beautiful is not preserved. Darkness spreads further.

There were Christians throughout history and in the last few years who did stand up, who said and did the right thing. Christian abolitionists who fought against slavery, white evangelicals who joined the civil rights movement, and 20 percent who voted against a political leader who routinely used racist and misogynist language and stoked xenophobia. They condemned evil and called for repentance and a return to what is good. Sadly, they are not representative of most people who check the "Christian" box when the pollsters call. And while many of the box checkers are likely "cultural Christians" and not actively practicing an orthodox faith, it is incumbent on those who are genuine believers to speak and act with clarity.

The proximity between evangelical Christianity and right-wing extremism in our time is both a heretical aberration of the true gospel and a natural progression of the corrupt leaders and structures within evangelical Christianity that have allowed the church to be exploited and abused. Yes, some of that exploitation is at the hands of extremist movements, but there are certain pervasive elements of American evangelical Christianity that make it uniquely vulnerable to that manipulation and ultimately, to corruption.

Let's dig a bit deeper into the white power and militia movements before turning to nationalism and evangelicalism in the following chapters. These forms of extremism deserve a deeper look due to their prominence in the US, their collision with conservative and libertarian politics, and their collision with Christian culture.

WHITE SUPREMACIST EXTREMISM AND THE WHITE POWER MOVEMENT

Racial and ethnic extremism is one of the oldest forms of extremism. As we know, social identity theory suggests we think more positively toward people like us, and our treatment of people different from us is directly related to a motive to protect or enhance ourselves.[9] That we have this natural bias does not make us extremists, nor does it make us racists. However, it can help explain why this form of extremism is globally and historically pervasive.

According to the Anti-Defamation League (ADL), *white supremacy* is a term used to characterize various belief systems central to which are one or more of the following key tenets:[10]

1. Whites should have dominance over people of other backgrounds, especially where they may co-exist.
2. Whites should live by themselves in a whites-only society.
3. White people have their own "culture" that is superior to other cultures.
4. White people are genetically superior to other people.

Historically, US government programs and policies sanctioned discrimination and violence toward Native Americans, Blacks, Mexicans, Central Americans, Chinese, and Japanese, to name a few.[11] For example, from 1828 to 1838, over eighty thousand Native Americans were forcibly removed from their native lands and sent to the far west.[12] In 1882, Congress passed the Chinese Exclusion Act barring Chinese immigrants for ten years, after white workers organized violent protests against Chinese immigrants they claimed were lowering wages.[13] In 1944, the US Supreme Court upheld the executive branch's internment of US citizens of Japanese descent after the bombing of Pearl Harbor.

And sadly, such government programs and policies were often supported or enabled directly by the church. One such example that is just coming to light: hundreds of thousands of American Indian and Alaska Native children were removed from their homes—many forcibly or coercively—and placed in boarding schools operated by the US government and churches.[14] The purpose, as articulated by Richard Pratt, the founder of the first government-sponsored boarding school, was to "kill the Indian, save the man."[15] To achieve this, they used tactics now considered physically, psychologically, and spiritually abusive. Though the research is ongoing, at least several hundred children died at these boarding schools.[16] At least fourteen Christian denominations ran boarding schools, with government funding going primarily toward Catholic, Presbyterian, Episcopalian, and

Congregationalist churches. The indoctrination into the Christian faith was seen as a key part of "civilizing" Indian and Alaska Native children.

Today, white supremacist extremism in the US is primarily not state sponsored. But it took longer than it should have and was not without significant struggle and pushback from the dominant culture. Because white supremacy is a broad and complex problem, when we want to refer to the extremist, violent version of it, we use the term *white power*. *White power* refers to the "broad affiliation of Klansmen, neo-Nazis, sovereign citizens, Three Percenters, posse comitatus members, some skinheads, some militia groups, and similar groups who seek the violent overthrow of the United States through a race war."[17]

But it's impossible to examine the current white power movements without understanding their historical background and the explicit or implicit support they originally received from the government and the Christian faith.

Historic White Supremacist Extremism

While there are earlier examples of white supremacist extremism, the Civil War period is generally the moment where we see extremist ideologies become more cohesive, leveraging Christian Scripture, leaders, and symbols to justify hostile action against Blacks.

These ideologies were built to justify slavery before the Civil War and later to support the "Lost Cause" myth. They divided more than the North and the South—they divided churches. Baptists, Methodists, and Presbyterians experienced denominational splits from the 1830s through the 1850s. The Southern Baptist Convention (SBC), now the largest evangelical denomination in the United States, was founded to protect Southern slaveholders.[18] A study conducted by SBC in 2018 reported in detail that all founders of the SBC's theological seminary were slaveowners and that faculty and trustees used Scripture to justify slavery. For example, they asserted that "God himself instituted human slavery," and that Africans were appointed as slaves for all time based on their interpretation of the "curse of Ham," an incorrect and racist interpretation of Noah's blessing and curses on his sons in Genesis 9.[19]

In the aftermath of the Civil War, a traumatized country attempted to rebuild. The Lost Cause myth framed Southerners as righteous victims, defending the aggression of the North and glorifying Southern culture. The authors of the 2018 SBC study explained that by 1900 this was the standard interpretation of the Civil War for whites across the US, in both the North and the South, and it powerfully shaped identity and values and "reshaped Christianity itself into a civil religion."[20]

This helps explain how the second wave of the Ku Klux Klan (KKK) became so mainstream.

The KKK: The Original White Christian Nationalist Organization

While the KKK was founded in the aftermath of the Civil War and was responsible for numerous acts of violence, including murder and violent assaults, the first wave was short-lived. In 1869, after pressure from the federal government, they disbanded, and KKK violence from various chapters came to an end in 1871.[21] In its rebirth in 1915, we see a glimpse of patterns now leveraged by modern extremists, particularly in efforts to build support from the mainstream. A socioeconomic crisis, with large waves of immigrants fleeing World War I, strained the job market and created the opportunity to scapegoat an "other."[22] Second, the movement leveraged the latest media and technology, capitalizing on silent movies[23] and leveraging a public relations firm to publish its propaganda.[24]

And finally, the movement tapped into concern of rapid moral and structural changes. The Roaring Twenties were perceived to be an age of liberalism. Women gained the vote and threw off the constraints of the Victorian era. Flappers, short hair, short skirts, and ongoing violations

of Prohibition,[25] all seemed indicative of a moral crisis to older generations and those with conservative tendencies. The 1920s KKK argued
that they were defending an endangered nation, defending the "morality and the values of 100% Americanism" from the changes taking
place in the US,[26] and their movement was saturated in Christian
teaching and symbology. It sounds very similar to the rhetoric we hear
today from those promoting MAGA and nationalist movements.

Capitalizing on the fact that white supremacy was the predominant view of Americans by then, particularly those with political
power, the KKK had a presence across the US, not just in the South,
with membership between 1.5 and 4 million at its height in 1924. One
in thirty Americans belonged to the KKK.[27]

This iteration of the Klan framed itself as a nativist fraternal organization. They perfected their in-group to be "white, protestant, native-
born Americans."[28] Intimidation and violence were still prominent, but
their numbers allowed them to be influential in traditional politics as
well. They campaigned against Catholics and Jews running for office
and helped elect at least sixteen senators and eleven governors—both
Republicans and Democrats.[29]

It was so mainstream that in August 1925, thirty thousand
people dressed in the trademark KKK hoods with unveiled faces and
marched down Pennsylvania Avenue in Washington, DC. Hugo Black
and Harry Truman, who were running for the US Senate at the time
(they would eventually become a Supreme Court justice and a president, respectively), both joined the KKK, "as they joined other fraternal orders, because it had become a politically desirable thing to do."[30]
Their extensive political power at a local and state levels also allowed
KKK's extremist tactics—voter intimidation and violence—to go
uninvestigated for decades.

For a variety of reasons, including leadership scandals and the
Great Depression, the KKK waned in the 1930s. By the late 1940s,

they even made the attorney general's List of Subversive Organizations along with other totalitarian, fascist, and communist organizations.[31]

The final KKK growth period occurred in response to Supreme Court decisions and the civil rights movement. Anxiety over racial integration in local schools led to membership of around one hundred thousand.[32] While the 1920s movement was done with political power and arguably, in coordination with government policy, the 1950s version of the KKK opposed the government's efforts to integrate society. In this third wave we begin to see the shift in tactics that represent more modern white power movements, including more violence, going beyond lynching and beatings to include bombings and coordinated shootings.[33]

While local law enforcement turned a blind eye, the FBI became more engaged in confronting violent white supremacy, which led to declines in membership. Subsequent iterations of the KKK were never as publicly prominent.

American Nazism: White Nationalism and Fascism

American Nazism started in the 1930s, thanks in part to the German government secretly funding the German-American Bund, a group that promoted antisemitism and anticommunism while also promoting German heritage and culture. Germany's invasion of Poland in 1939 abruptly stifled the growth of Nazism within the United States.[34]

Nazi is shorthand for National Socialist (German: Nationalsozialistische), the first two words in Hitler's political party: National Socialist German Workers Party. The primary word to focus on is *national*—the ideology takes nationalism to a racial/ethnic extreme. Tapping into the post–World War I grievances of humiliation and economic struggle created an opening for messaging around "true" and "pure" Germans, which laid the groundwork for the removal of all "undesirables," including Jews, in the 1930s.

Socialist and *Workers* in the party name are a bit misleading. Whether you examine the historical party or today's Neo-Nazis, which carry labels such as National Socialist Movement or National Socialist Vanguard, they are not advocating for the far-left political ideology of socialism. This is best understood as a political ploy to garner support from the working class in the 1920s along with beliefs in conspiracies that capitalism—especially banking—is orchestrated and controlled by Jews and foreigners. Their opposition to "Jewish" capitalism does not drive them toward the opposite side of economic theory. Nazis were vehemently anti-communist and anti-Marxist. They were also against classical liberalism, which holds equal rights for all as one of its key principles.

Hitler's Nazi government was fascist—they "advocated ultranationalistic policies, usually espousing ethnocentric ideas of racial superiority, esp. anti-Semitism," and leveraged totalitarian dictatorship to achieve their vision.[35] It was a political ideology manifested as an authoritarian and totalitarian state.[36]

After World War II, several Neo-Nazi groups formed political parties, but the association with Nazism made it difficult to develop a large following in the US. Attempts at rebranding had minimal success. They borrowed from Hitler's party name, calling themselves the National Socialist White People's party and changed their slogan from "Sieg Heil" to "White Power."[37] Their focus shifted to promoting "an all-white America" and "eradicating control of American Jewry over American culture, finance, and politics."[38] While their ranks were small, their ideology persisted and influenced other movements—including Christian Identity and today's Neo-Nazis.[39]

Christian Identity

When you first hear "Christian Identity," you might think it's a fringe Christian sect with some weird doctrine, but it is an extremist group that has had outsized influence over the white power and militia movements. A Methodist minister from Southern California who was also active in the KKK helped shape Christian Identity into an antisemitic extremist ideology and made it popular in the US. Generally they believe that those who currently identify as Jews are not actually true Israelites. Rather, today's Northern Europeans—Celtic, Anglo-Saxon, Germanic, and Nordic peoples—were biologically descended from the "lost tribes" of Israel—the ten tribes that made up the Northern Kingdom of Israel and were taken into captivity during the Assyrian invasion (740–722 BC). The most extreme narrative suggests not only that Jews are not Israelites, but also that they're literally children of the devil. There are several variations to this story and no solid agreement among followers about which is the correct interpretation. The point is not in the details, but rather having a "theological" justification for hating Jews and nonwhites.

Christian Identity theology is considered by orthodox Christianity to be heresy. They take texts out of context and leverage them to promote inherently racist and antisemitic beliefs. The number of followers is relatively small, yet it has an outsized influence on the white power and patriot movements. Terrorism expert Jessica Stern asserted in the early 2000s that "Identity Christianity has become the dominant religion of the racist right in America."[40] While it is less prominent today, it's ideological threads persist among today's domestic violence extremist actors.

The Modern White Power Movement

Experts believe that there is a rhythm to violent extremism in society. Peaks of extremism typically follow war and economic downturns. Wars create trained warriors with valued skills, some of whom are burdened with reintegrating into society as changed, and often traumatized, people.[41] War also leaves veterans and the general population disillusioned about their government and society writ large.

Meanwhile, economic downturns create uncertainty and opportunities for grievances, which extremists leverage for recruitment. We see this in the repeated waves of the KKK after the Civil War, World War I, and, to a lesser extent, World War II. It also occurred for the white power and militia movements after Vietnam, the first Gulf War, and the global war on terrorism and 2008 financial crisis.

Today's white power movement came of age in the post–Vietnam War era. Christian Identity and KKK members, Neo-Nazis, and skinheads begin to intermingle and adopt elements of one another's ideologies, narratives, and symbols.[42] Unlike after the world wars, there was an added humiliation for some in returning home. Grievances were leveraged by leaders of the KKK, Christian Identity, and Neo-Nazis groups, who were veterans themselves, and used to recruit active duty personnel and military veterans to their cause.[43]

The early 1980s were a critical turning point for the white power movement. The fractured white supremacist movements came together in 1983 for the Aryan World Congress. Their gathering—which might be better thought of as summer camp for white supremacists—had been happening since 1975 at the compound of the Aryan Nations (a Christian Identity–based group) in Hayden Lake, Idaho.[44] Participants came from across the US and Canada and from Germany. Before the 1983 congress, Klan and Neo-Nazi groups primarily conducted vigilante violence, which they claimed supported the government. After the Aryan World Congress, there was what historian Kathleen Belew calls a "tectonic shift" in their goals and tactics.[45] Court testimony from witnesses present at the Congress reported that there was a private, heavily guarded meeting of white power leaders.[46] It is believed that this meeting is when the decision was made to declare war on the government.[47] A year later, one of the more violent groups, the Order, issued a written declaration of war.[48]

The tactics used after the Aryan World Congress set the stage for the next decades of activity. The first was the creation of a computer-based social network to share propaganda and coordinate action, and the second was "leaderless resistance"—leveraging cell-style terrorism tactics, which would make it difficult for the government to infiltrate and prosecute.[49] These two shifts in tactics were largely successful both in stymying law enforcement disruption and in blinding the American public to the dangers and insidious nature of the white power movement.

Forty years later, the average American views the attacks at the Pittsburgh Tree of Life Synagogue, an El Paso Walmart, and a Buffalo Tops grocery store as episodes of a "lone wolf" attacker who is mentally disturbed. But these are not isolated incidents. These attackers were following the leaderless resistance model, a model they were exposed to through internet-based spread of white power propaganda.

The Unite the Right rally in Charlottesville, Virginia, in August 2017 demonstrates the continuing prevalence of white power groups. The driver who murdered Heather Heyer by driving his car at high speed into a crowd of counterprotesters was photographed earlier in the day carrying a shield with the emblem of Vanguard America—a Neo-Nazi group.[50] A variety of white power symbols were visible at the attack on the Capitol on January 6, 2021, and court records indicate that several people who were indicted or convicted of crimes related to the January 6 attack held Nazi views.[51]

As with other ideologies, there is a spectrum of extremism. The Patriot Front, a Texas-based group launched in the aftermath of Charlottesville, primarily focuses on intimidation through hate-filled rhetoric at protests and counterprotests and by "stickering"—placing racist, antisemitic, and anti-LGBTQ+ banners, flyers, and stickers on campuses and in cities across the country.[52] While other groups, like

The Base, Atomwaffen Division, and the National Socialist Order,[53] run training camps and have plotted a variety of attacks.[54]

Today's white power movement believes an apocalyptic race war is coming—one that will set whites against Jews, Blacks, and all other minorities. Some are passive in their belief, much like militias—they want to be prepared but not necessarily to instigate it. Others, especially those who adhere to an accelerationist ideology, may believe it is their job to bring about society's collapse. They often look for natural opportunities, such as protests, civil unrest, or a January 6–type mass political violence moment, to contribute further to the breakdown of society. It will be through that war—they believe—that the US government will be overturned and a white nation can be established.

Christian symbols, culture, and beliefs continue to influence the white power movement. While there are fewer Christian Identity churches and organizations than in the 1990s, researchers identified their ideology as ever present in the online milieu of Neo-Nazi and neofascist extremists. For example, researchers found a moderator of a large channel on the social media platform Telegram, who self-described as a "White Christian Nationalist," leveraging Christian Identity propaganda in their online discussions and channels. In their examination of popular channels on Telegram, there were frequent claims that "the Holy War is imminent, alleging that, 'we are in a spiritual war fighting for our souls.'"[55] Others asserted that "the entire purpose of Christianity is the preservation of the White race."[56]

The Role of Antisemitism in Nationalism and White Power Movements

If racial and ethnic extremism is the oldest form of extremism, antisemitism is the oldest and longest running subcategory of hatred against a specific people group. Antisemitism, defined as "hostility or discrimination against Jews as a religious, ethnic or racial group," dates back millennia.[57] In the fifth century BC, the world power of the day, the Persian Empire, "sought to destroy all the Jews."[58]

As a group of people, Judaism is small. In 2020 it was estimated that Jews made up 0.2 percent of the global population.[59] The United States hosts the largest concentration of Jews outside of Israel, but that is only around 2.4 percent of the US population.[60] But they receive an outsized portion of attacks and hatred. Jews are the most frequently targeted by domestic extremists.[61] More than 60 percent of religion-based hate crimes are against the Jewish community, according to the FBI.[62] In 2022, the ADL tracked the highest number of antisemitic incidents since they began data collection in 1979.[63]

Antisemitism is pervasive across many forms of extremism. The white power movement, antigovernment extremists, and even the more recent QAnon and vaccine conspiracies leverage antisemitic myths in their ideologies. And there are many myths: Jews are disloyal, greedy, or have too much power; they are guilty of blood libel; the Holocaust never happened. These myths are recycled across time and cultures to undergird antisemitism.[64] You likely have heard them, even if you didn't recognize them as antisemitic. For example, common coded language used today to criticize "globalists" and "the elites" are euphemisms for Jews and allude to the myth that they are powerful and controlling the course of events from behind the scenes.[65]

In modern times, nothing has influenced antisemitic conspiracies more than the fake and plagiarized publication *The Protocols of the Elders of Zion* in the early years of the twentieth century. Originally published in Russia, it purports to be notes from a meeting that never happened, laying out the Jewish plan for global domination. It may have been used to set the stage for violent actions against Jews, called pogroms, in the Russian Empire from 1903 to 1906.

By the 1920s, *The Protocols* had been translated and spread throughout Europe, Britain, the United States, and the Arab world. It was quoted extensively in Nazi propaganda and referred to in Hitler's *Mein Kampf.*

In the United States, Henry Ford bought the *Dearborn Independent* newspaper out of paranoia that Jews would take control of the media.[66] He published a weekly series based on *The Protocols* called "The International Jew: The World's Problem" on the paper's front page. The series was later turned into a four-volume book. Ford was so prominent in antisemitic propaganda that he was mentioned by Hitler in *Mein Kampf* and received the Grand Cross of the Order of the German Eagle by Nazi Germany in 1938 for his "humanitarian ideals."[67] Ford and his book were named in the Nuremberg trials as a radicalizing factor for one of the Nazis being tried.[68]

In the white power movement, the myth of Jews seeking global control is framed as the Zionist Occupational Government (ZOG)—a particularly anti-internationalist, antisemitic, and apocalyptic set of beliefs that developed during the Cold War. Historian Kathleen Belew explains that "white power activists believed that the Jewish-led ZOG controlled the United Nations, the U.S. federal government, and the banks, and that ZOG used people of color, communists, liberals, journalists, academics, and other enemies of the movement as puppets in a conspiracy to eradicate the white race and its economic, social, and cultural accomplishments."[69] In the 1990s, the phrase *New World Order* replaced the term *ZOG* to appeal to a broader audience that was concerned with "malevolent internationalist forces, including the United Nations, global finance, nations, and technology" conspiring to take over the world.[70] For white supremacist extremists, the New World Order "included both the old idea of ZOG and a broader international conspiracy of elites (sometimes Jewish) that intended to enslave the US population."[71]

ANTIGOVERNMENT EXTREMISM: THE PATRIOT MOVEMENT AND MILITIAS

It is a distinctly American ethos that focuses on the individual and their liberty. Thus, cultural context is important when we examine antigovernment extremism. Arguments for limited government or governmental power being held closest to the people (at a local or state level) are distinctly conservative and embedded in our country's founding. Conservatives generally believe that less government is better and distrust the federal government to do things well. On this latter point, it's not just conservatives—trust in Congress, the Supreme Court, and the presidency has been trending downward over the last decade and is currently at an all-time low.[72]

This is why the antigovernment extremist movement may be one of the more dangerous in our present moment. With such strong distrust and frustration with government, it could be easy to recruit people into extremism. But we also need to be *very* clear that being frustrated with your government, holding a traditional conservative view of the Tenth Amendment, and believing that the federal government has exceeded the powers given to it under the Constitution are not in and of themselves extremism.

Tax Protests Lead to Vigilante Justice and Militias

Collectively known as the patriot movement, tax protesters, sovereign citizens, and militia members believe that the government has been subverted by conspirators and replaced with an illegitimate government. Their goal is largely to "restore" what they perceive to be legitimate government.

The oldest element of the patriot movement was a protest of the new federal income tax in the 1930s. By the 1950s and '60s, when it became clear that attempts to repeal the Sixteenth Amendment would not pass, other strategies beyond protests were needed. Initially, it took the form of the John Birch society, tax evasion, and fraud. But the movement moved into extremism when William Potter Gale founded Posse Comitatus in the late 1960s and "urged the use of vigilante justice to protect the citizenry from an unlawful, tyrannical government."[73] Gale's manifesto advocated for organizing local "Posse" groups, the county sheriff as being the only legal law enforcement officer, and establishing "common-law courts."[74] Gale brought to the tax movement his antisemitic Christian Identity ideology, which weaved in beliefs about the ZOG conspiracy, and concluded that this made the US government illegitimate and argued that the highest form of American authority was at the county level.[75] Their actions include threatening law enforcement agencies, attempting citizens' arrests of legitimate law enforcement personnel, assaulting an IRS agent, and killing two US Marshals.

The Militia Movement

The militia movement was born out of the tax protest and white power movements in the 1980s with significant crossover among them. Both the white power and the patriot movements were heavily influenced by the antisemitic Christian Identity beliefs. Christian Identity believes Jesus will return only after a period of tribulation (known as a post-millennial eschatology). Perceiving that their country and the white race are in crisis led some to believe that the end was near. These apoc-alyptic beliefs drove some to the conclusion that they needed to be prepared to defend and provide for their family whenever that "bad day" appears. Through membership in a militia, followers could conduct paramilitary training and practice survivalism—growing their own food, making their own soap and clothing, and stockpiling food, water, medicine, and weapons.[76]

It's best to think of militia members as being on a spectrum. At the benign end of the spectrum are people and groups who largely view what they do as "grown-up Boy Scouts"[77]—a way to have community with likeminded individuals who glorify an imaginary past and train together to be prepared, "just in case." On the other end of the spectrum are people fueled by anger and hatred toward a government that they believe has exceeded its constitutional limits and been taken over by globalists and the New World Order; they are waiting for (or perhaps are willing to start) a civil war where they can burn it all down and start fresh.[78] Somewhere in the middle, the bulk of militia members may engage in some criminal activity but generally view their involvement in the militia as a defensive activity, not offensive. This spectrum is by design; it allows for easy recruiting, and once people are pulled in, propaganda and conspiracy theories will further radicalize some—perhaps even to plot murders and terrorist attacks, or at least embrace the white power movement. Others will remain in the benign part of the militia.

Unauthorized, private militia activity—including activities reserved for state militia and law enforcement activities—is outlawed in all fifty states.[79] The term *militia*, as used in the Second Amendment and in various state laws, "refer to able-bodied residents between certain ages who may be called forth *by the government* when there is a specific need; but private individuals have no legal authority to activate themselves for militia duty outside the authority of the federal or state government."[80] The US Supreme Court in 1886 and more recently in 2008, in a decision written by conservative justice Clarence Thomas, explained that the Second Amendment does not prevent the states from prohibiting "private paramilitary organizations."[81]

So even benign membership in a militia—not seeking proactive violence, but just trying to "be prepared" and protect their family and neighborhood—is illegal if they engage in law enforcement activities without being called upon by the government.

Through the militia movement, the war that the white power movement declared on the government at the 1983 Aryan Nations

World Congress found a way to go public in a more palatable, less obviously racist way. The militia movements leveraged many of the same symbols and logic from the white power movement but shifted its language to broaden the appeal. Instead of railing against a Zionist Occupational Government, they referred to a New World Order.[82]

The movement was extremely active in the mid-1990s, gaining momentum from multiple real-world events: the end of the Cold War and the loss of a unifying external enemy, the signing of North American Free Trade Agreement (which was blamed for job losses and framed by some conservatives like Pat Buchanan as an attack on "national sovereignty" and a step toward one world government), and a successful push of gun control reform.[83] But the sieges in 1992 at Ruby Ridge in Idaho and in 1993 in Waco, Texas—the federal government admitted the former was handled inappropriately;[84] the latter is enshrouded in a mythologized narrative of twisted facts[85]—seemed to provide the proof that the feds really were coming for you and your guns. The call to defend your family, your neighbors, and your community became an easy sell.

After a period of relative quiet in the post-9/11 period, militias began to grow in popularity again in 2008. The Great Recession, combined with fatigue and disillusionment over the War in Iraq, likely explains some of the increase. Further, the election of our first Black president was used to fuel conspiracies that the president was planning on confiscating guns and was part of the New World Order—conspiracy theories that were often broadcast on mainstream conservative platforms. Finally, the rapid growth of social media allowed people to spread ideas and conspiracies anonymously and widely.

Usually, militias did not support mainstream Republicans. But that changed with Trump. They saw an outsider willing to disrupt the system, talking about things they cared about: shutting down immigration and banning Muslims. With the embrace of Trump, militias became more accepted in mainstream conservative culture. They even provided "security" at Trump rallies and for other Republican candidates.

This current militia cadre attracts a noticeably younger group compared to their 1990s counterparts. White power adherents make up a relatively small proportion of the ranks of the militia now.[86] There are also more people of color involved than in the 1990s, but it remains predominantly male, and there are undercurrents of misogyny and white supremacy in some chapters.[87] Amy Cooter, a sociologist who studies militias, explains that "Whiteness and masculinity are central features, though not often clearly obvious ones—in the rearview nationalism of militia members' values."[88]

The most prominent militia activity in recent years was their involvement in the attack on the Capitol on January 6, 2021. Militia members from the more organized Oath Keepers and Three Percenters to the more street-gang-style Proud Boys, among others, have been indicted and several have been convicted for seditious conspiracy—a charge that means two or more people conspired to overthrow the US government.

After January 6, militias have lost membership, "gone dark" in their communications, and instructed local chapters to focus on local activities and issues. Not unlike in the late 1990s, law enforcement investigations have caused many to rethink their involvement in militias. However, many have continued and channel their energy into quasi-legitimate political protests around anti-COVID measures, Stop the Steal, QAnon, and protesting drag queen story hours and transgender rights.[89]

The increase in rhetoric from politicians suggesting that the federal government is being weaponized against Republicans or against the American people continues to drive antigovernment sentiment.[90] When politicians say, "If it can happen to me, it can happen to anybody" and the implication is that what has happened to them is unjust, we should expect that the quiet will not last.

I recently had a conversation with a colleague who works with people attempting to exit extremist groups, primarily those involved in the white power movement. How and why people disengage and deradicalize is still something the prevention community is trying to better understand. She pointed out that while the go-to answer is frequently "empathy" or "love"—which are true and powerful—what is often forgotten is the role accountability plays. Usually something catches up with them. It causes them to reevaluate whether a life of hate and violence is really what they want. Sometimes they lose a job because an employer discovers racist tattoos, or a loved one sets a boundary and they can no longer be in a relationship with them while they participate in the movement. They are held to account for their behavior, and this leads to the openness to consider changing.

For Christians, this is core to our beliefs. We believe we will be held to account by the Lord someday. It is in recognizing our sin and our inability to ever atone for it that we can then see and receive God's great love for us. It is seeing both God's truth and his love that brings heart change.

Christianity is the backdrop against which many domestic violent extremist movements in the United States and Europe build their ideologies and leverage grievances. Making ourselves aware of these ideologies and how they pervert Christianity and leverage conspiracy theories and the political system is an important way we can help stop the spread of extremism. We also must examine and acknowledge the ways we wittingly and unwittingly tolerated extremism in our midst.

Accountability is a necessary step to enable our community to heal.

FIVE

TODAY'S CHRISTIAN EXTREMISM
Trends Driving Radicalization

*Radicalization appears to be a process in which individuals are destabilized
by various environmental factors, exposed to extremist ideology, and
subsequently reinforced by members of their community.*
—MASON YOUNGBLOOD[1]

One way researchers examine vulnerability is through categories of push and pull factors.[2] Pull factors are personal or individual; they can be internal (i.e., psychological) but also include the peer group, associates, or networks that may expose them to extremism. Push factors are external to the individual (endemic or environmental) and often impact a community or whole society, such as societal crises (e.g., 9/11, COVID-19, war, the 2008 financial crisis) or other political or socioeconomic events. Push and pull factors interact with each other. An external event can lead to internal changes (e.g., humiliation, loneliness, or psychological distress). While the impact of push and pull factors varies across individuals and there is no one path to radicalization, we can observe that certain societal or community trends may have greater destabilizing impacts on a large number of people. And when your community amplifies and reinforces grievances and calls for hostile action, the result, research has shown, is a contagion of extremism.[3]

What destabilized our communities? How did our communities get exposed to extremist ideology? And what were the reinforcement mechanisms that created the contagion effect that was clearly on display on January 6, 2021, and continues today?

CULTURAL VULNERABILITIES

The American experiment was premised on the idea that civil society (i.e., nongovernmental associations) would come together to work on common interests and shared goals in the spaces unmet by government and industry.

I spent the better part of my career working on public policy issues at the federal government level. Whether the topic was homelessness, poverty, education, or preventing violence, I was acutely aware of how complex such challenges were. Yes, there are systemic factors that aggravate the situation—some of which government is well positioned to address. But behind each statistic is a human being with not only practical needs but also emotional, spiritual, and psychosocial needs to be met. Government does not do "heart" issues well. I love that we are a country that governs by the rule of law, but when people are hurting they need grace and encouragement, not bureaucracy and doing things by the book.

Alexis de Tocqueville marveled at the young United States' propensity toward forming associations to solve problems. He noted that such associations form bonds within the community and help individuals break out of the human tendency to be self-focused: "The only way opinions and ideas can be renewed, hearts enlarged, and human minds developed is through the reciprocal influence of men upon each other."[4]

Somewhere along the way, this feature of the American experiment changed. Now the vast majority of Americans glorify the rugged individualism myth, increasingly "bowl alone" (or, more recently, "scroll alone") and reject the idea of interdependency. Lacking an in-person community of recognition that helps form us and helps us flourish, we become lonely and unmoored. I believe this failure to put our hands to work for bettering our communities and our country has created voids that tribalism, politics, polarization, and extremism fill.

Fraying Bonds and Lost Connections

Two years before COVID-19 forced us to retreat to our homes, journalist Johann Hari released a book exploring the causes of depression and anxiety. This was a personal journey for him—he had been diagnosed with depression and anxiety in the late 1990s. Hari's book chronicles a three-year investigation into nine scientifically backed causes of depression and anxiety. He finds a common theme throughout the six of the nine, which inspires his book title: *Lost Connections.*

Disconnection from people, disconnection from meaningful work, disconnection from meaningful values, disconnection from the natural world, disconnection from status and respect, and disconnection from a hopeful and secure future have been scientifically linked to increases in depression and anxiety.

In 2018, when Hari released his book, the medical community was suggesting that depression and anxiety were nearing epidemic levels—particularly for youth and young adults. Between 2008 and 2018, eighteen-to-twenty-five-year-olds had experienced a 183 percent increase in anxiety.[5] We do not have too many research studies yet about the impact of the COVID-19 pandemic on mental health, but we do have surveys. In May 2023, Gallup released a report showing that between 2017 and 2023 there was an 8.4 percent increase of adults who at some point in their life had experienced depression; 18 percent of adults said they were currently depressed.[6]

COVID-19 was the great accelerator, creating tremendous pressure that our already fraying and disconnected society could not withstand. It broke us. And it broke our relationships, families, communities, and churches. As we take stock of the impact and try to rebuild, we would be foolish to assume it was *just* a pandemic. As Hari and many others have exposed, our disconnection from people, values, meaningful work, and so on is not good for the human soul. It leaves us depleted, anxious, and depressed.

As a conservative, I'm predisposed to laud the role of the individual and minimize the need for help from the government or others. I feel guilty when I cannot do it all on my own and need to ask for help. Likewise, coming out of the American evangelical culture, I was taught to view Christianity through an individualistic lens, as primarily a relationship between me and Jesus. Yes, being in a small group was important for accountability, but that was about it—so I thought. These views miss the depth, richness, and joy of community, but worse, they're making us sick.

In May 2023, US surgeon general Vivek H. Murthy released an advisory titled "Our Epidemic of Loneliness and Isolation."[7] Surgeon general advisories are designed to make the public aware of new evidence about potential harm to the public's health. The most famous was the 1964 report that informed the public that smoking causes lung cancer. By issuing this advisory, he effectively declared loneliness a public health crisis.

And the evidence backs this up. A lack of connection to people not only causes anxiety and depression, but it is also associated with a "greater risk of cardiovascular disease, dementia, stroke, . . . and premature death. The mortality impact of being socially disconnected is similar to that caused by smoking up to 15 cigarettes a day, and even greater than that associated with obesity and physical inactivity."[8]

Here are some of the findings from the advisory:[9]

- Americans have become less socially connected over a period of several decades.

- From 2003 to 2020 the average time spent alone increased by twenty-four hours per month.
- For the same time period, the amount of time respondents engaged with friends socially in person decreased twenty hours per month.
- For people age fifteen to twenty-four, "time spent in-person with friends has reduced by nearly 70 percent over almost two decades."[10]
- The number of close friendships has also declined over several decades. In 2021, 49 percent of Americans in 2021 reported having three or fewer close friends. In 1990, only about a quarter (27 percent) reported having three or fewer friends.
- In 2018, only 16 percent of Americans reported they felt very attached to their local community.

Relatedly, beginning in the early 1990s, we began to see a steady uptick in people religiously affiliating as "Nones"—that is, they have no religion. The Nones went from 6.3 percent of the US population in 1991 to 23.7 percent by 2018.[11] To put this into context, by 2018 the number of Nones was about the same as the number of Roman Catholics (23.1 percent) and evangelical Protestants (21.5 percent) in the US.[12] A more recent study suggests we are amid the "largest and fastest religious shift" in our country's history.[13] Sixteen percent of adults have dechurched in the last twenty-five years. That means almost 40 million people used to go to church but no longer do. The authors of that study, Jim Davis and Michael Graham, are pastors, and they make a compelling argument in their book, *The Great Dechurching*, that in addition to the concern for the souls of those that have left, this trend will hurt our communities, culture, and country.

The surgeon general's advisory asserts the same concern:

*In 2020, only 47% of Americans said they belonged to a church, synagogue, or mosque. This is down from 70% in 1999 and represents a dip below 50% for the first time in the history of the survey question. **Religious or faith-based groups can be a source for regular social contact, serve as a community of support, provide meaning and purpose, create a sense of belonging around shared values and beliefs, and are associated with reduced risk-taking behaviors. As a consequence of this decline in participation, individuals' health may be undermined in different ways.**[14] (Emphasis added)*

One of our cultural vulnerabilities is our disconnection from people and things that give us meaning. And I believe that our lack of healthy communities creates openings for some to be more susceptible to extremist ideology.

Society-Wide Upheaval: Great Uncertainty

We are living amid an epoch shift. Mark Sayers calls it "the gray zone"; others call it a liminal age.[15] The idea is that we have left behind the world we knew, but we have not yet entered the world to be. "[Gray zones] contain the influence of both the passing and forming era—it makes gray zones confusing and contradictory."[16] The gray zone intensifies the past eras' traits, almost as if segments of society are clinging to the past and hoping they can prevent the inevitable change. But it also contains elements of what is to be in the coming era.

Samuel Huntington, the late political scientist, calls it a moral convulsion and observed they happen about every sixty years in the United States. David Brooks, writing about this phenomenon in 2020, observed that across America's four previous convulsive moments, there are shared features: "People feel disgusted by the state of society. Trust in institutions plummets. Moral indignation is widespread.

Contempt for established power is intense. A highly moralistic generation appears on the scene. It uses new modes of communication to seize control of the national conversation. Groups formerly outside of power rise up and take over the system. These are moments of agitation and excitement, frenzy and accusation, mobilization and passion."[17]

Brooks parallels Sayers's observations—as the convulsions recede, "new norms and beliefs, new values for what is admired and disdained arise. Power within institutions gets renegotiated."[18]

This is where we find ourselves: in the middle of changing eras, a moral convulsion.

Part of this changing of eras is a result of drastic technological advancements—leading to changes in how we communicate, live, and work. A 2017 McKinsey study suggests that "50 percent of the activities that people are paid to do in the global economy have the potential to be automated by adopting *currently demonstrated* technology."[19] The study was conducted before ChatGPT broke into mainstream conversations and disrupted markets and the internet.

In his book *Them: Why We Hate Each Other and How We Can Heal*, former senator Ben Sasse points to this upheaval as a driver behind our great uncertainty. Sasse makes a good case that automating certain jobs does not mean that jobs vanish. "*Most jobs* will begin to look *significantly* different. It is more accurate, then, to speak not simply of jobs lost and gained, but also—and primarily—of *jobs remade*."[20] But he also acknowledges that as a society, we are not doing a good job of preparing people for that disruption, and the disruption is likely to have a greater impact on older workers.[21] And social psychologists fear it will "usher in a staggering level of cultural disruption."[22]

These observations from Brooks and Sasse were made about life before COVID-19, before the 2020 summer of protests, before January 6, 2021. It reflected the upheavals and disruptions of globalization, 9/11, the 2008 financial crisis, and social media. Brooks considers the

events of 2020 an acceleration of the moral convulsion trend. "They
flooded the ravines that had opened up in American society and
exposed every flaw."[23]

For all of its blessings, the "American way of life" offers a false
sense of control. The past decade has exposed that lie for millions of
us. Job losses, losing trust in our institutions, a growing isolation and
loneliness, the inability to get ahead, or just a nagging sense that life
isn't what we dreamed it would be—all of this has shaken our world.

It is human nature to seek answers and look for something to
put our hope in during this season of great upheaval. Too many of us
found answers in politics and the belief that we could fix things if we
regained control or if we could exact our revenge.

Society-Wide Attack: Foreign Enemies Sow Discord

Beginning in the mid 2010s, Russia began laying the groundwork to
inauthentically influence Americans through social media.[24] By 2020,
Iran joined the effort, as did Lebanese Hizballah, Cuba, and Venezu-
ela.[25] According to publicly available, unclassified intelligence assessments and congressional testimony, Russia's aim is to "sow discord
in the U.S. political system through what it termed 'information
warfare'"[26] so that there is not enough political will to counter their
strategic aims. In 2016, Russia also attempted to gain access to election
infrastructure but was unsuccessful.[27]

This is not a new tactic for Russia. Soviet-era "active measures"
called for using the "force of politics" rather than the "politics of force"
to erode American democracy from within.[28] What is new is the methods Russia uses to achieve these objectives.

A leaked internal Facebook report found that "Facebook's most
popular pages for Christian and Black American content were being
run by Eastern European troll farms . . . professionalized groups that
work in a coordinated fashion to post provocative content, often

propaganda, to social networks."[29] The Eastern European troll farms referenced in Facebook's internal report are most likely the primary "proxies linked to Russian intelligence," which the US intelligence assessment stated pushed influence narratives. In February 2023, the head of Wagner, the Russian private military company that has been designated by the US government as a significant transnational criminal organization and sanctioned accordingly,[30] admitted to founding the Internet Research Agency (IRA), the most infamous troll farm known to have interfered in American elections.[31]

Troll farms coordinated content that reached 140 million Americans monthly—that's nearly half of all Americans. Not because 140 million Americans were following pages curated by troll farms, but because "Facebook's content-recommendation system had pushed it into their news feeds."[32] For comparison, according to *MIT Technology Review*, which obtained the internal Facebook report, the Facebook page with a US audience with the second largest reach was Walmart at 100 million. The troll farms' pages combined to form the largest pages for Christian Americans (twenty times larger than the next largest) and African Americans (three times larger). They also created the second largest page for Native Americans and the fifth largest women's page.[33]

The topic of disinformation has become politicized in recent years, particularly around concerns about the government arbitrating truth. But even more than concerns that the opposing political party is obsessed with disinformation, we should be concerned that foreign nations attempted to interfere in and influence our elections. An authoritarian dictator whose intentions to invade sovereign countries to rebuild the Russian Empire have been revealed and whose evil is on full display—abducting thousands of children,[34] beheading soldiers,[35] and other documented war crimes[36]—started orchestrating active measures ten years ago to sow social discord and weaken our society.

The Big Sort and the Law of Group Polarization Set the Stage for Extremism

In 2004, a journalist discovered that Americans had spent the three previous decades sorting themselves into red or blue areas, down to the neighborhood.[37] The Big Sort, as it became known, was enabled by the comparatively great wealth of Americans, which allowed freedom humans previously could not enjoy—the ability to choose where you lived and to make that choice based on preferences about your lifestyle and beliefs. By 2016, it was clear our geographic sorting had deepened.[38] The sort was not originally tied to anything political; it was a self-segregation "by lifestyle."[39] But time will tell whether, over the course of the pandemic, the sort became more drastic and explicitly based on politics. I wonder what the data will show us in a few years.

It turns out that not only does living in homogenous communities promote groupthink, according to the law of group polarization, but we also become more extreme in our views when we gather with like-minded people.[40] Cass Sunstein, a law professor who published a paper on this phenomenon, concluded that "this general phenomenon—group polarization—has many implications for economic, political, and legal institutions."[41] Among other societal ills, Sunstein directly connects polarization to extremism and radicalization. David French, in his book *Divided We Fall*, considers this the best explanation for why the Big Sort has had "such a practical, malignant effect on American politics."[42]

The Big Sort also leads to a stunning misunderstanding of the "other." More in Common, a nonprofit that seeks to understand the forces driving us apart, find common ground, and bring people together to tackle shared challenges, has been studying our polarization for most of the last decade.[43] They identified a sizable "perception gap" in what we think the other side thinks. For example, when you ask whether they agree or disagree with the statement "Most police are bad people," 85 percent of Democrats disagreed. But Republicans imagined that only 48 percent of Democrats would disagree—a perception gap of 37 percentage points.[44] Democrats assumed only 51 percent of Republicans would admit racism is still a problem, but in fact 79 percent of Republicans agreed with that statement; a perception gap of 28 percentage points.[45]

The Big Sort has removed people who have different lifestyles and experiences from our lives, and we are left with caricatures of the other side. Notably, the same study found that people who watched more news had a wider perception gap (they assumed worse of the other), unless they were watching news on one of the broadcast television networks (ABC, CBS, NBC).[46]

It is not that the other side doesn't hold some "extreme" views; it's that we assume the majority of the other side hold those views. And it turns out that it is only a minority on the left and a minority on the right who hold those extreme views. The minority extremes tend to be loud and leave an outsized impression. More in common calls the middle ground the exhausted majority.[47]

The perception gap is dangerous. It allows extremists and those incentivized to fuel outrage to sow false narratives about the threat the "other" poses.

The Identity Trap, Cancel Culture, and Chilling Speech

In 2017, antifa and others protested a planned speech by alt-right personality Milo Yiannopoulos that was to be given on campus at the University of California–Berkeley.[48] The resulting melee resulted in $500,000 in property damage on campus and in the town and multiple injuries.[49] Violent protests on a college campus are worthy of condemnation but also not without historic precedence. It's the response of the university—or rather, their lack of response—that represents a concerning trend. Greg Lukianoff and Jonathan Haidt, examining the 2017 event in their book, *The Coddling of the American Mind*, asserted that "the failure of UC Berkeley to openly discipline any of the students who engaged in violence or vandalism . . . taught the protestors an important lesson: Violence works. Unsurprisingly, the Antifa activists built on their success by threatening more violence in response to campus invitations to conservatives David Horowitz, Ann Coulter, and Ben Shapiro."[50]

A month after the Berkeley riots, Charles Murray, a scholar at the American Enterprise Institute, a conservative public policy think tank, was giving a speech at Middlebury College when he was interrupted by protests. One of the professors hosting Murray was shoved and pushed so hard she suffered whiplash and a concussion.[51] Her injuries required six months of physical therapy.[52]

One of the arguments made by these violent protesters was that the words of the slated speakers had caused harm to them. Their violence was justified "as a legitimate form of 'self-defense' to prevent speech that they said was violent."[53]

Another trend on the rise in the mid-2010s was "cancel culture." Lukianoff, in his book *The Canceling of the American Mind*, defines cancel culture as "campaigns to get people fired, disinvited, deplatformed, or otherwise punished for speech that is—or would be—protected by First Amendment standards and the climate of fear and conformity that has resulted from this uptick."[54] He provides a survey of the effects it has had on society in the last ten years—from "upended lives, ruined careers, and undermined companies" to destroying trust in institutions and deepening our polarization.[55] He argues that cancel culture is not "moral panic" but a "dysfunctional way members of our society have learned to argue and battle for power, status, and dominance."[56]

In his book *Live Not by Lies* Rod Dreher explores the cancel culture phenomenon as a "soft totalitarianism" that has taken over the United States, "masquerad[ing] as kindness, demonizing dissenters and disfavored demographic groups to protect the feelings of 'victims' in order to bring about 'social justice.'"[57] He sees many of the same concerning trends we've examined in this book—"widespread loneliness, the rise of ideology, widespread loss of faith institutions"—and warns that they are making us vulnerable to "militantly illiberal ideology."[58] Specifically, he asserts the "intellectual, cultural, academic, and corporate elites are under the sway of a left-wing political cult built around social justice" and that they are "dividing humanity between the Good and the Evil."[59] You either agree with the elite's schema of social justice and are "Good" or you will be demonized, excluded, and persecuted, Dreher asserted.

Dreher is not alone in his observations of drastic culture change in academia and corporate America. Lukianoff and Haidt, a liberal Democrat and centrist Democrat, respectively, devote a significant portion of their critique in *The Coddling of the American Mind* to academia and make a case that creating "safe spaces" from microaggressions and triggering and practicing "common-enemy identity politics" is weakening the next generation and our country.

Yascha Mounk, a center-left political scientist and professor at Johns Hopkins University who has been studying the rise of populism and the crisis of liberal democracy, offers the clearest explanation I've seen so far of the observations Dreher, Lukianoff, and Haidt were making in the mid 2010s, in his book *The Identity Trap*. What started as an effort to appreciate the cultures and experiences of minority groups has become an obsession with group identity. Some call it identity politics, and others call it woke; Mounk suggests we call it "identity synthesis"—an ideology built from postmodernism, postcolonialism, and critical race theory intellectual traditions that is "centrally concerned with the role that identity categories like race, gender, and sexual orientation play in the world."[60] He shows how it started taking over college campuses in 2010 and how by 2020 a "niche academic theory" had reshaped the landscape of business, media, and government—even our local schools.[61]

To the casual observer, the resulting concepts, policies, and norms of identity synthesis ideology may not seem to be related. Identity synthesis leads to assertions that speech is a form of violence and therefore preventative violence is justified as a form of self-defense, as the students at the "Milo riot" in 2017 claimed. It says that you can never truly understand someone from a different racial or ethnic background, and thus the one who has more privilege should "defer to the factual assessments and political demands of those who are comparatively marginalized."[62] It claims that you cannot appreciate someone else's cultural food or celebrations, for that is cultural appropriation. And there is even a movement to reinstitute forms of segregation, which Mounk calls "progressive separatism." There are schools that have "introduced race-segregated affinity groups, some as early as kindergarten."[63]

Mounk's thesis is that identity synthesis is a trap and one which will worsen society:

> *The lure that attracts so many people to the identity synthesis is a desire to overcome persistent injustices and create a society of genuine equals. But the likely outcome of implementing this ideology is a society in which an unremitting emphasis on our differences pits rigid identity groups against each other in a zero-sum battle for resources and recognition.*[64]

This trend that started on college campuses and has spread to businesses, neighborhoods, and schools is partially responsible for our deepening polarization and "us versus them" mentality. The speed at which these changes occurred is certainly part of what many of the right feel is so disorienting. It was not infrequent to hear of a well-intentioned person attempting to use what they thought was the correct term or framing about a matter only to be viciously derided by a work colleague or perhaps on social media for their "backward" thinking. It left many feeling like it's best not to say anything at all for fear of getting wrong. Others have the opposite reaction to the bullying from the left—they instead double down and embrace the labels.

Mounk, Haidt, and Lukianoff are calling out the ways in which the left is contributing to our societal challenges and offering healthier paths forward. Some intellectuals and commentators on the right applaud and draw attention to these efforts. But many more view the antics of the left as useful fodder for stirring up anger and outrage. They obsess over the flaws of progressives and lose themselves and the principles of their argument in the process.

We see this even among the intellectuals of the right. Dreher's book, for example, which spent weeks on national bestseller lists, employs catastrophizing rhetoric that belies the foundational elements of extremism. He closes his descriptions in fear, telling his readers, whom he calls Christian dissidents, that they need to open their eyes and mount a resistance before they lose control. While I'm not suggesting that he is advocating for violence, in the broad uptake of his book, we see the potential mainstreaming of a moral justification for extremism.

NO LONGER THE MAINSTREAM: THE CHRISTIAN AND CONSERVATIVE COMMUNITIES' RESPONSE TO RAPID SOCIAL CHANGE

Perhaps the most relevant aspect of the epoch shift described above is the waning of a dominant Christian culture and the waning of dominant white culture. These rapid changes are disorienting and, sadly, create space for narratives that stoke grievances. Some interpret these changes as a loss of power, control, and significance. They see the cancel culture phenomenon as rejection and disrespect of their values and beliefs. Certain incidents—especially when amplified by the media—can feel like a group humiliation. These are all high-risk factors for radicalization.

Walking on Eggshells

A direct result of the cancel culture and identity trap trend is a growing sense that its best to just hold your tongue. A *New York Times / Siena College* poll taken in 2022 found that more than 55 percent of Americans did not share their views out of concern for "retaliation or harsh criticism."[65] The same poll indicated that people felt less free today than ten years ago to speak on politics and race. The director of the research institute that conducted the survey stated that "rather than being a marketplace of ideas . . . many of us walk on eggshells."

A Cato Institute survey conducted in 2020 showed an even worse result—62 percent indicated they self-censor.[66] But more critically, what we see in the Cato survey is that those with moderate, conservative, or strong conservative views self-censor at much greater rates than liberals and strong liberals: 77 percent of conservatives and strong conservatives (the rate was the same for both) believe others will find them offensive, so they self-censor. Only 42 percent of strong liberals and 52 percent of liberals shared the same fear.

The 77 percent do not feel comfortable sharing their opinions at work, at a community event, or in the bleachers while watching Little League or soccer games. While privately, among close friends or confidants, they may express their true feelings or positions, they generally keep quiet in public settings. They genuinely fear social marginalization and, worse, retaliation. Forty percent of Republicans with a college degree and 60 percent with a post-graduate degree worry that their political views could harm them at work.[67] Only 23–25 percent of Democrats worry about this across identical educational attainment levels.

No Longer the Mainstream on Sexuality and Gender

Certain teachings in historic orthodox Christianity contradict mainstream values. In some ways, this is not new: the 1960s sexual revolution championed values that are considered sinful according to the Bible, and the early church lived among a very liberal Roman sexual ethic. The most recent shift has been the culture's embrace of homosexuality, gay marriage, and transgenderism.

Most of the people I know in Christian communities that adhere to a biblical view of marriage, gender, and sexuality also practice the principles of the imago Dei—"the truth that all people are made in God's image and granted human dignity, bodily purpose, and inviolable rights."[68] Serious Christians share society's concern about high rates of suicide, depression, and anxiety among transgender and nonbinary people.[69] They also practice loving their neighbor—there is no caveat to that command. It does not say to only love people who believe what you do. It is a command to love and care for people across religions, races, ethnicities, tribes, and even positions on gender and sexuality. I realize that my in-group of believers does not represent all Christians and certainly not cultural Christianity and today's brand of conservatism. But I thought it important to point this out before we talk about how this cultural change is creating fear in the Christian community.

About ten years ago, the questions were about whether you were required to bake a cake or provide other services for a same-sex wedding. Now it is about the use of pronouns. There are teachers, doctors, and others in the private sector who have been fired for not using the student's, patient's, client's, or colleague's preferred pronoun.[70] I do not know the merits of their cases, whether they genuinely were expressing a religious belief or if they're just obnoxious people trying to "own the libs," but that's really not my point. The issue remains: these stories get around the conservative and Christian community and create fear for those who hold sincere religious beliefs about gender identity.

It's common in certain types of churches to hear pastors speak about the coming day when they will be jailed for teaching Scripture. I don't attend churches that preach that way anymore, but in the past, I would usually hear those sermons in the lead-up to elections. Their logic is that at some point, the Supreme Court will assert that the First Amendment's protection of religion does not allow for the discrimination on the basis of sexual orientation or gender identity. They assert that a pastor, in the near future, who teaches that the Bible says marriage is between one man and one woman may be arrested and thrown in jail.

I do not mean to minimize the very real challenge the Christian community has in navigating the rapid changes in our post-Christian culture. But I believe that the example above qualifies an example of catastrophizing—"a cognitive distortion that prompts people to jump to the worst possible conclusion, usually with very limited information or objective reason to despair."[71] It is also a known symptom of people with anxiety, depression, or PTSD. Catastrophizing is used in both conservative and progressive media today as a tactic for capturing the attention of their audiences and increasing ratings.

Society's mainstream views on marriage and gender have changed quite rapidly. The reality is that the law is still trying to figure out how to balance the First Amendment rights to exercise religion and have free expression for Christians and other religious practitioners, while also protecting the rights of those who, for most of history, were marginalized and discriminated against. I have faith that given time, we will find a way to honor both perspectives, but until we do, many people will fear being fired or discriminated against for not holding to the newly adopted mainstream view.

A Six-Way Fractured Response from the Christian Community— Who Is Most at Risk for Extremism?

As Christians have grappled with societal changes and their loss of mainstream influence, the responses have varied widely. Michael Graham and Skyler Flowers observed that the dramatic cultural moments we've shared over the recent years are interpreted differently by different groups of evangelicals. Where evangelicals previously found unity in Christ, increasingly different groups "are becoming incomprehensible to one another."[72] They label this phenomenon a fracturing and developed six categories to help leaders diagnose and discuss the different "lens" used by the fractured parts. I've summarized their six fractured groups below:[73]

1. *Neo-fundamentalist evangelicals* have a deep concern that political and theological liberalism is invading the church. There is some overlap and co-belligerency with Christian nationalism, but neo-fundamentalists do so with more theological vocabulary and rationality.

2. *Mainstream evangelicals* emphasize the fulfillment of the Great Commission—the final charge Jesus gave to his followers to spread the "good news" and make disciples of all nations. They share some concern for the secular right's influence on Christianity and agree that Christian nationalism is dangerous, but they are far more concerned by the secular left's influence.

3. *Neo-evangelicals* are doctrinally evangelical but may no longer use the term. They embrace a winsome and moderate alternative to the rhetoric they see from neo-fundamentalists

and mainstream evangelicals. Within the church, they are highly concerned about conservative Christianity's acceptance of Trump and its failure to engage on topics of race and sexuality in helpful ways. This group feels largely homeless in today's world.

4. *Post-evangelicals* have fully left evangelicalism and rejected the evangelical label, yet are still churched and likely still agree with the Apostles' Creed and Nicene Creed. They are more vocal in their critiques of neo-fundamentalists and mainstream evangelicals and are primarily concerned with matters of injustice, inequity, the secular right, and to a lesser extent the radical secular left.

5. *Dechurched (but with some Jesus) people* have left the church but still hold to at least some orthodox Christian beliefs.

6. *Dechurched and deconverted people* have left the church and are completely deconverted with no vestigial Christian beliefs.

I believe that neo-fundamentalist evangelical churches are likely the greatest contributor to radicalization within the church right now. Both neo-fundamentalists and mainstream evangelicals, as a group, probably experience more exposure to extremist narratives than the other four groups. As we will explore, mainstream evangelicals have multiple factors that make them vulnerable. Most, of course, will not radicalize. However, Graham has noticed a concerning trend in the last year: mainstream members moving into the neo-fundamentalist category, and neo-fundamentalists leaving Christianity altogether to join Christian nationalist movements or other radicalized political efforts. This is not to say that individuals in other categories couldn't have their own individual vulnerabilities that may make them shift and then gain exposure to extremism, but as a group, they tend to be strongly antagonistic to the on-ramp narratives that lead to extremism.

The Christian Nationalist Response

There is another segment of reactions which those outside the church might consider "Christian," but within the church, we would consider them overtly political groups (not faith groups). These groups co-opt Christian elements and are heretical in their idolization of America, a party, or a candidate. Groups like Turning Point USA and the ReAwaken America Tour are more political than faith based. Yet, prominent pastors and church leaders embrace them as legitimate expressions of Christianity. Celebrity pastor Mark Driscoll, who used to be a theologically conservative "young, restless, and reformed" movement leader, is participating in Turning Point USA events.[74] There is even a network of Patriot Churches now.[75] The people attracted to these movements tend to be deeply angry over the world changing beneath their feet. They feel rejected, disrespected, and humiliated. They used to have significance and power. They used to abide by societal norms and had success in doing so. But those norms have changed and so has their influence.

As uncertainty, anxiety, and grievance have taken hold in our society and the "power" that comes from being the dominant culture wanes, many in Christian culture have turned to worldly tools to seek power. Perhaps too few church leaders are offering the Bible's answers to trials. Or perhaps—as Graham and Flowers's research suggests—some of our "churched" people are rejecting the Bible's answers.

THE NARRATIVE AND THE NETWORK: THE ROLE OF THE OUTRAGE INDUSTRIAL COMPLEX IN CATASTROPHIZING AND REINFORCING OUR GRIEVANCES

For extremism to take root, a vulnerable individual needs to be exposed to the extremist ideology and needs a community to reinforce it, often through significant repetition. We call these factors the narrative and the network. The rise of media as entertainment or infotainment in

the 1990s created the echo chamber necessary for reinforcing grievance narratives.

Marc Ambinder, writing for the *Atlantic* in 2009, coined the
term *outrage-industrial complex*. At the time he was commenting on
the nature of partisan politics: "There are people in Washington who
have the job of manufacturing outrage; who get paid to take offense,
or to find ways to take offense, and to broadcast their outrage to
others." Outrage is the "default emotion" of politics and is "incapable
of distinguish[ing] between what hurts and what harms."[76] Ambinder
was writing just before social media hit a tipping point and was available in the palm of our hand.[77] Facebook's like button debuted a few
days before his article . . . the concept of social media virality was just
beginning.

Fifteen years later, the outrage-industrial complex has grown
exponentially. It is no longer limited to election cycles, politics, and
the nightly news—though they remain core drivers. If you routinely
watch a cable news network or use X (formerly Twitter), YouTube, or
Facebook—you are likely participating in it. But it doesn't stay online.
It has infected our communities—from how we treat restaurant workers and flight attendants to our participation in school board meetings
and churches.

With growing frequency, prominent leaders in media, politics,
and religion take legitimate grievances and catastrophize them, turning them into existential threats. These personalities may not actually
believe their own narrative. But as any fundraiser or political operative knows, the way to raise money, pack an auditorium (or stadium),
or get out the vote is to create a crisis and leverage fear and anger. The
result is a narrative that by itself may not be extremist, but it sets up
the permission structure for hostile action, including violence.

It often starts with overgeneralization and catastrophizing. And
then it becomes increasingly personalized. They are coming for *you*.

For example, in response to legal action against the former president, Republican politicians suggested that federal law enforcement was being weaponized—not only against the former president but against all Republicans.[78] Senator Marco Rubio suggested that funding for new agents at the IRS, an agency that is woefully understaffed and leaves $600 billion uncollected every year, was designed to come after "us"—meaning Republicans.[79]

During a March 2023 opening monologue when he was still anchoring his prime time show on Fox News, Tucker Carlson said: "They're targeting specifically *anyone* who is religious, *humiliating* them in front of their children. Now, why are they doing this? Well, because on some level, all governments *hate* religious people because it's competition. . . . *Anyone who sincerely believes in God is a threat*" (emphasis added).[80]

The conservative infotainment echo chamber is the network that provides fresh angles on core narratives—repeating grievances, finding slightly "new" anecdotes to tell the same stories of hostility and disrespect, and painting a picture of a threat to the community's success or survival. And as the community absorbs these narratives with little to no alternative perspectives, the community experiences the effects of the law of group polarization: they become more extreme in their viewpoints and more susceptible to suggestions that they need to do more to address the threat. The conservative community that regularly consumes right-wing infotainment is primed for radicalization.[81]

EMBRACING HOSTILE ACTION

Recall that under our definition of extremism, hostile action includes harassment and discrimination, both of which have become commonplace in political dialogue and infotainment of late.

The response of some influencers and leaders to uncertainty and rapid societal change is to agitate and scare their followers about the "other." They do this for power, money, and votes, resulting in a culture of constant fear and rage. You only need spend five minutes on X to see that some conservatives and Christians have crossed into the lower end of the hostile action spectrum with their words and contempt.

From there, it's not a far distance for some to adopt an extremist mindset—whether as part of a violent extremist movement or simply being willing to entertain violence as an option to achieve their aims, an option that could be exercised in the right circumstances—like when your president tells you to fight for your country or you won't have a country anymore.

We can see it in the data. We can see it in the increasingly hostile rhetoric, more melees, hate crimes, and terrorist attacks. But for a while, they just seemed like blips—an incident here, an attack there—and they were easy to explain away as the work of a lone wolf or a mentally unwell person. They may have acted alone and they may also have needed mental health support—but they were swimming in a culture that tolerated and promoted extremism.

If there is a moment, a year, to pinpoint the completion of the extreme becoming mainstream on the right, it is 2020. Extreme ideas from white supremacists, antigovernment militias, and QAnon became the right's mainstream. Lies about antifa, COVID-19, and Marxists in the Democratic Party and Black Lives Matter movement become "facts" in the alternative universe of the right. And the rhetoric throughout 2020 increasingly suggested violence as a legitimate course of action.

That was the moment when extremists mobilized to violence and a mass political movement turned violent under the belief that their country and way of life were facing an existential threat.

It was also the moment when some churches crossed the line from cultural syncretism with the Republican Party through political activism to outright extremism: equating members of Congress and Vice President Pence as the Pharisees, as a brood of vipers, and of Satan.

The phrase "Not Pontius Pilate but Pontius Pence" became prevalent. (Note the outright and unapologetic idolatry in this adage as a horrifying bonus.)[82]

TODAY'S CHRISTIAN EXTREMIST MOVEMENT

There are probably plenty of other labels beyond Christian extremism appropriate for the movement we are witnessing today. My purpose in calling this movement *Christian* extremism is to be direct. Violent extremists and political parties have infiltrated and manipulated the Christian faith. They leverage legitimate grievances, false conspiracies, and the perception that Christianity or "Christian culture" is under attack to build an ideology with heretical moral justifications that hostile action, including violence, is necessary. And sadly, many leaders and followers within the Christian church have let them.

Today's Christian extremist movement is made of up of mostly cultural, and some genuine, Christians who believe that out-groups (i.e., progressives, liberals, Democrats, elites, the federal government, the "deep state," globalists, international institutions, immigrants, Muslims, secularists, Marxists, Black Lives Matter, wokeists, and proponents of critical race theory) pose an existential threat to their way of life. They feel that those who hold the power—institutions of higher learning, government, business, and cultural institutions—are hostile to their Christian values and that a day is quickly coming when they will be persecuted for adhering to the traditional Christian values that they feel made the country great. This is fueled by grievance and conspiracies. Threads of those conspiracies are borrowed from the white power and militia movements, which, if revealed, might surprise some of their adherents. Their stated motive for needing hostile action is to "protect" what they perceive to be their *Christian* way of life.

The movement is large, disparate, and fluid. It was visible on January 6 and by most estimates continues to grow, wrapping itself in the signs, symbols, rhetoric, music, and texts of Christianity. No solid organizational structure or hierarchy binds the movement together, but there are influencers and leaders who reach a variety of overlapping audiences. Some of these influencers have financial backing to provide them the ability to organize and spread propaganda. Those in the movement hold a range of beliefs about what level of hostile action is permissible and what the end goal is.

There is no internal consensus among those for whom violence is an option on what to call themselves. The labels they most frequently use are MAGA or patriot, neither of which I'm comfortable using because there are millions of people who also claim those labels and absolutely reject hostile action, including violence, as a solution. I disagree with President Biden's branding of all MAGA as extremists and semi-fascists based on both the facts and the harm it is likely to cause.[83] Given the current us versus them context—we don't need to further feed the narrative that all MAGA or all people who consider themselves patriots are extremists.

Increasingly we are seeing organized white power and militia extremist groups attempt to intermingle with conservative political activists to recruit them into their extremist movements. They do this by showing up at protests and engaging in online forums discussing "culture war" issues. They use activities protected by the First Amendment to recruit people to their more violent extremist views. In 2022, several people involved in white power and militia groups sought to gain power through MAGA and Republican politics. In 2023, self-proclaimed Neo-Nazis attended rallies in support of a Franklin, Tennessee, mayoral candidate; the candidate not only refused to dissociate herself from the white supremacists on multiple occasions, but she also later posed with one of them and posted it on social media.[84]

Historian and militia expert Robert Churchill offered this analysis in 2022: "There is a convergence of apocalypticism, coming from the [militia] movement, and from QAnon and from Evangelical Christianity. What we really saw on January 6 was not just the [militia] movement but a whole broader phenomenon."[85] I agree and will add to Churchill's assessment: it is the nationalist movement within evangelical Christianity—often called Christian nationalism or white Christian nationalism—that is creating risk for more violence as it converges with these other movements. Just as earlier manifestations of white power and militia movements wrapped themselves in Christian Identity theology, violent extremist movements are finding common cause with those evangelicals who ascribe to Christian nationalism. It is this convergence that has led me to sound the urgent alarm that is this book.

And it is increasingly clear that this convergence is not isolated to the United States. The presidents of Hungary and Russia are actively leveraging Christian symbols, culture, texts, and clerics to promote ultranationalism and at times extremism. They've justified atrocities (for example, the illegal invasion of Ukraine) and created out-groups of immigrants and political enemies.[86] Of particular concern in our home country is the small but relevant percentage of Republicans and conservatives who appear to support Viktor Orbán and even Vladimir Putin—viewing them as "strong men" willing to push back against the evil, godless secular culture.[87]

When we bring in the international context, we realize this is a transnational movement, heretical to orthodox Christianity and aligning itself against the classical liberal values of Western civilization.

SIX

A CORRUPTED FAITH

How Pursuit of Power Made Us Vulnerable to Extremism

I confess that the original reason I started this path of mapping how evangelicalism became vulnerable to extremism is that it scared me how close I came to being caught up in it. And I wanted to understand why people I had respected and friends I cared for did get caught up in it. Why did some of us resist and some of us succumb to our group's radicalization? Why did so many reject the peaceful teachings of our faith, opting instead for a false sense of power and control?

No single factor led to the moment we're in. I've spent the years since the invasion of the Capitol immersed in study of this question, and I still discover something new every few weeks. There are a lot of reasons we're broken, and there are lessons to be learned from our failures.

The process of digging deep has humbled me. As Aleksandr Solzhenitsyn frames it:

> *Gradually it was disclosed to me that the line separating good and evil passes not through states, nor between classes, nor between political parties either—but right through every human heart— and through all human hearts. This line shifts. Inside us, it oscillates with the years. And even within hearts overwhelmed by evil,*

one small bridgehead of good is retained. And even in the best of all hearts, there remains . . . an uprooted small corner of evil.[1]

At the Good Friday service at our church, we read through Matthew's passion. At the point at which Pontius Pilate asks the crowds, "What should I do then with Jesus?" (Matthew 27:22 CSB), we in the audience were to answer the reader as the crowds did that day: "Crucify Him." It is deeply unnerving.

Christians are catechized to say "It was our sin that nailed Him to the cross." But if we examine our hearts honestly, we know that when we imagine ourselves at the cross, we picture ourselves as one of the few disciples who remained loyal—John the beloved disciple or Mary Magdalene. The reality is that if we had been there, the overwhelming odds suggest that we would have been chanting "crucify him" with the mob.

I offer these observations not to judge but to help us understand how we are vulnerable to extremism. I have spent times in places of darkness, and I know there remain corners of my soul—beliefs and biases, stubborn anger and willfulness—that have yet to be exposed to the light. I pray that they will be, as painful as I know it will be. It is in this trying process that we are refined, by God's grace, into the likeness of Christ, the Prince of Peace.

> *The United States, unlike any other nation in the world at the time, claimed to be defined by a set of ideas; and those ideas have proven to be the most successful for ordered liberty, for the peaceful transfer of power, and for human flourishing in the history of human civilization.*
> —PAUL D. MILLER, *THE RELIGION OF AMERICAN GREATNESS*[2]

THE IDOLATRY OF AMERICAN EXCEPTIONALISM

I believe that the United States of America is exceptional. I think the story of our founding is unique in history. I cannot help but be amazed by what we have overcome and that we're about to celebrate 250 years of independence.

I also believe that America in the past and present was and is full of sin. Ours is a story of failing to live up to our values and beliefs and yet still striving to be a "more perfect union." I think being able to admit that as a country is part of what makes the American experiment exceptional.

Further, I believe that part of the reason the United States is blessed is because that "set of ideas that proved to be the most successful for ordered liberty" included principles of human rights that were a gift that originated from the spread of Christianity.[3] Consistent with what the Bible teaches, I believe that God, in His sovereignty and providence, blessed America in our founding and continued existence—but not because we are valued more by God, are morally superior to others, or have somehow earned it. It is a gift of grace.

The view I'm describing is called open exceptionalism, a term coined by John D. Wilsey, assistant professor of history and Christian apologetics at Southwestern Baptist Theological Seminary, in his book *American Exceptionalism and Civil Religion.* Open exceptionalism can acknowledge that America has a unique story, but it can also acknowledge our failures and the places where we are not living up to our values. It acknowledges that the values to which we hold fast are in fact universal values, and no country can claim exclusive rights to them. And part of our story includes inspiring and promoting other peoples and countries to embrace these values of freedom, liberty, and equal rights.

In contrast, closed exceptionalism interprets America not only as blessed but as God's chosen nation, the new Israel. Closed exceptionalism is not new. From colonial times, there were people who believed America to be the New Israel and a Christian nation. It's the backstory to Christian nationalism.

Here's how scholars Gorski and Perry describe the deep story for American Christian nationalism is: "America was founded as a Christian nation by (white) men who were 'traditional' Christians, who based the nation's founding on 'Christian principles.' The United States is blessed by God, which is why it has been so successful; and the nation has a special role to play in God's plan for humanity. But these blessings are threatened by cultural degradation from 'un-American' influences both inside and outside our borders."[4]

This deep story—which Gorski and Perry demonstrate is untrue—undergirds the versions of civic religions that Americans have adopted over the centuries. It supports the religion of the Lost Cause, which, as we saw in chapter 4, led to the mainstreaming of the KKK in the 1920s. And in the 1950s, this deep story becomes a crucial framing for how to view America in the fight against the Soviet Union.

Coming off the twin challenges of the Great Depression and World War II, Americans returned to church in the late 1940s.[5] It's difficult to know how much of that return was a peace dividend—a desire to return to normalcy—and how much of the religious surge was a way to deal with new anxieties of the Cold War and potential nuclear annihilation. Either way, President Dwight Eisenhower and the Reverend Billy Graham took advantage of the increased religiosity for their respective careers.

Graham leveraged the apocalyptic threat of nuclear war to win souls. Two days after news broke of the first Soviet nuclear test in 1949, Graham preached: "God is giving us a desperate choice, a choice of either revival or judgment. There is no alternative! . . . The world is divided: into one side we see Communism . . . [which] has declared against Christ, against the Bible, and against all religion! Unless the Western world has an old-fashioned revival, we cannot last."[6]

Both Eisenhower and Graham believed that religion set America apart from communism and that by embracing faith more publicly, they could rally America to stand strong against the Soviet Union. "By framing the Cold War as a moral crisis, Graham made himself useful to Eisenhower," explains historian Kristin Kobes Du Mez.[7] It affirmed that deep story of good and evil: "Communism was 'the greatest enemy we have ever known,' and only evangelical Christianity could provide the spiritual resources to combat it."[8]

Eisenhower initiated the National Prayer Breakfast and worked with Congress to add "one nation under God" to the Pledge of Allegiance and "In God We Trust" to US currency. When signing the legislation that added "under God" to the pledge, Eisenhower stated: "In this way we are reaffirming the transcendence of religious faith in America's heritage and future; in this way we shall constantly strengthen those spiritual weapons which forever will be our country's most powerful resource, in peace or war."[9]

In *One Nation under Graham: Apocalyptic Rhetoric and American Exceptionalism*, Jonathan Redding argues that the apocalyptic setting of the 1950s, with the threat of nuclear war hanging in the shadows, and Graham's interpretations of the books of Daniel and Revelation combined to "cement the idea of 'America as a Christian nation' among evangelical voters."[10] And the corollary idea is perhaps as important: "the fall of America will yield global destruction culminating in the events foretold in Scripture" (the end times).[11] These themes were preached and leveraged by both religious leaders and politicians over the next seven decades, and they are the backdrop to many of the arguments Christian Nationalists make today.

The Church's Embrace of American Exceptionalism and Christian Nationalism Can Lead to Extremism

Aside from it being biblically incorrect, closed exceptionalism and Christian nationalism pose three major dangers relevant to our topic of extremism.

The first is that adherents use the mantel of "chosen" to argue they have a "unique moral status," which allows them to justify atrocities (supremacy of the white race, colonialism, slavery, and Manifest Destiny to name just a few).[12] It creates the "us vs them" through which they view the world. And it inherently frames America (or rather, those who get defined as "American") as good and everyone that is not included in that category as evil.

In Dr. Paul Miller's book on Christian nationalism, he shows that American nationalism has an "us" that is usually a narrowly defined identity based on ethnic sources (shared culture, heritage, and ethnicity—primarily Anglo/Western European) and religious sources (primarily Protestant Christianity).[13] In the spectrum of American nationalism—there are those who emphasize the Anglo side in an exclusionary way, which leads to racial identitarian movements that see, "Western civilization and American identity as a function of European DNA."[14] These views would be considered white nationalism and are found throughout the white power movement. On the other side of the spectrum are those that primarily emphasize the culture and religion, their Christian heritage—which is Anglo-Protestant, but not in a racially exclusive way. These adherents would say that, "anyone can assimilate to Anglo-Protestant culture, regardless of race or ethnicity."[15] Note the attitude though, "an unstated presumption that Christians are entitled to primacy of place in the public square because they are heirs of the true or essential heritage of American culture, that Christians have a presumptive right to define the meaning of the American experiment because they see themselves as America's architects, first citizens, and guardians."[16]

The second problem is that it sets the stage for a false gospel. Closed exceptionalism "conflates American identity with Christian identity and treats the good of one as the good of the other," Miller argues.[17] If you are an American—you are chosen, therefore you don't need personal salvation from Jesus; you're saved just by being an American. Further, Christian nationalism makes the nation the thing that is worshipped instead of God. This is idolatry. This is not just my opinion—academics that have studied nationalism—like Paul Miller, John Wilsey, Andrew Whitehead, and theologians—like the late Rev. Timothy Keller and Russell Moore—have come to these conclusions.[18]

The third is a problem inherent with all idolatry. Since you are anchoring you hope not on Christ, but on something human and you will inevitably find yourself in constant fear of loss. Specific to Christian nationalism, you fear losing your "chosen" status and going into exile. The Old Testament tells the story of what happens to Israel when they disobey God and refuse to repent—they are displaced from the land and scattered across the Babylonian Empire. Even when a remnant returns to Israel a generation later, Israel is never restored to its former glory. It remained a vassal or client state until Jerusalem is destroyed by Rome in 70 AD.

You can see this fear in the prominence of certain scriptures being used in evangelicalism. Since the Civil War American leaders have applied 2 Chronicles 7:14 to the United States: "If my people who are called by my name humble themselves, and pray and seek my face and turn from their wicked ways, then I will hear from heaven and will forgive their sin and heal their land." Eisenhower and Reagan were sworn in with the Bible open to this verse. The problem? That verse is God speaking to ancient Israel, specifically, King Solomon, about his plans to fulfill His covenant with Solomon's father, David. A covenant which has since been fulfilled in Jesus Christ.

Now that does not mean we should not pray. Nor does it prevent God from hearing the prayers of believers and choosing to "heal the land." But Americans cannot claim 2 Chronicles 7:14 as a covenant promise for the United States.

Christian nationalism is a "prosperity gospel for nation-states," says Russell Moore.[19] What happens when the prayers to heal our land seem to go unanswered? What happens when America becomes less and less religious? When our prosperity has been lost? When the country seems to be hostile to traditional Christian values? Miller observed that, "as Christian power has waned, Christian nationalists have become all the more assertive in staking claim to America's status as a chosen people and a Christian nation."[20] This is the problem with wrapping the cross in the flag, with God and country religion, with worshipping our Nation. It offers a false gospel, which is destined to fail because all false gospels do.

This idolatry has created pathways for on-ramping to extremism. Where the Christian faith should be a protective factor for someone experiencing uncertainty or a life crisis, instead—it creates an ideology that justifies the need for hostile action. Several of the most prominent adherents of American Christian nationalism do just this.

Two Examples of Christian Nationalist Arguments Nearing the Extremist Line

While Christian nationalism is a popular topic at the moment and the subject of academic research from theological, sociological, and political angles, there is not consensus on what the label actually means. The "backstory" on Christian nationalism I shared above from Gorski and Perry is at odds with how some proponents of Christian nationalism have explained their views. Take, for example, the vision of Christian nationalism of Andrew Torba, founder of Gab, and Andrew Isker, a Minnesota pastor, in their very short book, *Christian Nationalism: A Biblical Guide to Taking Dominion and Discipling Nations*. They explicitly debunk closed exceptionalism and clearly state that they do not idolize or worship America. Their stated goal is not to overthrow the US government, but "to build a parallel Christian society, economy, and infrastructure which will fill the vacuum of the secular state when it falls."[21] They are motivated by an interpretation of the Great Commission that it is the Christian's responsibility to set up God's Kingdom on earth to "take dominion in His name."[22] Though not explicit, they appear to align with Christian reconstructionism, dominionism, and theonomy as popularized by R. J. Rushdoony and Gary North. (Reconstructionism believes that it is the Christian's "responsibility to challenge the anti-Christian character of society and culture" and "seek to change society in ways that will bring it into conformity with the teaching of Scripture."[23] The theonomic Christian reconstructionist believes that nonceremonial Old Testament law should govern society.)

Meanwhile, Stephen Wolfe, a PhD from the reformed Presbyterian tradition, wrote a five-hundred-page theoretical book on Christian nationalism. His vision includes advocating for the return to the sixteenth- and seventeenth-century practices of churches, specifically for a "Christian prince" to rule and be able to put to death heretics, or perhaps "banishment or long-term imprisonment may suffice as well."[24] Wolfe's version of Christian nationalism is unapologetically misogynistic, and while he states that his is not a white nationalist argument, he uses language that is frequently leveraged by historic and current white supremacists and Nazis.[25]

Though they are coy in how they frame it, Torba, Isker, and Wolfe use language implying that a fight is necessary. Torba and Isker speak of spiritual warfare but drop in references to the sword as well.[26] Wolfe lays out an academic argument for resistance, even violent resistance. He goes so far as to explain that Paul's instruction in Romans 13 to "be subject to the governing authorities" (v. 1) is contextual. It would be "absurd" for Christians with their small numbers to revolt at that time. Paul's "silence on revolution cannot be construed as a denial of its permissibility," Wolfe argues.[27] At the end of his argument on the right to violent revolution, he states: "It is to our shame that we sheepishly tolerate assaults against our Christian heritage merely sighing or tweeting performative outrage over public blasphemy, impiety, irreverence, and perversity. We are dead inside lacking the spirit to drive away the open mockery of God and to claim what is ours in Christ. . . . But we do not have to be like this. We have the power and right to act. Let us train the will and cultivate our resolve."[28]

It would be a whole other book to counter the theological errors and political impracticalities of Torba, Isker, and Wolfe's books. My point in briefly highlighting them is that, first, there are many *takes* on what Christian nationalism is, and according to sociological studies and polls, those voices don't necessarily reflect what the average American seems to mean when they talk about Christian nationalism.[29] Thus, if you find yourself engaging with someone who says they are a Christian nationalist, ask questions. There is a wide spectrum of beliefs; some are more concerning than others. Second, some people are making arguments suggestive of hostile action and, in the case of Wolfe, literally laying out a theological and moral justification for violence in the name of Christianity. I do not believe that most American Christian nationalists support violent solutions, but you can see from these examples that the argument is being made.

———

What is the American church's role in this? I see two primary errors. Too many churches promoted an Anglo-Protestant civic religion in America. Perhaps they didn't outright express Christian nationalist ideology, but their actions demonstrated support of it: the American flag in the sanctuary during worship service; patriotic songs sung on the Sundays of Independence Day, Memorial Day, and Veterans Day. It is understandable how the generation processing the trauma of World War II and angst of the Cold War and potential nuclear apocalypse found comfort in a patriotic faith, and how we turned back to our churches after 9/11 and wanted reassurance that God was on our side. But for many, patriotism turned into idolatry, and this false gospel leaves souls in peril. Many Americans now think they have Christian salvation solely because they are patriotic Americans. We should care that many have never heard the Truth.

The second error is silence. I was in my late thirties before I heard a sermon pointing out the idolatry of Christian nationalism; they didn't use the term *Christian nationalism*, but that's what the pastor was describing. The events of the past ten years have led to more books and teachings on this error. But I know there are still many pastors and Christian leaders facing the uphill battle of seeing their congregants one hour a week, while the news or "conflict entrepreneurs" catechize them 24/7. Do not let this silence you. We need your voices pushing back against the idolatry of Christian nationalism.

MISDIAGNOSING THE PROBLEM: THE PURSUIT OF POWER AND SUPREMACY THROUGH MORAL MAJORITY POLITICS

By most accounts the 1950s was the height of civic religion in the United States, and then it began to decline. As the civil rights movement gained momentum and challenged institutions and structures, white Christians were split, largely along geographic lines. Unsurprisingly, the South—still believers in the Lost Cause religion—opposed integration. The North, and some national organizations and figures—like the National Association of Evangelicals, *Christianity Today*, and Billy Graham—were what Du Mez calls "cautious supporters"; they were "wary about moving too fast," which might exacerbate "extremists on both sides."[30] The civil rights movement could have been an opportunity for the church to promote the teachings of Jesus and acknowledge the sins of the past and repent; instead, historians note that after the passage of the Civil Rights Act of 1964, most white

Christians were ambivalent. Du Mez argues that this ambivalence "is key to understanding the role race would play within evangelical politics more generally, but backing away from their support for civil rights, . . . they ended up giving cover to more extremist sentiments within the insurgent Religious Right."[31]

While it does not come to fruition until Ronald Reagan's election, it was in the late 1960s and early 1970s—the heart of our last American "moral convulsion," a season of great upheaval and uncertainty as cultural norms were changing about race, sex, and women—that we see the stage set for political alignments to shift. Political strategists saw opportunities to leverage the Christian voting bloc that Eisenhower rode to the presidency.

When I was learning about Republican politics in the 1990s, the story I was told said that the *Roe v. Wade* decision rallied evangelical Christians and Catholics into the Moral Majority, which helped Ronald Reagan win in 1980. It's now well documented and confirmed by the architects of the Religious Right themselves, Paul Weyrich and Richard Viguerie, that "family values" was a cover for the real wedge that created the Republican majority. Race was the "wedge that split off white evangelicals from the Democratic Party."[32]

By the 1970s, it was clear that politicians couldn't be overtly racist. Most Americans knew the times had changed; racism was wrong—or at least socially unacceptable. Gorski and Perry identify three shifts Weyrich and Viguerie made to the White Christian nationalist narrative: (1) they picked up on the apocalyptic rhetoric that Billy Graham popularized (we will touch on this more in a section below); (2) they "gradually shifted from white supremacism to 'color-blindness'"—using terms like "welfare queens" and "culture of poverty" as dog whistles and laying out a case that racism is a heart matter, something that laws or paying reparations cannot fix; and (3) they focused on sexual purity and family values.[33]

Part of what allowed this union between evangelicals and Republican politics to occur was the decline of traditional Christian denominations and the rise of the independent church, evangelical and charismatic movements, and parachurch organizations. In the absence of denominational oversight and accountability, there was more freedom for these new movements to form associations and alliances with other cultural forces, including with politics.

The great realignment of the white church with the Republican Party changed the country's politics, but it also changed the American church. Christian leaders realized, and perhaps some followers subconsciously understood, that secularization and diversification of society was leaving them with less prominence. They needed to be organized to ensure that their values were maintained in the public square. Jerry Falwell formed the Moral Majority, James Dobson formed the Family Research Council, Pat Robertson formed the Christian Coalition, and Tim LaHaye started the Council for National Policy and the American Coalition for Traditional Values.[34]

While fearmongering has often been a tool of preachers to promote conversions and repentance, it is usually focused on the fear death, of hell, or the fear of an external threat like nuclear apocalypse that might bring about your demise sooner than you think. As American Christianity become associated with only one side of the political spectrum, the fear that was stoked was not of eternal damnation but of losing our country and the dangers coming from the other political party. It was whitewashed in the language of preserving morality and trafficking in the fear that God might "remove his blessing" from America; the pursuit of power at all costs was justified to "protect the faith." "Taking our country back" for God isn't a new sentiment. It's been baked into the religious right from the beginning. *They* are coming to get *us*, and *we* need to "stand up and defend" *our* way of life.

This is also when Christians created their own subculture—a sure sign they were on the road to no longer being the dominant mainstream culture. This played out not only through political action organizations but also industries designed to help marriages and families navigate changing times; the creation of the homeschool and private school movements; the development of the Christian music, book, and movie industries; and the rise of celebrity Christianity.[35] While the evangelical church pushed back hard against perceived changes in sexual morals within society, they embraced other "softer sins," like consumerism and idolizing money, comfort, control, and power.

It was a mutually beneficial relationship if the key metrics are power and control. Republican political operatives used Christians for votes and money. And Christians gained access to power and "wins" on policy matters.

The melding of faith and politics created a generation of "church" people fixated on preserving traditional morals and virtues, protecting their children from the "declining culture"—while completely missing the purpose of the gospel—to shine the line of Christ into the world.

I'm not suggesting that the cultural changes of the past sixty years don't have a downside, but it is time the church stops obsessing over the moral decline of society as if it is somehow new and a threat to God. The entirety of the Bible points to man's depravity and his inability to save himself. Jesus' last command to his disciples was not to ensure that we commiserate over how messed up the world is but rather to go and tell the good news that he created a way out of the mess. We should not expect a culture that does not know God to adhere to His values. That the world is hurting and in need of a savior is the crux of our worldview. We shouldn't be shocked by it.

The Bible says we are to "Seek first the Kingdom of God" (Matthew 6:33), not an earthly kingdom, not the security of what we think made America great, obtained by any means necessary. Instead of bemoaning the consequences of a sinful and godless society, the church should be more concerned about the sin within and the lack of fruit being produced by the church. We should lament how poorly the church has carried out its mission to spread the good news, make disciples, do justice, love mercy, walk humbly, and seek the flourishing of our communities.

BIBLE QUOTERS, NOT READERS: BIBLICAL ILLITERACY AND THE LACK OF CHRISTIAN FORMATION

We live in a remarkable moment in history. Humanity has more knowledge and access to information than ever before. We have access to an incredible trove of information about Jesus and the Bible: more Bibles in print, electronic, audio, video, and other formats; more translations; more Bible studies; more scholarship; better technology to aid archaeologists in helping to confirm fragments of the scriptures and historical context; and an unending feed of commentaries, sermons, devotionals, and discipleship programs. What was once limited to those with education and wealth is increasingly accessible to all people, including those with disabilities and in the remotest parts of the world.

Within the next ten years, the Bible will be translated into every language used on Earth.[36] That's over seven thousand languages.[37] The promise God made to Abraham that "all the peoples" (Genesis 12:3 CSB) and "all the nations of earth will be blessed" through Him (Genesis 18:18, 22:18, 26:4, 28:14 CSB) and the vision from Revelation 7:9 that "a vast multitude from every nation, tribe, people, and *language*, which no one could number, standing before the throne" (CSB) of God and Jesus is being fulfilled in our lifetime.

And yet, the irony of our nation and our generation is while we have more resources to understand the teachings of Christian Scripture, we have also experienced the greatest declines in biblical literacy.

David Nienhuis, writer of a book on how to read the New Testament, observed that his students struggled with biblical material "because they have been trained to be Bible quoters, not Bible readers."[38] I can relate to his description. In some of the churches I attended, sermons were for guidance on Christian living, with a verse as a proof text. They were not about experiencing the character of God and spreading His light. Nienhuis noted: "They have the capacity to recall a relevant biblical text in support of a particular doctrinal point, or in opposition to a hot spot in the cultural wars, or in hope of emotional support when times get tough. They approach the Bible as a sort of reference book, a collection of useful God-quotes that can be looked up as one would locate words in a dictionary or an entry in an encyclopedia."[39]

There are many contributing factors to the decline in biblical literacy. Certainly, what we explored in the previous section—the unholy union of evangelicalism and Republican politics, which created a subculture of Christianity focused on culture wars and politics instead of the Bible—is a key one.

Another thread may be tied to seeker-friendly or seeker-sensitive churches, which became popular in evangelicalism in the 1990s. It was a consumer-driven model of church. Anything that seemed stodgy and stiff, like pews or liturgy or hymns, was removed from the experience in favor of comfortable chairs, coffee bars, and sermons that ran like clockwork—literally, a countdown clock showed the time to the second to make sure everything started and ended on time. If church could be run like a successful business and take advantage of modern marketing techniques, it could reach new people and win souls.

The largest and most famous seeker-friendly church during this era was Willow Creek Community Church in the Chicago area. Their services reached twenty thousand people a week at one point.[40] They conducted a study of themselves and six other churches in 2007 and assessed that while they were "successfully meeting the spiritual needs of those who describe themselves as 'exploring Christianity' or 'growing in Christ,'" a significant number of those who identified as "close to Christ" or "Christ-centered" were disappointed with the church.[41] Some of the critiques included a sense they were "not being fed" or "stalled in their spiritual growth," and that they "wanted more meat of the Word of God."[42]

The seeker-friendly movement carries on, though it is not nearly as celebrated as it was twenty-five years ago. Having spent time in several of these churches, I can say that they have their merits. They do a great job of welcoming people who are skeptical of the faith or who might otherwise be uncomfortable in a traditional church. They tend to emphasize God's amazing love for us and as a result tend to be very warm and welcoming regardless of your background. One such church played a pivotal role in helping me come back to my faith. Many people have been blessed by their ministries.

But I wonder if the weaknesses exemplified in the Willow Creek study may plague many other churches in our country, and if such weaknesses may have contributed to the vulnerabilities in some that were exploited a decade later by politicians and extremists.

God's purpose for the church is to shine the light of Christ into the world and to light a path to our transformation into the image of Christ or, as Jesus put it, to make disciples. It is not to get more people through the church door. A healthy church points congregants to God, so that He can transform hearts and minds to move from natural selfish tendencies to a life of service to God and to others. There, the Bible tells us, we find truth and joy.

The "vision" laid out in the New Testament for what it looks like to mature in our faith was to become more and more like Jesus. There are volumes of books on how to become more "Christ-like," so I hesitate to oversimplify, but since Jesus did, I think we can be safe in boiling it down to living out the greatest commandment: "'Love the Lord your God with all your heart, with all your soul, with all your strength and with all your mind,' and 'your neighbor as yourself'" (Luke 10:27

CSB). The ultimate example of Jesus modeling this for us was through his suffering and death on the cross.

Jesus gave us several tools to aid us in maturing in our faith. The Bible is a core one. The finding that the churches were not teaching the "meat of the Word of God" may imply the churches were not equipping their congregants with the tools to study the Bible themselves or in a small group. Or it may mean that sermons did not teach the full text of the Bible over time. (Topical sermons or sermons with three steps to improving your life with biblical wisdom are a common feature in some churches.) Or it may mean that the churches avoided in-depth discussions on some of the tougher topics, such as what does it mean to deny yourself and take up your cross daily (Luke 9:23) or that "in this world you will have trouble" (John 16:33 NIV)? How are we supposed to "count it all joy" when we have trials (James 1:2 CSB) or "rejoice in our sufferings" (Romans 5:3 CSB; 1 Peter 4:12–13)? Any model of the "Christian life" that does not account for suffering is incomplete and may leave the follower disappointed or disillusioned when difficulties and tragedy inevitably arise.

It's not just a lack of biblical knowledge that can leave us vulnerable. God designed Christian formation to occur in and with community— rejoicing, overcoming challenges, providing comfort and encouragement, even mourning together. We were not designed to live alone. If we lack a strong attachment to a biblical community, what happens when difficulties arise? Who will help remind us of what we believe? Who will pray for us to have strength to endure?

A healthy church should come alongside those who are suffering and bear their burdens in both spiritual and practical ways. If a church is not routinely teaching on the role of suffering and trials in the life of a Christian, it may subtly convey to the one suffering that they must be doing something wrong. And it may prevent someone from turning to their church community for help.

There are other weaknesses in American Christianity that created openings for not maturing in our faith: an obsession with celebrity within the church that becomes idolatrous[43] and an overemphasis on individualistic "personal salvation," which misses the part of the gospel about redeeming the whole of creation and subsequently lacks seriousness about the command to love our neighbor.

Jesus taught a parable about the good news of the gospel being scattered over four different types of soil (Matthew 13:3–9; Mark 4:2–9; Luke 8:4–8). Only in the good soil did the seed produce a crop. The seed sown along the path never took root; it was eaten by birds. The seed that fell upon the rocky places, where the soil was shallow, sprang up quickly but was scorched and withered when the sun came up because it had no roots. And the seed that fell among the thorns grew but was choked by the thorns.

It is the latter two soils that we in the American church are wise to contemplate. Jesus explained their meaning to his disciples: the rocky soil describes someone who hears the word and at once receives it with joy, but since they have no root, it lasts only a short time. When trouble or persecution comes because of the word, they quickly fall away. Meanwhile, the thorns represent the worries of this life and the deceitfulness of wealth, which choke out the word and make it unfruitful.

I do not fully understand why our community was so vulnerable, why we forsook the Bible's teachings to gain earthly power. But I believe part of that answer was the lack of a deep transforming relationship with God.

HISTORIC SINS AND PRIDEFUL BLINDNESS

Very likely, some of our biggest weaknesses stem from our historic sins and lack of repentance. In this book, we're barely scratching the surface of the sins of our country: colonization, Manifest Destiny, atrocities exacted on Native Americans and indigenous peoples, Japanese internment camps, the scourge of slavery and racism and Jim Crow laws and segregation and their harrowing consequences that we still feel today. These sins left tremendous scars on our nation that remain unhealed even now. A growing field of study is showing evidence that experiencing trauma literally changes our DNA and that those genetic changes are passed on to children who did not experience the original trauma.[44]

As we examined in chapter 4, American churches used the Bible to justify Jim Crow laws, segregation, and resisting the civil rights movement. The second wave of the KKK was led by a former Methodist minister and included prayer at their big marches in Washington, DC.[45] The fact that they used the symbol of the cross lit on fire to instill terror should alone cause us to weep.

But many conservative strains of Christianity embrace sanitized history. "We are the greatest country in the world," we are told. "Don't dwell on the 'minor' things; after all, *we* didn't do it, and what can we do to fix it now? Plus, look at all the good we have done!" We are told that those who come forward in humility and repent or seek restitution are weak, or they are Marxists fixated on power structures. But this ignores the ways of the Kingdom of God: the meek and the poor in spirit are the blessed ones.

Repentance takes great courage. Looking at the dirtiest parts of our history with humility and seeking to reconcile or restore systems, communities, and people that were hurt by it is the way of Jesus. This is what it means to be a peacemaker. Though it cannot erase the original harm, it creates a bridge to the renewed flourishing of our community.

Some denominations and churches have done the hard work of looking at their history and repenting. In the 1990s, parts of evangelicalism sought racial reconciliation. Intentional church planting led to a tripling of multiracial churches, from 6 percent to 19 percent over a twenty-year period. Jemar Tisby, who grew up around the movement, confesses that at a certain point it felt like the effort was working.[46]

He points to the killing of Trayvon Martin by George Zimmerman as the event that changed the momentum toward reconciliation. Zimmerman was acquitted. The #BlackLivesMatter hashtag was first used in response to the acquittal. If it had just been one killing, perhaps things could have gone back to where they were, but that is not what the last ten years have been. In 2014, a white police officer killed a Black man, Michael Brown, in a dispute on the street. This officer was acquitted as well, which sparked outrage. There were protests in 150 cities.

An awareness dawned on many in the church and conservative movement. We thought racism had been pushed to the far margins of society—but it had never left.

Some churches made efforts to listen. A survey conducted by Lifeway Research in 2016 indicated that 90 percent of pastors agreed that their congregation would welcome a sermon on racial reconciliation. But four years later, that had dropped to 74 percent.[47]

What changed? The roots of radicalization had taken hold and were fertilized abundantly by right-wing politics and an amoral media. The MAGA movement tapped into the simmering angst of white grievance. The country was ripe for populism.

Any progress being made on racial reconciliation, even if it was on the surface, was stopped in its tracks.

By 2020, grassroots political operatives[48] were already laying the groundwork for lauding anti-wokeism and making critical race theory (CRT) a boogeyman. The movement was so well orchestrated that the Southern Baptist Convention's six seminaries unanimously passed a resolution declaring that "affirmation of Critical Race Theory, Intersectionality, and any version of Critical Theory is incompatible with the Baptist Faith & Message."[49]

Even the protests of the murders of George Floyd, Ahmaud Arbery, and Breonna Taylor were co-opted by the MAGA movement for its "law and order" message.

I personally disagree with CRT and, as I think I demonstrated in the previous chapter, have grave concerns about the identity synthesis trap that has taken over some institutions and spaces. But we in the church should still be working to address racial injustice and the long-term effects of our country's sinful history. Doing so is not Marxist; it is the way of Jesus.

> *Wherever we find women treated with disdain in Jesus' name, we also find a single-minded pursuit of political power and a lust for violence.*
> —JARED STACY[50]

AUTHORITARIANISM, HYPERMASCULINITY, AND MISOGYNY

In response to the rise of feminism in the 1960s, evangelical church culture sought to elevate and encourage "traditional womanhood." Regardless of your theological interpretation of women's roles in the church, the reaction to feminism drastically overcorrected. It led to hypermasculinity, misogyny, authoritarianism, and countless stories of sexual abuse in the church.

As a woman who grew up in a theologically conservative culture, I can tell you that I was not exposed to a church that taught that my value before God as equal to that of a man until I was in my late twenties. My parents, thankfully, taught me I was made in God's image and that God esteemed me as much as a man, but the culture and churches I grew up in did not affirm those teachings. I was not taught how radical Jesus' esteeming of women was—absolutely turning upside down the paternalistic hierarchy of the Roman world. I was not taught about the apostle Paul's many affirmations and praises of women co-laboring in the sharing of the gospel.[51]

I *was* taught about the need to reclaim masculinity and femininity. That to help men to "step up," it was important that we women stepped back to give them space to fulfill their God-given duties. After all, we can cause them to stumble not only by what we wear, but also by challenging them intellectually. No, I'm not exaggerating—that was counsel I was given on multiple occasions by well-meaning Christians.

Personally, I didn't fit the mold of a "godly woman" because my interests were not in preparing meals and serving in the nursery. (Both noble callings and, ironically, things I enjoy doing now.) But when I was younger, those were the *only* ways women could serve in our church. And the message that we were a stumbling block to men was repeatedly drilled into us. One weeknight in college, after getting my hair cut much shorter than I was used to, I attended an event at our church with a special guest speaker. Halfway through the program I was passed a note from an "older sister in Christ" telling me to stop touching my hair because it was causing her twelve-year-old son to "stumble." I have no doubt I was distracting, but the framing was off-putting and the anonymous nature of the note left me wondering: how do you even know that I'm a fellow "sister"? You can let someone know their behavior is distracting without having to frame it as causing someone (a twelve-year-old, no less) to be sexually tempted. These experiences were a part of why I pulled away from the church for a time.

When I stepped back into the church in my late twenties, I struggled for nearly a decade to reconcile conservative cultural Christianity's messages about womanhood with what I saw in Scripture.

And then there was the #MeToo movement. When #MeToo launched in Hollywood, #ChurchToo grew quickly—and is still ongoing—exposing sexual abuse across churches and denominations.[52]

In the last few years, two historians have written complementary accounts of how the Bible has been interpreted through the lens of American culture and rocked the evangelical world: Kristin Kobes Du Mez's *Jesus and John Wayne: How White Evangelicals Corrupted a Faith and Fractured a Nation* and Beth Allison Barr's *The Making of Biblical Womanhood: How the Subjugation of Women Became Gospel Truth.*

I'm grateful for their scholarship. Not only did it help me process my personal experience in the church, but it made it easier for me to connect the dots to our topic.

Because the church overcorrected, because authoritarianism and hypermasculinity were lauded as what it meant to be a good Christian, more Christians have become susceptible to misogynistic extremist ideologies, including white supremacy, incel culture, and extremist forms of Christian nationalism.

———

Our faith should have provided protective factors to resist radicalization. Even as society is experiencing great uncertainties and unprecedented crises and perceiving threats, our Scriptures offer guidance to walk through suffering and humiliation. Our Savior offers refuge. Our faith traditions offer comfort. And when we are weak, the Christian community should offer us encouragement to persevere. We do not need hostile action to address perceived threats, because we believe a sovereign, all-knowing, and all-powerful God is for us (Romans 8:31).

In the summer of 2023, the former southern Baptist pastor and now editor of *Christianity Today* Russell Moore summed up our current state:

> *American Christianity is in crisis. The church is a scandal in all the worst ways. We bear responsibility for that. Some of us contributed to it. Some of us were crushed by it. We cannot will it away by shrugging our shoulders and saying, "That's just the way people are." But however many hucksters and grifters lead this movement, sinners still find in Jesus someone who is not. . . . Evangelical Christianity as we know it might not survive. American evangelicalism might not be there for the future. But someone will be. As long as there's a church, there will be people within*

reminding everyone else that the Spirit blows where he wills, and
that there's hope, no matter how far gone a person goes, to be born
again.[53]

We should grieve the church's pride and pursuit of power, which
left us vulnerable. But we do not lose hope. Our hope is not in the
American church or evangelicalism. Nor is it in a godly politician
returning the country to more "normal" and sane times. Our hope
is in Christ alone. Our path forward requires disentangling our faith
and identity from politics and working within our church communities to remind Christians where to anchor our hope. And from there,
we work to bring our communities back to the path of peace.

Part II

THE PATH BACK
TO PEACE

SEVEN

UNTANGLING OUR HOPE AND IDENTITY

The Need for Significance and Belonging

The people who walked in darkness have seen a great light; those who
dwelt in a land of deep darkness, on them has light shone.

—Isaiah 9:2

ACKNOWLEDGING THE DARKNESS

December 2020 was the first time I deeply understood Advent. The evangelical churches of my youth were not liturgical or observant of church calendars. When I was a child, the four-week period leading to Christmas celebrated as Advent meant counting down the days until you could finally open the presents!

As an adult, I knew it had a deeper meaning—remembering the centuries-long wait the faithful had for the Messiah's first coming and being reminded that we're waiting for His return. But it felt a bit like a history lesson, and didn't seem very relevant to my life.

In the wake of the 2020 election, something shifted for me. People weren't snapping out of it. The fog didn't lift. By mid-December, the anger and bitterness both in the church and in the political party in which I'd invested my entire career were getting worse.

One of the benefits of "betraying" one's political side is that you are psychologically freed up to see the parts of the history of your side that have been painted in a bad (or misleading) light or purposefully

glossed over or ignored. It was in this space, particularly in wake of
the horrific murders of Ahmaud Arbery and George Floyd and the
tragic killing of Breonna Taylor, that I realized how poisoned my own
mind had been from the echo chamber of right-wing infotainment.
It had hardened and blinded my heart toward suffering and injustice.
This wasn't injustice somewhere "over there," in another part of the
world. This was right here, in the cities where I've lived and worked.
And I didn't see it. And in realizing my own ignorance and my sin
of self-centeredness, pride, blindness, hard-heartedness—and the list
could go on—the impossibility of helping others to see weighed heavy.

"How do we make progress on racial injustice when half of the
country is conditioned to believe Black Lives Matter is a front for
Marxism or reflexively retorts 'Blue Lives Matter' or 'All Lives Matter'
instead of focusing on the actual problems?" I wrote to a mentor two
days before the election. "I suppose—in getting involved in the political side for the first time in 20 years, I've started to catch a glimpse of
how broken it all is—and I don't see a reason for much hope."

In the days that followed, my hunch that there wasn't much hope
was confirmed. Desperate for someone to tell me otherwise, that it's
not as bad as it seems, I talked with seasoned conservatives, political
operatives, and church leaders. "What do we do now?" I asked.

It was unnerving to see people with decades' more experience
than I possess not have answers to this question. They, too, sensed
that the institutions we grew up with and had been relying on for the
last seventy years were irreparably broken, and not just political institutions, but our entire culture, especially religious culture. And while
none of them were giving up (they all were looking to contribute in
some way to rebuild), no one was foolish enough to suggest that we
humans could fix it.

I expect the kingdom of this world to be dark. Scripture tells us
that over and over again. But that darkness had overtaken the thing

that was supposed to offer light in the world: the church—or, perhaps more accurately, those who claim to be the church. And that shook me.

The communities that had lectured me for years about principles and virtues abandoned them because they had fixed their eyes on a worldly enemy and pinned their hope to earthly power instead of Christ.

I was angry at the lies and the liars misleading so many. I was angry at the injustices so many faced and experienced at the hands of the two belief systems that had been most important to me throughout my life: "conservatism" and "Christianity." And I was angry at the stoking of grievances that was leading many down a pathway of violence.

And so in December, at Advent, I found myself cross-legged on my bedroom floor, letting the darkness wash over me.

It is difficult to really fathom how long Israel waited for their Messiah. At Jesus' birth, the people of Israel had been waiting for six centuries. Without looking it up, do you even know what was happening in world history six centuries ago?

This is well before the United States was founded, before the Enlightenment, before the Reformation, before America was even "discovered" by Europeans. Six hundred years ago, it was the end of the Middle Ages and start of the Renaissance. In 1422, King Henry V died and King Henry VI became king of England at nine months old. Later the same year, he became King of France. In 1440 Gutenberg invented the printing press. Leonardo da Vinci was born in 1452. And in 1453, Constantinople, known as the capital of the world at the time, fell to the Ottoman Turks.

For six hundred years Israel was in some form of captivity and waiting for the Messiah to redeem them. And before that captivity set in, the prophets warned the people and pleaded with them to repent. The prophets saw the darkness setting in.

Isaiah was watching the spiraling decline of his nation. His prophecy warned of coming invasions and Israel and Judah's devastation. If we zoom out, we see this pattern throughout the scriptures. Man fails. It seems all hope is lost. But God.

Each successive step in God's redemptive story is a nail-biter. God makes promises, darkness creeps in, humans' depravity appear to disrupt the plan, and then miracles happen, preserving the way for the Redeemer to come. This happens over and over again: preserving Noah and his family through the flood; calling Abraham out of Ur to make of him a great nation and waiting years for a child to be born in order to fulfill that promise; providing for Israel's eleven sons during a great famine through their brother, Joseph, whom they sold into slavery; raising up Moses to lead the enslaved Israelites out of Egypt; providing the law and dwelling with the Israelites in the wilderness to teach them how to be God's people even after multiple instances of rebellion. All these stories have moments that cause even the most faithful to doubt how God will keep his promise. And yet, God keeps the covenant, even when humans fail.

When I allowed myself to sit with the gravity and reality of the season our country finds itself in, the optimist in me found it difficult to have authentic hope grounded in any human logic. Anything I came up with sounded like platitudes.

Lament is the expression of regret, sorrow, or unhappiness. Ancient cultures were much better at it than the modern Western world. With the exception of stoic philosophers and cultures, most of the globe throughout the millennia mourned through rituals and ceremonies that would last days or weeks. Public emotion was not only required but performed ceremonially. Some may dismiss such performative actions as meaningless, but I think we were created to grieve and lament together—and we've lost that art.

As societies have modernized and medical knowledge has advanced, humans have increasingly been separated from the "normal" human experiences of birth, pain, suffering, and death. A person born two hundred years ago had a life expectancy in the midthirties. If you survived to your midthirties, you would have buried many loved ones, including, likely, some of your own children.

When pain and despair do enter our lives, our stunted emotional muscles panic and we stay stuck in alternating realities of denial and seeking distractions to anesthetize the despair. We hold a false belief that if we only work hard enough or read enough or find the right thinker, we humans can fix the problem.

The blessings of progress have also robbed us of the communal experience of lament in suffering, pain, and death.

The closest experience I recall in recent times to communal lament occurred in the aftermath of September 11, 2001.

In the first few months of the COVID-19 pandemic, there were also attempts at communal lament. There were campaigns about being "alone together." Churches held virtual lament services. But we quickly got tired of the sadness and fear. Anger feels more empowering when life is uncertain. I wonder if much of the polarization and unrest we have seen the last few years is a direct result of our society getting stuck in the anger stage of grief.

For the Christian, there is good news in the lament. It leads us to the cross and the ultimate reconciliation and restoration of the world to God. We don't get to that hope without first experiencing the lament.

It's when He enters the brokenness that healing and hope are possible.

HUMBLING OURSELVES

There is a principle in the military, intelligence, and first responder communities that always being ready requires taking care of your home front first. If you or your family are not safe, then your ability to carry out your critical duties will be impeded. On airplanes, we're told to put our own oxygen mask on first before helping those who need assistance.

We can apply this principle to addressing the sin that is plaguing our community, as Jesus taught: we need to remove the log out of our own eye first, before attempting to remove the speck out of our brother's eye (Matthew 7:5).

If we want to restore peace in our community and build resilience to extremism, we need to examine ourselves first. How did *I* contribute to the brokenness, the darkness, we find ourselves in? Wittingly and unwittingly? With clear eyes, we can see our own vulnerabilities and the places where our hearts are steering us to act and live in ways that are inconsistent with what we say we believe.

Self-examination is considered an important spiritual discipline and a critical part of our spiritual formation and maturation.[1] Self-examination is done for the purpose of improving and healing. It is not only used in the spiritual context. Entire sections of bookstores are taken up with self-help approaches that usually involve some version of examining ourselves and our goals and desires for the purpose of ridding ourselves of bad habits or achieving the next level of performance.

Christians view self-examination as a practice to be done in partnership with the Lord, who knows us and searches our heart and mind, and with the support of a loving community. This process can be uncomfortable, but it's a discipline the American church tends to underemphasize, so we may not have much practice with it. Culturally, we are action oriented and impatient. We avoid pain when we can. It requires patience, humility, and sitting with ambiguity and paradox—not always knowing what the right next step might be. There is a mystery to it. Sometimes we are called to be still, and sometimes we are called to act.

There are a great number of books by both modern and ancient saints that can help you learn the spiritual discipline of self-examination. For some suggestions, visit the resources section of PathBackoPeace.org.

The Needs That Drive Us

There are over a hundred risk factors that researchers believe create vulnerability to extremism.[2] A study released in 2022 examined the interaction of fifty-four of them to identify those that are most likely to create pathways to radicalization. Radicalization is not linear. As the authors of the study put it, "There is likely no single driver of radicalisation, rather it is the crystallisation of personal and situational characteristics, converging in time and space, which results in radicalisation, for some."[3]

In order of strength, the top factors included being disrespected, psychological distress, a recent crisis, witnessing verbal statements in support of violent extremism, and feeling like a helpless victim.[4]

This research explored connections between the different risk factors. For example, they found that having certain cognitive susceptibility factors in the background (specifically, chronic stress, obsessive thinking, and isolation) and *then* having a crisis (specifically, interrupting the pursuit of a life goal) created one of the shortest paths to exposure to extremism. In this pathway, the exposure usually occurred through receiving propaganda online.

What should humble us is that many of these factors—a crisis, being disrespected, or psychological distress—are not things we can prevent. In fact, most people will at some point face all of these factors in their life. We can only control our responses to them. The goal is not avoiding them, but putting in place protective measures that will help us when we do encounter them.

In chapter 2, we examined three main pillars that motivate radicalization: needs, narratives, and networks—also known as the 3N model. The social psychologist behind this model, Arie Kruglanski, argues that the underlying need or motivation that drives one to be open to radicalization is the quest for significance.[5] But activating that quest often occurs as a result of other unmet needs, such as dealing with societal uncertainty, lacking social cohesion, and experiences or perceptions of rejection or humiliation at an individual or group level. Such experiences threaten our security, our sense of belonging, and our sense of significance.

The desire to feel safe, to belong, to be recognized, to be loved, and to have purpose and significance is part of the human experience. For millennia, religions provided answers to the needs for belonging, love, and significance. As religion becomes less prominent in Western society, these answers have come from ideologies, philosophies, and other secular sources.

Of the three needs—security, belonging, and significance—our culture's standard for significance has changed the most drastically in the last century, even within the last twenty years. Celebrity culture and the ability to project an image of "living your best life" (even though that image is a lie) make meeting our culture's definition of significance impossible.

Earlier, we explored how we are situated in an epoch shift—a liminal age—transitioning out of what has been but not yet sure what we are stepping into. This comes with unprecedented uncertainty and anxiety amid rapid change. If you have not yet had the experience of your identity being threatened, at some point you will. If your earthly foundations have not yet been shaken, they likely will in the future.

From a Christian perspective, we believe these needs are to be met in our identity as a child of God.[6] But we often substitute with other things, which may even be good things. When we make "good things into ultimate things," that is "primarily idolatry," says Tim Keller, and if we "build our life" on them, "they will drive us and enslave us."[7]

In *Counterfeit Gods*, Tim Keller distinguishes between surface idols (such as money, sex, career, relationships, family, and politics) and the deeper motives, or root idols, behind those surface idols. These are power (success, winning, influence), approval (affirmation, love, relationships), physical and emotional comfort (privacy, lack of stress, freedom), and control (self-discipline, certainty, standards).[8]

Most interesting for our purposes is when Keller takes the four root idols and identifies their "greatest nightmares"—several of them line up with known risk factors associated with radicalization: a root idol of power fears humiliation, approval fears rejection, comfort fears stress and demands, and control fears uncertainty.

Humiliation and rejection are two of the primary triggers for the "quest for significance," which Kruglanski asserts is the greatest need in those that radicalize.[9] Individuals who fear uncertainty tend to be more anxious and more likely to perceive a threat when others might consider the circumstances benign. In this way, individuals with low uncertainty tolerance seek out ways to control the circumstances, which creates a cognitive opening to extremist ideology that falsely provides black-and-white thinking and certainty.[10]

When our root idols are threatened, it increases our risk factors and threatens our sense of significance, belonging, and security. Our idols make us vulnerable. We need to find them and uproot them.

The Narratives That Shape Us

Narratives are the stories we tell that give life meaning and create our individual motivation. The narratives we believe help us interpret life and significantly inform the way we perceive reality. A Christian worldview is a type of narrative; as Christians, we would consider it a "master narrative."[11]

In the context of extremism, narratives are the ideology. They tell a story about the in-group's plight or crisis (the hero) and the evil of the out-group (the enemy), and make a case for a solution involving hostile action (a quest).

I believe our cultural narratives are broken cisterns. They seek to meet our needs, but they cannot hold clean, safe water for us to thrive.

These broken cisterns of cultural "truths" make us sick from contaminated water and languishing from thirst. And some of them are particularly grievous for laying the groundwork that can make us vulnerable to extremism.

The Myth of Owning Yourself

Self-belonging is our modern age's primary narrative, and it is leaving so many of us vulnerable. Two of our primary psychosocial needs are a need for significance and a need for belonging, and yet we're being told that all you need is yourself, follow your dreams or your heart's desires, and you can make yourself significant.

In Alan Noble's book *You Are Not Your Own*, he explores this "fundamental lie of modernity," the notion that to be human is to *belong to yourself* and our greatest purpose is to "be the best me I can be." He shows that the "Responsibility of Self Belonging" is crushing us. It requires us to forge our own identities and values and find ways to prove our significance and justify ourselves. It's exhausting. And it leads to anxiety and despair.[12]

We explored several cultural narratives in chapters 5 and 6 that likely led to our community's vulnerability. As you examine yourself, consider which of these narratives may be influencing you. To build resilience, we need to understand the full implications of belonging to Christ, for Christians, and belonging to each other, for everyone. Though we cannot fix society's narrative, we can choose to live differently and in so doing be a blessing to our community, offering hope to a society in despair.

The Networks That Expose Us

Our unmet needs and narratives of untruths may create vulnerability in us that could make us susceptible to extremism. But a key component of radicalization involves some type of repeated exposure to extremist spaces, people, or propaganda. Extremist grievances, memes, coded language, dog whistles, trolling, and ideology are increasingly being discussed in the "mainstream." Extremists are adept at marketing their beliefs to the unsuspecting in less offensive ways and taking advantage of crises to exploit fears and uncertainty.

I believe part of the reason more of the US population is expressing extremist viewpoints in recent years is because the social networks that provide our "epistemic authority"[13]—a narrative that defines our "truth," how things are and how things should be for us—increasingly provide the moral justification for doing *something* to "protect" ourselves or our way of life that they would otherwise believe immoral (i.e., use of force or violence).[14] Further, our social networks provide a "rewarding function"—respect and appreciation—when we comply with the group narrative.[15] This partially explains the difficulty in breaking away from our networks: we lose the respect and appreciation reward, and worse, we may lose our belonging, significance, and identity. It's easier to just stay quiet and tolerate it. And over time, toleration becomes agreement with these grievance narratives.

But our networks used to have some resilience to grievance narratives. What happened to allow these narratives to be entertained in the first place? Yuval Levin makes the case that as institutions have weakened, they have become more and more prone to manipulation. Institutions now provide a platform, not a role with instructions on how to contribute. Instead of being formative, they are performative.[16]

In his examination of churches as an example of failing institutions, Levin observes that some evangelical churches, instead of forming followers of Christ, are being used to platform culture wars and political activism. Similarly, some celebrity pastors are drawn to the allure of power and faux intimacy and are uninterested in the traditional functions of being a pastor of their church. Their focus is not on shepherding their local flock but using the platform of the pulpit to cultivate a following.

The local church is supposed to be the place where we are formed into disciples. If a church has a different motive—culture wars, celebrity, power, money—it will be difficult to be formed into a disciple of Christ. And by spending time networking with a deformed church, we are likely being exposed to grievances and narratives that could lead to vulnerability to extremism.

But we should also examine our motives in attending a church. If our motive is being part of a social club, raising our children with good morals, or advancing our political agenda, we are also part of the problem of our weak institutions.

Our country is desperate for a revival of meaningful institutions that help mold and shape us into adults with character, integrity, and competence. And it should start with our local churches.

A major challenge with some churches lies in teachings that reference bits and pieces of actual Truth but are applied to a distorted view of history and culture wars and lack biblical depth in proper context. Reading and studying full passages of Scripture and seeing their connection to the gospel will help us remain grounded in the truth.

I am wary of sermons or Bible studies that focus on politics or candidates or culture wars. There should be very clear lines between the ministry of God's Word and discussion of political beliefs. Why? Because Jesus, the Bible, and God's church are gifts to all people, not just Republicans or Democrats. Rampant partisanship intermingled with worship is a stumbling block that prevents unbelievers from coming to know Christ and stunts the growth of young believers.

I'm also wary of teachings that offer an "anti-vision"—that is, any vision of the Christian life, or life in general, that requires the existence of an earthly enemy. A teacher who overemphasizes earthly things to be feared (losing religious freedom, taking our guns, losing democracy, moral decay) and deemphasizes trusting God is not preaching the gospel. I'm not suggesting they be Pollyannaish about life. A proper teaching of God's Word should routinely come across passages that encourage believers to be prepared for trials and suffering, and frankly, at times, they should make us uncomfortable in a good, godly manner. But if in assessing our worldly challenges they never get to the hope we have in Christ, this will create fear and grievances that can leave people susceptible to radicalization.

Finally, I'm wary of teachings that lack nuance and assert only one way to interpret secondary and tertiary issues of doctrine. I think there is much beauty in practicing "In essentials unity; in non-essentials liberty; in all things charity."[17] The "essentials" generally cover who Jesus is and what he accomplished in his death and resurrection; salvation by grace through faith, not by works; and the authority of Scripture. I am not suggesting doctrinal minimalism. Secondary and tertiary issues do matter, and as you mature in your faith, you should wrestle with them and search the Scriptures for yourself to ensure you agree with what your church teaches, but if you find yourself in a place where someone suggests you are not saved if you don't agree with their stance on infant baptism or premillennial eschatology, or if you find yourself surrounded by people who are uncomfortable with you believing something different from what they do, this is a big concern. Our command to seek unity in Christ is clearly more important than doctrinal unity on secondary and tertiary matters, especially if the latter results in casting judgments and joining in "heresy" hunting.

Christ-centered churches will have healthy leaders who exhibit humility. They will practice love and compassion. When people are held accountable or "truth" is conveyed, it will not be done in judgment or condemnation but out of love for the people receiving the message.

Where Do We Get Our News? How Do We Vet Information?

The void left by formative institutions is being taken advantage of by profit-driven media and politicians, leveraging time and algorithms to form a false sense of "belonging" and "significance," not to mention addictive dopamine hits, via constant outrage.

If you are sickened by it, you likely have removed yourself from those groups. But how do we stay informed absent polarized news sources and echo chambers? This is harder than it should be. We're addicted to the dopamine hits. We like the sense of belonging to groups or listening to those who are seemingly like-minded. We need to rewire our brains to have longer attention spans that can allow us to sit still, be quiet, and think deeply. Instead of the churn of the daily news cycle or, worse, the constant swiping through TikTok, Instagram, or Reels, a key part of rewiring our brains is building habits of attention throughout the day that refocus our mind on the world around us and on God.

We might consider proactively changing our routine, so that the first thing we do in the morning isn't picking up the phone and scrolling through Instagram and X. There is growing consensus by those who study anxiety that our first set of activities in the morning should be tech-free (except for the coffee maker—that is a necessity).

In the context of choosing our information sources, spend more time reading books or long-form journalism than daily news or tweets. Just as our financial statements remind us where our priorities lie, our investments in time (including media consumption) show what is truly forming us. Jeffrey Bilbro suggests that "rather than diversifying our news feed or subscribing to papers across some artificial political

spectrum, we should subscribe aspirationally."[18] This means supporting newspapers, podcasts, and websites that *gather* communities to
which we want to belong. Believers should strongly consider spaces
that have values and perspectives that we want to have form us.

Evaluate the organizations whose information you subscribe
to. Does the institution have transparent standards and journalistic
ethics? How do they handle mistakes? (All news organizations make
errors; the question is, how do they make it right?)

Many organizations put their writers on podcasts now, especially
with long-form content. Listen to journalists and opinion writers; if
they lack curiosity, don't seek to understand others who disagree with
them, and don't from time to time change their opinion because they
learned something new, they are probably not worth our time.

Are the "Tribes" We Belong to Polarized?

Associating with a so-called tribe is normal human behavior. God
intended for us to live in a community, and belonging to healthy
groups is a part of that design. Living and serving our communities is
part of how we love our neighbor. And it helps to satisfy our needs to
belong, be recognized, and have purpose.

Our loneliness epidemic has made it difficult to find belonging in
communities we can trust. Between the decline of social trust, living
farther away from our extended families, and often lengthy drives
between school, church, work, and home, we have plenty of reasons to
be lonely—even without the screens that divert our attention from the
human beings in front of us. This has made it easier to join communities that give lip service to belonging but in reality have weaker real-
life ties and weaker accountability. In other words, they lack the depth
of true community.

Despite their lack of depth, such groups often make up our identity in our minds, such as the political party we associate with, our

cable news station of choice, the radio show or podcast we listen to. We
use these to characterize the tribe to which we belong, but in reality, all
we are is a consumer of their content—unless, of course, we decide we
need to be promoters of the content too. All the evidence shows that
social media makes us more anxious and lonelier, which is, of course,
concerning—those are vulnerability risk factors.

But the bigger concern is how much our networks participate in
the polarization cycle. The cycle of reacting to the "crazy" of the other
side drives us further and further apart. The resulting binary worldview passes moral judgment on the other group. "We" are good; "they"
are bad. If the groups with which we associate routinely practice narratives which imply the other is bad or evil—it might be time to find a
new crowd.

Watch out for groups that see outsiders as threats and encourage
hostile action to resolve their differences with others. For example, the
sweeping generalization that our school boards are out to indoctrinate
our children with Marxist ideas, backed up by thin facts and rampant
speculation, leads to community-wide fear.[19]

Watch out for groups that spend their time focused painting the
out-group as oppressors and the in-group as victims. Evidence is growing that "victimhood culture" is a contributing factor of the rise of
anxiety and depression, and I believe it is contributing to our vulnerability to extremism. Two sociologists studying victimhood culture
describe it as having three distinct attributes: "individuals and groups
display high sensitivity to slight," they "have a tendency to handle
conflicts through complaints to third parties," and they "seek to cultivate an image of being victims who deserve assistance."[20]

Find ways to check the assumptions your in-group makes about
their narratives—particularly when the narratives involve others. We
can do this by finding ways to build proximity to people outside of our

bubble, reading or listening to people from other groups, and maintaining a posture of curiosity.

Seek out people who are curious and want to learn. Seek friends and perspectives that offer charity to other perspectives (giving them the benefit of the doubt) and exhibit self-control in responding to people with different opinions.

Also, we can seek out real-life connections that have nothing to do with politics or other polarizing conversations. We can gather merely for the purpose of enjoying a hobby or benefiting our local community. Meeting and interacting with people from different perspectives and working together on common goals can help us rehumanize each other.

Unfortunately, we cannot eliminate our exposure to extremism. It's in the mainstream. But we can place ourselves in networks and institutions that will help us recognize it and repel its lies. Belonging to a community that values grace, kindness, and integrity provides multiple protective factors. It addresses the core needs of belonging and significance. It reduces a key vulnerability tied to extremism: isolation. Multiple perspectives allow us to see what we might otherwise be blind to. "In an abundance of counselors there is safety" (Proverbs 11:14). But most important, in such communities we grow deeper in Christ. The more we find our identity, belonging, security, and significance in Christ, the more resilient we will be to the lies extremism offers.

UNTANGLING OUR FAITH FROM OUR POLITICS

So here's a question for us to reflect on: are we interpreting our faith through the lens of our in-group, patriotism, or politics?

It should be the other way around. Faith first.

If we seek hope, belonging, significance, and security in our in-group, our party, or our country, we are staking our identity on it. When those things are threatened or fail, our identity is threatened.

We become open to narratives of existential threats to our existence and a need to do something to "save" our future or our children's future.

This is not the case if our hope is in Christ alone. With an anchor in Christ, we can still participate in politics and desire the flourishing of our city and country. But if politics fails (spoiler alert: it always does), it is not an existential crisis for us.

It is fine to be engaged in politics, but that should not be where we find our faith community. Our faith community should come first, and ideally it is diverse not only in race, ethnicity, and economic class but also in political opinions. After the Big Church Sort, this may be particularly challenging. But let's seek to be in a place where we can practice loving people who are different from us.

In pursuing Christ and His community (church), we will build resilience to the lies that lead to extremism.

EIGHT

LIVING IN THE AGE OF OUTRAGE

The Perils of Anger and Contempt

*Anger is an acid that can do more harm to the vessel in which it is
stored than to anything on which it is poured.*

—MARK TWAIN

According to a poll conducted in 2018, 84 percent of us believed that Americans were angrier than a generation ago and 42 percent said they were personally "angrier in the past year than they had been further back in time."[1] And this was before the pandemic.

Despite it being a moderate risk factor of extremism, anger's prevalence in our culture requires us to address it.[2] Anger and fear are serving as primary gateway drugs for the group radicalization that has occurred in recent years. When we are angry, it reduces our ability to reason logically; we are more prone to catastrophizing and all-or-nothing thinking. This leads us to be more open to false narratives that our significance and way of life are threatened.

UNDERSTANDING OUR ANGER

Some psychologists consider anger to be a secondary emotion that is used as a defense mechanism; it's a way to avoid other emotions.[3] It can allow us to feel powerful, restoring a sense of control (even though we probably are not in control), and the biological responses activated by anger can help us minimize physical or emotional pain.[4] Anger's dominance means we may not realize the reason behind it—such as anxiety, fear, or sadness.

Psychologist Paul Ekman, who pioneered the study of emotions and facial expressions, categorizes anger as one of the seven universal emotions. Anger "arises when we are blocked from pursuing a goal and/ or treated unfairly."[5] Incidentally, goal interruption is a risk factor for extremism.[6] "The primary message of anger is, 'Get out of my way!'" and it can manifest through a range of less-intense emotions (such as annoyance and irritation) to moderate-intensity emotions (such as frustration, exasperation, and argumentativeness) to the most intense emotions (bitterness, vengefulness and fury).[7] Ekman's common anger triggers include someone or something interfering with your goals, betrayal, abandonment, rejection, breaking of the law or norms, injustice, another person's anger, and someone trying to hurt us or a loved one physically or psychologically.

There are good and healthy aspects to anger. In his book *Good and Angry: Redeeming Anger, Irritation, Complaining, and Bitterness*, Christian psychologist David Powlison asserts that anger helps us recognize wrong and gives us energy to do something and to protect those being harmed and seek justice. Anger over abuse and injustice is righteous. If channeled appropriately, anger can be constructive. But the physiological effects of anger can make it difficult to carry out righteous anger in righteousness.[8]

More frequently, our anger is often driven by our pride and selfishness. Something has gotten in our way. The "evil" to which we are responding may or may not actually be evil. Further, our ways of handling anger—from irritation to rage—often sin against others.

There is a reason that half of the typical sins to avoid that Paul lists in his instructions to the church belong to the anger family.[9]

Most of Your Anger Isn't "Righteous"

Among those who believe we should "fight" for our "Christian heritage," our culture and virtues, we hear the frequent citation of Jesus' righteous anger in cleansing the temple of the money-changers by overturning tables and pouring out the coins (John 2:14–17).[10]

But we are deceiving ourselves if we think our anger is mostly righteous. Pastor and biblical counselor Robert D. Jones asserts that "most human anger is sinful."[11] He surveyed the Old Testament for the most common Hebrew word used for human anger (*aph*) and concluded that 89 percent of the references indicate sinful anger.[12]

Jones identifies three criteria in Scripture that demonstrate righteous anger:[13]

1. Righteous anger reacts against actual sin.
2. Righteous anger focuses on God and His kingdom, rights, and concerns, not on me and my kingdom, rights, and concerns.
3. Righteous anger is accompanied by other godly qualities and expresses itself in godly ways (i.e., self-controlled and confident).

Are we angry because such sin is affront to God? Are we concerned that our neighbors are under God's wrath, and, out of love, we want to help them see their enslavement to sin and the freedom that is offered in Christ?

I believe that much of the anger driving our community today comes from feeling rejected and humiliated and the fear of what more may come. Our root idols of power, control, approval, and comfort are threatened. We are scared that the trajectory of rapid change, which in one generation has gone from a dominant Christian culture to Christianity being viewed antagonistically, may lead to persecution.

Prominent among Christian nationalist advocates is a willingness to set aside the teachings of Jesus that call for patience, meekness, and turning the other cheek for calls to "stop being wimps" and "rise up to the battle God is calling them to fight" against "all forms of evil that seek to destroy us."[14] While they use the veneer of Christianity to provide moral justification for their anger, I do not think these groups are truly focused on God's Kingdom as much as they are focused about protecting their kingdoms, their in-group.

Keller suggests that we experience our most "uncontrollable emotions" when our idols are threatened. We become angry when the *evil* we're detecting is likely a threat to *our* kingdom.

———

Since our country's founding, anger has been leveraged by politicians and civil rights leaders to drive revolution, reform, and votes. Some of this is good, of course—righteous anger directed in a righteous manner is part of loving our neighbor, especially those marginalized in society (e.g., caring for the poor, widows, orphans, sojourners, and immigrants).[15]

But in America, we've mostly seen anger used to make a buck. "If it bleeds, it leads" was a concept coined by William Randolph Hearst in his competition with rival Joseph Pulitzer during the Spanish-American War. Both Hearst's and Pulitzer's newspapers used "melodrama, romance, and hyperbole to sell millions of papers."[16] This practice became known as yellow journalism and used sensationalistic stories that framed opinion as fact.

Anger is also one of the key emotions used to gain market share in the "attention economy." Fear, anger, shock, and awe keep eyeballs "tuned in" and fingers clicking. In 2012, researchers explored the virality of certain online content such as advertisements, videos, and news articles. Their conclusion was that content that evokes awe, anger, or anxiety was more viral.[17]

The goal of any free media (meaning you're not paying to access content or use the service) is to capture your attention and keep you there as long as possible so that you can be exposed to as many ads as possible; those ads drive the company's revenue. Over time, content creators heavily involved in social media (companies, media organizations, political activists, and influencers) learned that sensational headlines and emotional cues are more likely to gain clicks. More often than not, the content is designed to elicit negative emotions such as anger, hate, disgust, and contempt.

For social media, anger is money. This is not speculation. We have internal documents that state this, and whistleblowers have testified to this. Researchers at Facebook told Facebook senior executives that "our algorithms exploit the human brain's attraction to divisiveness."[18] Another internal Facebook study demonstrated that when you start a new, clean profile on a social media platform and don't post to it, within days your feed can be filled with content that promotes conspiracy theories, hate, and extremist groups.[19] One attempt, in 2018, by Facebook to "strengthen bonds between users and to improve their well-being" backfired; Facebook researchers discovered it made the "platform an angrier place."[20]

For this reason, multiple researchers and commentators have asserted that social media is a new form of yellow journalism.[21] While the mechanism is different—algorithmic sensationalism—the motive is the same: profit. The outcome is the same, too: outrage.

There is a case to be made that at least with anger there is a drive toward action. Setting aside whether our anger is righteous or not, at least when we have a drive to fix what's broken, there is a hope that the grievance that led to the anger can be addressed.

What happens when we no longer have hope that we can fix it? When we think nothing can be done, we become embittered.

Arthur Brooks makes the case that we're not angry; we have given up on anger. Americans have embraced a "culture of contempt." See if this sounds familiar to your experience. Contempt is "anger mixed with disgust."[22] It is derived from the Latin word for scorn and implies not a temporary frustration but an ongoing, "enduring attitude of complete disdain."[23] Contempt "seeks to exile . . . to mock, shame, and permanently exclude from relationships by belittling, humiliating, and ignoring."[24]

Contempt dehumanizes both the object and the expressor. Cultures of contempt set the stage for hostile action against their disdained and scorned out-group.

> *If then you have been raised with Christ . . . put to death therefore what is earthly in you . . . In these you too once walked, when you were living in them. But now you must put them all away: anger, wrath, malice, slander, and obscene talk from your mouth.*
>
> —COLOSSIANS 3:1, 5, 7, 8

PUT THEM ALL AWAY

How do we put anger and its associated vices away?

If our "daily habits reveal and shape our actual theology"[25]—then saturating our minds in content that increases our anxieties and grievances and provides a permission structure for anger, contempt, and hate will inevitably harden our hearts and make it very difficult to fulfill our primary commandments of loving God and neighbor. We need to stop participating in the things that drive our anger.

Practically, this means we should be wary of infotainment personalities with talk radio shows, TV shows, podcasts, YouTube channels, and X, Threads, and Instagram feeds that routinely traffic in performative outrage. You can recognize them by the catastrophizing language, absolutist all-or-nothing labeling, frequent exaggerations, and hyperbolizing of people or incidents. Some are particularly known for their outright deception—taking short clips out of context and packaging them with other visual and audio signals that leave the audience with the impression that what the person said was really evil, when in fact the context was something completely different. Outrage performers frequently cherry-pick an example from the out-group and overextrapolate its prevalence and influence.

It is also wise to keep in mind the motives of those to whom we expose our minds and hearts. The only goal is ratings. Ratings equal profits. Brooks pinpoints our "cultural addiction to contempt" as being "abetted by the outrage industrial complex for profit and power."[26]

Some news organizations and certain media personalities value good character and the virtues of truth and integrity, and they practice journalistic ethics and standards. And there are watchdog groups that routinely rate news organizations to identify where journalistic standards have been compromised. But in recent years, we have seen some news organizations become more willing to make compromises.

We should also be careful not to spread anger. This can happen directly in our engagements with others, but it can also happen online. Choosing to repost or share things that we cannot personally validate as true or that are intended to make fun of or express ill will toward other people could be spreading anger. We are particularly at risk of doing this within our in-groups. Over time, our in-groups develop shorthand ways of speaking about the other side. And we find it enjoyable to hyperbolize and exaggerate the other side's position. We poke fun at or even drive hate toward the other side.

Let me be more direct.

Asserting that all MAGA, Republicans, or Christians are racists or "a basket of deplorables" is slander—a false statement that damages their reputation.

Attempts to "own the libs" is a form of malice—you desire to see the other side suffer.

"Just asking questions" about conspiracy theories you have no firsthand knowledge about and no authority to investigate or act on, yet sharing your theory that politician A is a Satan worshipper and abuses children—that is slander.

Likewise, sharing a post or a meme that criticizes the "deep state" is a form of slander.

This last one really bothers me on a personal level. One might think it's harmless poking fun at the "system." But that system is made up of about 3 million federal civil servants. Even more people serve at the state and municipal levels. I am friends with many people who have served in federal and state government as career employees. I'm also married to one. Those characterizations and the general antipathy they've endured the last six years hurt them. It has made their jobs harder. Certain types of civil servants, such as law enforcement and election administrators, have seen increased threats of violence. Even their children have been threatened because of this rhetoric.

This rhetoric has damaged the church's reputation and created a barrier for spreading the gospel. Why should a civil servant be interested in what Christians have to say when the "Christians" they see on TV frequently demonize them without any evidence and blatantly lie about their intent?

Do not misunderstand me. In a democratic republic such as ours, the people have every right to hold their government accountable. Governments are made up of human beings and make mistakes. Governments can have blind spots. We can criticize our government and petition to have our grievances heard—but do it without malice or slander.

Let's put the anger away.

Changing our habits is hard. As we've discussed in other parts of this chapter, the transformation process can look and feel slow. If this is a challenging area for you, please take advantage of the resource section at PathBacktoPeace.org for books on uprooting anger.

In putting to death anger, we must cultivate mercy and grace in our hearts and with others. This not only builds resilience for us, but it also spreads in our communities. We have the ability to lower the temperature in our homes and workplaces when we respond to others' anger or stressful situations with calm and peace. As we work to identify and remove sinful anger and abide in Christ, we will, over time, bear the fruit of compassion, kindness, gentleness, and patience, which will in turn build peace in our communities.

NINE

OUTLIVING THE STUPOR OF EASE
Transforming Our Response to Suffering

Everyone agrees that the last few years have been hard. Really hard. When I ask people to pinpoint the start of the downward spiral for them, the answers vary. For some, it started with the 2008 financial crisis: the shame and emotional toil of having an underwater mortgage requiring a short sale or foreclosure or even declaring bankruptcy. Even if you did not lose a house or job, there was this sense of your life's momentum being stalled and that you'd never quite recover. For others it was anger and despair over the killings of Trayvon Martin, Michael Brown, and Eric Garner—will racism ever stop? For some families and communities, it was the 2016 election process, which deepened our polarization and drove people to bitterness and rage; for others it was the 2020 election cycle, the George Floyd protests, and fights over masks, vaccines, and whether to open or close schools during the COVID-19 pandemic. The hits didn't stop there. Another recession and financial crisis. January 6, 2021. Russia invading Ukraine. The 2022 election cycle. The Israeli-Hamas war. And the dread of another election cycle in 2024. When will it end?

Returning to the vulnerability to radicalization study, you'll recall that experiencing a crisis was one of the strongest factors associated with radicalization.[1] I think our decade-plus worth of crises and trauma and perhaps a culture that is weak in promoting resilience to adversity explain some of the increases in radicalization to extremism we've seen over the last decade.[2]

RESPONSES TO TRIALS AND SUFFERING

Our reactions to bad news, suffering, and trials are an excellent barometer for the health of our heart. It exposes where we have placed our hope. And in that reveal we may discover our theology to be weak, our actions to be perhaps sinful, and our heart's loves to be disordered.

Think back to the last time you faced a crisis, or the last time you were disrespected. (If you live with teenagers, this may be a near daily occurrence. For our purposes, try to think of examples outside of parenting, where the disrespect was unjust and deeply hurtful.) Think about the last time you experienced mental or psychological distress, which the American Psychological Association describes as "a set of painful mental and physical symptoms that are associated with normal fluctuations of mood in most people."[3] In lay terms, these are feelings of being anxious, depressed, troubled, confused, or out of the ordinary.[4] (Note that while psychological distress can accompany mental illness, experiencing mental distress does not necessarily mean there is a serious mental health issue.)

The Bible uses the metaphor of heat and drought for crises, and it is very clear that crises are not an "if," but a "when." Perhaps you are in the midst of one of these experiences right now.

Let's think back to March 2020, when we collectively had our worlds turned upside down. Regardless of your opinions of the pandemic and the government's responses to it, for everyone, there was a sudden disruption to our lives. Things were no longer as they were. Grief was universal. What was your response? Were you scared? Angry? In denial? Where did you seek peace and comfort? Where did you find hope?

The first few weeks I was fine. Twenty years of working in homeland security means I am used to watching disasters unfold, communities process the disruption, and the long tail of recovery. I could hold three truths in my mind without tension: (1) We were living through something extraordinary. (2) We were living through something universally human. Pandemics and disease are the norm for human beings; it's only been in the last hundred years or so that we've been able to medically protect ourselves from them. (3) God is still God—sovereign and good.

I was intentional about exercising more and taking walks with my family. That seemed a healthy coping mechanism.

But at some point, it got to me. Maybe it was when my husband was laid off just a few weeks after I resigned from DHS. When the landlord decided it was a good time to raise the rent. The tedious labor of packing, moving, and unpacking. Having to explain to the kids yet again why they could not play with their friend or go to a restaurant. Summer plans canceled. Celebrations for graduation, weddings, and retirement ceremonies postponed. Loved ones passing, and funerals unable to be held. Loss. Too much loss.

In April, I participated in a virtual lament worship service. I was so grateful for the opportunity to be guided in lament. Grieving can be an act of worship, and we needed it then.

It is healthy to have a suite of coping skills to endure the trials we all face as human beings. Sometimes we just need to make it through the day, the week, or the month—taking it one step at a time. Coping mechanisms help us do that.

But to be healthy and resilient, we need more than just techniques for coping; we need to be able to process the suffering and trials. We need to grieve, and we need to find something in which we anchor our hope for better days. As believers we can find solace in the fact that Jesus, while on earth, entered into grief with us.

There is another response we can choose when we face fear or danger. Instead of leaning into our initial fight-or-flight responses, we can choose to persevere through the suffering, to walk through it instead of trying to fly over it or walk around it. In these moments, we find hope by letting go of our very human need to understand and control things. We conquer difficulty by exercising our faith, knowing that we can trust Him, even when we can see no evidence of it with our human eyes. This is no doubt the harder road initially. Yet it is the path God invites us to, and it is the only way that we can truly persevere and be transformed through periods of suffering.

RESILIENCE AND GRIT

In homeland security, *"resilience* is the ability to adapt to changing conditions and withstand and rapidly recover from disruption."[5] The Department of Homeland Security is responsible for administering billions of dollars every year to help the nation be prepared for a bad day. The goal of those investments is to build resilience into our systems and infrastructure so we can quickly bounce back from a disaster—particularly catastrophic disasters. The homeland security community is constantly evaluating our protection, mitigation, response, and recovery plans; exercising those plans; and shoring up any gaps to ensure we are as prepared as possible. One of the best ways we prepare for the catastrophic events is by perfecting our responses to more frequent disasters—tornadoes, hurricanes, floods, and wildfires. We need the practice in responding to smaller disasters and learning how to recover quickly in order to be prepared for the larger ones.

Unfortunately, we might be doing the opposite of this principle in our parenting and for ourselves. In the last decade, educators and parents have become more aware of the dangers of "helicopter parenting." Overprotecting our children—particularly, saving them from having to solve problems on their own or from experiencing failure—is contributing to their anxiety and depression and stunting their ability to mature into functioning adults.[6] Age-appropriate adversity in childhood "provides opportunities to strengthen adaptive skills and self-regulatory capacities."

It turns out that stress is a good thing in the right doses. Much like lifting weights tears down muscle to build it back stronger, adversity strengthens our resiliency. But increasingly, American culture is about pain avoidance. We seek ways to be comfortable and feel like we're in control (even if it's a false sense of control). Any concept of having to endure pain is lost on us. The problem is, our avoidance of adversity—either by quitting when things get hard or distracting ourselves or numbing the pain away—weakens our ability to endure bigger crises.

Studies on resilience in children show that having "at least one stable and committed relationship with an adult"—such as a parent, caregiver or other adult—provided the "personalized responsiveness, scaffolding, and protection that buffer children from developmental disruption." Likewise, we know adults fair better in stressful situations when they have secure relationships, suggesting that a key part of resiliency is having strong relationships.[7] Other factors that contributed to resilience in children included building a sense of self-efficacy and perceived control, and mobilizing sources of faith, hope, and cultural traditions.[8]

Schools are increasingly emphasizing the importance of resilience and grit—learning how to push through adversity and not giving up.[9] They're creating opportunities for children to try hard things, set small goals, and keep persevering. These opportunities to "fail" and learning how to see "failure" with a growth mindset are a springboard for learning and for growing abilities.[10]

If you are a parent or educator or otherwise involved with youth, along with being a stable adult in their life who demonstrates unconditional love, one of the best gifts you can give your child is providing age-appropriate opportunities to practice persevering through adversity. If we can spread this gift across society, it will contribute to restoring peace in our communities over the next generation.

WHAT DO YOU BELIEVE?

A recent essay in the *International Journal for Philosophy of Religion* argued that the practice of religious faith has built into its nature resilience in the face of challenges.[11] Other psychological research has demonstrated that faith is used as a tool of resilience, which "can play an important role in individuals' lives in overcoming and coping with the challenges of their daily stressors."[12]

Yet we have individuals claiming to be people of faith who are not demonstrating resilience. Where is the disconnect? My hypothesis is we may have two challenges. First, we may be misunderstanding what the Bible says and thus have false hope about how our life should go. Second, we might lack experience in practicing our faith in the midst of trials, and thus we struggle to persevere.

Let's start with what we believe. Why does that matter? The Bible teaches us that renewing our minds is the key to transformation (Romans 12:2), and recent scientific research on the brain's neuroplasticity confirms the Bible's wisdom. When the Bible talks about our minds, it is not just focusing on our intellect or knowledge of Scripture (a left-brained activity). Rather, it is calling for us to adjust our moral and spiritual thinking to that of God's, an activity that requires both left- and right-brain activity. The positive and negative narratives we dwell upon transform us. Our actions and choices are a direct result of what we believe—even if it is subconscious. Believing a narrative that is simply not true leaves us vulnerable during crises.

David French suggests that many Christians view God as a "cosmic loss avoider guarantor,"[13] meaning that God exists to ensure we don't experience any loss or fear of loss.

Such false beliefs imply any crisis or suffering are the result of you sinning. You have done something wrong and God is out to "get" you.

This sentiment can show up without explicitly heretical teaching. The Western church is accustomed to comfort and power, thus we probably don't hear enough sermons on trials and suffering. Or when we do, they seem unrelatable.

The American church also has a reputation for superficiality in our interactions with fellow church members. We say we're "fine" when asked how we are. Our society's increased mobility combined with phenomenon of "church-hopping" means many of us have shallow relationships with others in the church. This limits our ability to share with others any struggles we might have, and—critically—we miss out on learning from those walking through a trial. We avoid deeper connections at our peril.

The Bible tells us that suffering should be expected of followers of Christ. We are told that to be Jesus' disciples we "must deny [ourselves] and take up [our] cross" to follow Jesus (Luke 9:23). In a world where we think of the cross as topping the steeple of a picturesque church or our favorite James Avery jewelry—it's easy to miss how violent and terrifying this metaphor is.

In Jesus' final teaching to his disciples, the night before he is crucified, he tells them that they will be hated by the world, rejected, and even killed by their own religious community (John 15:18–25, 16:2–3).

This is not the first time Jesus warns his disciples about the cost of following him. In Matthew 10, he warns the disciples of the violence he is ushering in: "Brother will deliver brother over to death, and the father his child, and children will rise against parents and have them put to death, and you will be hated by all for my name's sake" (vv. 21–22).

This is jarring because five chapters earlier, in the Beatitudes, Jesus is teaching "Blessed are the poor in spirit, for theirs is the kingdom of heaven" (Matthew 5:5) and "Blessed are the meek, for they shall inherit the earth" (Matthew 5:7). He takes the known Jewish law against murder and applies it to the heart: if you are angry or insult your brother, it is as grievous as murder (Matthew 5:22). If you lust, it is as grievous as adultery (Matthew 5:28). Love not only your neighbor, but also your enemy—and pray for those who persecute you (Matthew 5:44). And the intervening chapters are filled with healing miracles that clearly demonstrate his power over the fallen world.

So which Kingdom is it? A Kingdom of peace or of violence?

Jesus closes this part of the teaching with these words: "I have said these things to you, that in *me* you may have peace. In the *world* you will have tribulation. But take heart; I have overcome the world" (John 16:33, emphasis added). I love the contrast between what he is offering. When we are abiding in Christ, we find the peace. Earlier the same evening, Jesus used the metaphor of the vine and branches and explains that abiding in Christ brings joy. The world brings tribulation, hatred, even death. Abiding in Christ is peace and joy.

This wasn't news to the saints who went before us. But those of us living in modern Western "Christendom" over the last century have gotten quite used to being the mainstream and enjoying the power, comfort, control, and approval (or adoration) that comes with it. For those of us blessed to have lived an "easy" life, it is critical that we renew our minds with this truth: trials, suffering, and persecution are an expected part of being faithful followers of Jesus.

Not only should we expect it, but the Bible teaches that we should *rejoice* when we encounter trials! This is so countercultural, the opposite of the American Dream world we live in. We are *so* good at avoiding pain. Trials are to be avoided or managed with distractions and anything that can numb the pain.

Trials expose what our heart believes about God, not just what we *think* we believe. It takes our hypothetical theology and makes it real. Do we *really* believe what we say we do about God?

He is good.

He is sovereign and all-powerful; in Him all things were created and are held together (Job 42:2; Acts 4:27–28; Colossians 1:16–17).

He is mighty to save (Zephaniah 3:17).

He sees you. He loves you. He has called you by name; you are His. He takes great delight in you. He will quiet you with his love and rejoice over you with singing (Genesis 16:13; Isaiah 43:1; Zephaniah 3:17).

You are blessed, chosen, beloved, and redeemed (Ephesians 1:3–7; Colossians 3:12).

He is with you wherever you go. He will never leave you nor forsake you (Joshua 1:9; Isaiah 43:1–2; Hebrews 13:5).

He is near to the brokenhearted and saves the crushed in spirit; he binds their wounds and heals them (Psalm 34:18; Psalm 147:3).

Every trial has a purpose; He will bring good out of it for those that love God (Romans 8:28).

Sometimes there is a big disconnect between what our heads claim to believe and what our hearts actually believe. We can pray for the Lord to strengthen our hearts; we can also choose to act in faith on what we know in our heads to be true, even if our heart is fearful.

There is a reason why "fear not," "do not fear," and "do not be afraid" are among the most prevalent commands in Scripture. God knows that to be human is to have fears. The fallen world we live in is uncertain and, at times, dangerous. Evil is real. And we are limited. Despite all of our efforts to gain power, control, comfort, and approval to assuage those fears, it is never enough to keep us completely safe.

During my most difficult trials, these are the truths I would say out loud, sometimes multiple times a day. I would ask God to help my heart catch up to my head. And I needed the support of fellow believers reminding me of these truths and encouraging me to persevere.

As difficult as those trials were, I am grateful they exposed the lies I was believing and in which I was wrongly placing my trust and hope. And can I tell you? God was so, so gentle with me. He would allow a smaller trial to prepare me for a bigger one. Having a track record of surviving the crisis, the humiliation, the anxiety, and the sadness, and seeing God provide—daily, sometimes hourly—for the need I had at a particular moment helped me walk through the next one more steadily, with confidence and hope. Moments of peace washed over me in the midst of absolute turmoil, when I had been reeling moments before. The hair on my arms stands up thinking about those moments when God becomes very real, very . . . present: experiencing the Spirit providing peace that surpasses all understanding (Philippians 4:7); having the courage to speak truth and knowing the right words to speak, despite the cost; having the love to show kindness to someone who is difficult to love. These trials—as hard as they were—strengthened and deepened my faith. The real treasure, though, was my deeper relationship with the Lord.

Suffering is a gift—though it is a very painful gift that can threaten to destroy even the strongest and most faithful among us.

But when the crisis, humiliation, anxiety, or depression arrive at our doorstep and we run to God with our pain and heartbreak, when we are humble and open to His refining work in us, when we lean in to our brothers and sisters in Christ to support us in prayer and in other practical ways, we persevere and endure, one painful, dark, and ultimately transformative step at a time.

This is the path of a disciple. This is the path of abiding in Christ and experiencing the joy and peace in Him while the world rages around us. And it is in abiding in Christ that we build resilience to the lies that lead to extremism.

TEN

FROM RADICALIZATION TO RECONCILIATION
Healing Our Church

P art of the American church is sick. We have too many Christians and ministry leaders who live and teach in full-scale opposition to the fundamental principles of the Christian faith and in outright rejection of Jesus' way to His Kingdom. We've elevated ourselves to the role of God in declaring how one cannot vote for this or that political party and be a saved Christian. We've elevated our politician, our party, or our infotainment host as a prophet and savior.

We have professed believers participating in culture wars, rejoicing in the slander and malice of their out-group, spending more time lamenting about America's morality problems than building meaningful relationships with God and with others. They explicitly reject Jesus' calls to turn the other cheek, love our enemies, and pray for those who persecute us, and instead call for "taking America back" and even laying out "moral" justifications for violence.

A significant part of the American church has failed to carry out our core mission as given to us by Jesus: to make disciples. We are supposed to be helping people become more and more like Christ in our daily lives. Instead, we have scattered seeds of the good news, but we have not encouraged deep growth in good soil. This lack of maturity and encouraging each other to follow Jesus' model of loving our neighbor by laying our lives down for one another leaves us vulnerable. When our significance has been threatened, our sense of belonging shaken, or our security is at risk, undiscipled, immature Christians or, tragically, people who think they are saved but aren't are easy prey for narratives of tribalism, contempt, and extremism.

In many instances, it's not uneducated Christians causing the damage. Christian seminaries and seminarians and churches and pastors are, under the guise of "standing up for what is right" or "for America's Judeo-Christian values," wittingly stoking the fires.

Our community actively participates in fearmongering for the sake of preserving our power, comfort, approval, and control. Some of our pastors preach how *they* (fill in the name of your out-group) or this idea (fill in the name of the latest cultural trend, moral outrage, or academic concept) pose an existential threat to our "Christian" way of life. They have moved into the lower end of the hostile action scale of extremism on their various platforms, including social media, TV, and even sermons—using slander, malice, derisive labeling, and speaking of others with contempt or derision. Further, their influence may indeed cause others more vulnerable to take the next step into violence.

Some are even worse to those inside the church that dared to question if this was the way of Jesus. They are quick to publicly label other believers as heretical when their theology or politics differs from their own. They believe that "discrediting their opponents and weakening or destroying their institutions" in order to "enforce *our* order and *our* orthodoxy" is their "moral duty."[1] They have blatantly criticized "winsome" Christianity as being incompatible with our present moment.

All these things are sinful and in and of itself are damaging to the church. Sadly, many who do not believe in Christ often find substantiation in rejecting faith in response to the behavior of Christians and their churches by pointing to culture warriors and online battles carried out in public between believers.

It is plausible that absent the convergence of events from the last ten years, we would have remained like the frog in the water, going from a balmy bath to a simmer and eventually a slow boil, a progression so slow that we wouldn't be aware that we needed to hop out of the pot on the stove. Instead, the church's failure to address sexual abuse, misogyny, racism, and, worse, its attempted coverups, combined with deepening polarization from the past two election cycles and a devastating pandemic, have led to the church's implosion.

The poor handling of the challenges of the past decade has drawn a sharp and obvious contrast between what people claim to believe about Jesus and how they actually live. The church's rejection of Jesus' teaching in our daily life, far from making America great again, is contributing to the faster downward spiral of our nation—and I don't mean our country's sexual ethic. I mean the growing despair and nihilism that is at the root of much of our violence. The church's failure has created the vulnerability to extremism.

Instead of being an antidote to extremism, American Christian culture has provided fertile soil for extremism to grow.

TO GO OR TO STAY AND HELP

In 2021, Tim Alberta, a political journalist and pastor's kid, traveled the country to explore how evangelical churches navigated 2020. He highlights the story of two pastors in suburban Detroit, both leading "predominantly white, Republican congregations" but using very different approaches to COVID-19 and the other challenges of the era. One of his observations was that after decades of a narrative that "courageous, God-fearing Christians" are pitted "against a wicked society that wants to expunge the Almighty from public life," something drastic had shifted. Both of the pastors "believe there is a war for the soul of the American Church—and both have decided they cannot stand on the sidelines. They aren't alone. To many evangelicals today, the enemy is no longer secular America, but their fellow Christians, people who hold the same faith but different beliefs."[2]

I do not envy the job of pastors over the past few years. In 2020 alone, twenty thousand pastors left the ministry. In the fall of 2022, 41 percent of pastors considered quitting in the past year; up from 29 percent in January 2021.[3] While we do not know the extent of the pre-pandemic desire for quitting, we do know that the annual attrition rate across Protestant denominations was 1–2 percent.[4] The top three reasons given for wanting to quit were stress, loneliness, and political division.[5]

I don't know if the survey categories adequately capture the emotional toll of the past few years. The connections we build with people in our church is (or should be) more deep, intimate, and vulnerable than relationships in other institutions. A church built on God's grace and love is the ultimate "safe space." We come alongside one another when we are grieving or struggling, and we confess sin and hold one another accountable. These are relational ties that we believe go beyond this world; we believe we will see these people in the next life. We share the same Savior and Holy Spirit; we are members of one body. And then people started to leave. Sometimes without explanation. Sometimes with severe emotional abuse toward ministry leaders. The breaking of these relationships feels like betrayal. And it has been particularly difficult for those in ministry.

So before we talk about if we need to confront our pastors, or how we discern whether we should leave our church, let's start from a place of compassion for those in ministry.

The Big Church Sort

Beginning in 2020, we started to see the church version of the Big Sort we discussed earlier and the role it plays in polarization—where evangelicals increasingly became incomprehensible to one another.[6] They self-sorted or fractured into six categories—neo-fundamentalists, mainstream, neo-evangelicals, post-evangelical, dechurched, and deconverted—on the basis of (1) COVID-19 restrictions (or lack thereof), (2) the response to the protests of George Floyd's murder, (3) the election, and (4) conspiracy theories (the 2020 election being stolen, QAnon, etc.).[7] Churches that took combative stances on pandemic restrictions or stolen elections saw their numbers increase dramatically, and this during a season when most churches lost congregants. One of the churches Alberta examined went from one hundred to fifteen hundred people in attendance per weekend within a year.[8]

Those who tried to stay neutral on issues did not fare well. People wanted their pastor to "pick a lane." As Alberta reported, "a strictly apolitical approach can be counterproductive; their unwillingness to engage only invites more scrutiny. The whisper campaigns brand conservative pastors as moderate and moderate pastors as Marxists."[9]

Michael Graham observed that "big tent" churches and paraministries are feeling the greatest tension of the moment. He suggests that before 2015, churches—and quite frankly all of us—had more elasticity. But after the past decade, particularly after 2020, we are like a rubber band that can easily snap. Today, most churches can handle being made up of no more than two adjacent subgroups. So, neo-fundamentalists and mainstream evangelicals could belong in a church together. Mainstream and neo-evangelicals could do church together as well. Likewise neo- and post-evangelicals. But if you start to mix neo-fundamentalists and neo-evangelicals, you are going to get some fireworks. Likewise, mainstream evangelicals and post-evangelicals in a church community will find themselves in deep tension.[10]

Consequently, he believes that the American church is in the process of a sorting process as people are trying to find a church that "best fits their animating and core concerns," a process they believe is well underway but will continue for the next two to five years.

I have attended solidly mainstream evangelical churches—that second category—most of my life, probably with a few neo-fundamentalists mixed in. In 2015, my husband and I started attending what you could probably consider a neo-evangelical church with some post-evangelical mixed in. We didn't realize it at the time, but when we returned to Washington, DC, in 2017 and went back to our mainstream evangelical Bible church, the one we had started attending together shortly after we had married, something felt off. They had a good kids program, we still had friends there, and I was too busy at work to build a new community, so we stayed.

Until 2020—when the unspoken majority political views of the church started to be more outspoken. Virtual Bible studies were being derailed as people used the gathering to complain about the "liberals" and spout the most recent talking points from Rush Limbaugh or Tucker Carlson. Jokes were made from the lectern, such as "Christ commands that I have to love my neighbor, but does that really mean I have to also love liberals?" One sermon explained that Joe Biden would die soon, so the person you were really voting for is Kamala Harris and you need to think about that. (It was not clear what they meant. Was it that Harris was a woman? A Black woman? Or more liberal than Biden?) We were completely shocked that this was said on a Sunday morning. While it was out of character for the person who said it, it was the moment we realized we couldn't stay.

I was already emotionally raw from friends and associates questioning my decision to speak publicly about my concerns about Trump, asserting that I had left the faith or had blood on my hands (a reference to abortion). I needed to be in a church where I could worship my Savior and not think about politics.

When we departed, there were no hard feelings. We are grateful for their ministry to us and our children. Our departure was not out of anger. The tension we were sensing had been building for a while, and it was best for our family's continued spiritual growth for us to find a new local church.

Yet, I'm saddened that the church finds itself at a place where such boundaries are needed. The Body of Christ should have diversity of viewpoints and experiences. The more singular-minded and sorted we become, the less we grow as disciples, and the less salt and light we can be in the world. You may have an important role to play in helping mainstream evangelicals see the dangers of neo-fundamentalism and Christian nationalism and strengthening their trust in God.

That said, if you find yourself in a church that is not adjacent to your worldview, it may be wise to find a church where you can worship without having to keep your guard up about politics and culture wars. Such departures are sad and maybe even painful and should be done after a season of prayer and seeking God's guidance.

MINISTERS OF RECONCILIATION

Whether we feel called to stay in our church or we've found a new church, we have been given a ministry of reconciliation (2 Corinthians 5:18). While we often think of that ministry as externally facing—reconciling the world to God, and it is—I believe our generation's call may be to first bring the message of reconciliation to the church. How do we do that? We plead for Jesus to intercede for his bride—the church—as he did for Peter and the disciples on the night of his crucifixion: "I have prayed for you that your faith may not fail" (Luke 22:32). And we start with repentance—expressing sincere regret and remorse for our wrongdoing. Even if we have not personally participated in any of these sins, the Bible lays out a pattern of the faithful repenting on behalf of their community.[11]

Our community needs to acknowledge the sin of our idolatry—the worship of patriotism, a political party, a politician. We need to repent of our fear and paranoia that the country is changing. Repent of our worship of an American Dream that our children's and grand-children's lives will be better than ours. All of the pitfalls we've already examined, vulnerabilities that derive from our needs for significance, belonging, and security that when misplaced on earthly idols cannot sustain the weight of our need; the narratives that sow grievance and lead us into idolatry; and our networks that traffic in outrage and grievance—all of these things need to be addressed in our church community. As each individual has different propensities, so too our communities will likely have certain weaknesses that make us more vulnerable.

Don't buy into the argument that admitting your sin or exposing the church's sin hurts the spread of the gospel. This is a lie. Christianity is not facing an existential threat. But we are a stumbling block to the lost finding God when we do not acknowledge our sin and ask for repentance. They already see it. They know we're hypocrites. The more "radical" thing is to be humble. To admit when we've screwed it up and ask for forgiveness. That is countercultural. That is not the way of the world. That is the way of Jesus.

Some in our community will reject our calls for repentance.

The vast majority of people in the church are not radicalized, just vulnerable. When lovingly confronted with the Truth that their behavior is not aligned with Jesus' teaching, many will be convicted and repent.

On the other side of repentance, the model we see in Jesus' counsel to Peter is to "strengthen [our] brothers" (Luke 22:32).

In the church we talk about this as Christian formation or disci-pleship. The goal of discipleship is to be formed into the image of Christ (2 Corinthians 3:18; Galatians 4:19). James Bryan Smith wrote about theologian Dallas Willard's model of formation. Willard viewed formation as "putting on the 'mind of Christ'" by "adopting the narra-tives of Jesus on key issues like the character of God the Father, the nature of human person as an embodied soul, and the reality of the present kingdom of God. Dallas taught that disciplines such as prayer, solicitude, and Scripture memorization are only *one part* of the formation process. The second part is the work of the Holy Spirit, and the third is learning how to see life's trials and events in light of God's presence and power."[12]

Did you catch Willard's framing? Becoming Christ-like means "adopting the narratives of Jesus." In being formed into the image of Christ, we take on His way of seeing the world, His narrative. When those narratives are in place, there is little room to be vulnerable to the false narratives of extremism—even when we go through trials and uncertainty, and even when we're rejected—because Jesus' narrative has answers for all those experiences and our unmet needs. His narrative offers a "solution" for our crisis, a solution that Jesus has already handled. Jesus' narrative is the ultimate protective factor.

So how do we help our church put on the mind of Christ? Certainly, all of the pitfalls we examined for ourselves are things our fellow brothers and sisters in Christ likely struggle with: vulnerabilities that derive from our needs for significance, belonging, and security; mistakenly looking to earthly idols to meet those needs; exposure to narratives that sow grievance and lead us into idolatry; and spending time in networks that traffic in outrage and grievance. All of these things need to be addressed in our church community.

But there is more we can do in our local churches.

Learn Church History, Mourn the Church's Sin, and Seek Justice

Ecclesiastes tells us that there is nothing new under the sun (1:9). The father of history, Thucydides, asserted that "events of future history will be of the same nature—or nearly so—as the history of the past, so long as men are men." There is even some scholarship that says there is a cyclical nature to history—and that it repeats every four generations!

The adage "history repeats itself" may be right. Mark Twain offered an alternative suggestion: "History doesn't repeat itself, but it does rhyme."

Our culture is notoriously historically illiterate. A 2018 study found that only one in three Americans could pass a multiple-choice history test made up of questions about the American Revolution, Civil War, and Declaration of Independence taken from the US citizenship test, so this might take some intentionality on our part.[13]

While our times seem unprecedented, our ancestors also endured times of great disruption, anxiety, and chaos. Our faith would be strengthened to see how God provided for past generations during their "unprecedented" times. We benefit from understanding the challenges the early church faced from both heresy and persecution. Helping people see that the saints who have gone before us have endured similar things will encourage us to press on.

Knowing church history also helps us avoid mistakes, because "most of the bad ideas out there are bad ideas that have been tried in the past."[14]

Further, to be ministers of reconciliation to the broader community, we must see our historic and present sin. We should be prepared to acknowledge publicly past sins that the secular world already knows about. And when present sin is revealed, we should lament and mourn with those who have been harmed. We should repent on behalf of the church. We should be quick to ask the Lord to reveal how our systems or blind spots allowed such harm. And we should seek justice—including through civil authorities—where earthly justice can still prevail. We find solace in knowing that wherever earthly justice fails, God's justice will prevail.

We are people of the Truth. We should not lie out of fear over what the world will think. I appreciate that for some, this propensity to hide our sin comes from a place of genuinely wanting the world to hold God and Jesus' name in high esteem. We should mourn. But we should not fear that God isn't strong enough to overcome man's failing.

In an era of #ChurchToo, it is past time for the collective church to genuinely lament with victims, examine ourselves about why we are so vulnerable to abusing the marginalized, offer reparations where we can, and seek justice—through both civil authorities and church discipline.

We have a responsibility to know our history and seek justice on behalf of those who have been harmed by the church.

Practice the Way of Jesus: Being Intentional in Community

We need to intentionally build and live in community with other Christians. It helps us let go of the false idol of self-sufficiency and push back against our culture's concept that we belong to ourselves. Being present in a local body allows us to experience the gifts of the full body of Christ. We weren't intended to be able to do it all. We are not meant to sojourn alone. Within the body of Christ, we fulfill our needs for significance and belonging by offering our strengths to the local body and serving with the body in the local community. Other believers need your God-given gifts. Likewise, our needs for belonging and security are met in receiving and enjoying the strengths of others.

Most significantly, it's part of God's design to sanctify us within a body of fellow sinners who also need God's grace. It is the iron-sharpening-iron method. Hanging out with fellow believers—much like connecting with family at Thanksgiving—can be frustrating and uncomfortable. God does not remove the friction. The friction is what sanctifies us. When we let people in, conflict is inevitable. The blessing of belonging comes with a responsibility to practice love.

If our quest is for a frictionless life, we will be doomed to immaturity in Christ. Becoming more like Christ comes from being in the local body. From the giving of our gifts and receiving of others' gifts. From learning together and praying together. From watching prayers be answered, rejoicing with those with cause to rejoice, serving those who are in need, walking with those who are suffering, and grieving alongside those experiencing the curses of a fallen world.

We also need to intentionally build community with people who are different from us, communities that hold different perspectives and have different experiences. When I meet people, fellow believers, who are dismayed at the current state of the American church, I ask, "What allowed you to see it? Why are you not living in fear? Why are you not deceived as others in your family or community are?" I'm looking for how they gained protective measures. Inevitably, part of the answer comes from having proximity to people who are different from those in their community of origin. Friendship is the most powerful. Experiencing different cultures and ways of seeing the world through travel and books seems to also provide some protective factors if one is curious and humble enough to seek out understanding of the "other."

Proximity to those different from ourselves cultivates gratitude and humility and protects us from "othering."[15] It rehumanizes individuals who are otherwise labeled, painted with a broad brush, or, worse, made the enemy by your community of origin. As we said at the beginning, it is normal and natural for us to have in-groups and out-groups. Experiences that allow us to develop relationships with different out-groups build resistance to any extremists' attempts to dehumanize the out-group. When you know someone personally who is a Democrat, Republican, Christian, Muslim, homosexual, immigrant, Border Patrol agent, hippie, transgender individual, IRS agent, law enforcement officer, member of the military, journalist, member of the clergy, or fill-in-the-blank person, instead of that label, to you they are Linda, Matt, Rio, Jemar, and Angelica.

And we can help our local churches experience the benefits of proximity by deepening our appreciation, love, and service to the global church. A healthy appreciation for the global church creates humility and builds inoculation to the idolization of American Christianity. The "Americanized" church has many weaknesses that are easier to see and repent of when we experience the power of the gospel outside of our country's culture.

Adopting Jesus' Narrative: An Invitation to the Step into the Kingdom

The most frequent critique I hear from unbelievers about their perception of the church is that we don't even pretend to practice what Jesus taught about the ways of the Kingdom. Twenty years ago, the critique was hypocrisy—that we would pretend to follow God's rules and hide our failures as much as we could.

Not so today. Today you see treatises exploring why it is not simply permissible but necessary to ignore Jesus' call to meekness (Matthew 5:5) and Paul's call to gracious speech, patience, and meekness (Colossians 4:6 and 12). These explanations overemphasize and misinterpret Jesus overturning the money changers' tables in the temple (Matthew 21:12) and calling the Pharisees "whitewashed tombs" and a "brood of vipers" (Matthew 23:27, 33).

This is the core of repair work that needs to be done.

We do this by identifying the ways we are clinging to the world's system and letting go to instead hold fast to Jesus' narrative. Sometimes we read Jesus' teachings and think, *How poetic! How beautiful this vision of righteousness! Can't wait to get to heaven to enjoy this.* This is one of the weaknesses of some parts of the American church's narrative. It focuses on the goal of individual salvation. Once that box is checked, we either think we're good—no further action necessary—or we attempt to use God or "Christianity" to obtain our "good" goals.

Some false narratives prioritize earthly blessings (health and wealth gospel). Some focus on exercising "dominion" and lay out the case for Christianizing the country. Some pay lip service to sanctification—following a list of moral rules and making sure our kids don't succumb to the culture's lies—but turn out more like the Pharisees, not actually becoming more Christ-like.

These gaps in our gospel demonstrate that we are blind to our identity in Christ, God's provision, and God's process—so we strive to find earthly things, even Christianized earthly things, to meet our needs of significance, belonging, and security.[16]

Jesus' narrative offers to fill those needs. It's an invitation to transformation.

Let's help our church communities hear Jesus' invitation and teach them what it means. By adopting Jesus' narrative we accept his invitation into living with *His* Kingdom's virtues and values. We take off the world's, our culture's, and our idols' values and replace them with Jesus'. In doing so, we put on the mind of Christ and through the work of the Holy Spirit become more like Christ—more holy, more righteous in our conduct, more at peace, more merciful, more generous. Or, as Paul frames it, "being transformed into [His] image from one degree of glory to another" (2 Corinthians 3:18).

Tools of Transformation: Spiritual Disciplines

There are a number of Christian discipleship practices that can help us learn to step into this invitation. There are the ones you probably think of: prayer (individually and corporately), gathering to worship together, reading Scripture daily, and the sacraments of baptism and communion. Then there are the ones that the "really spiritual" people do: meditating, fasting, practicing silence, liturgy, and participating in the church calendar (Advent, Lent, Christmas, Easter, etc.). There are excellent classics to read, such as Brother Lawrence's *The Practice of* the *Presence of God*, Richard Foster's *Celebration of Discipline*, Dallas Willard's *The Spirit of the Disciplines: Understanding How God Changes Lives*. And, depending on your faith traditions, you may enjoy devotionals from Thomas Merton, Henri Nouwen, and Eugene Peterson.

Consider learning more about one of the spiritual disciplines, and pray about whether one or two might be helpful for your community to practice together. Certain practices may seem antiquated, particularly if you come from a nondenominational church. But that may be precisely why exploring them may be healthy. Tish Harrison Warren encourages such disciplines because they offer a counterformation to our culture's proclivities, like impatience. Practicing the liturgical calendar, for example, requires "mak[ing] space—lots of space— for waiting. . . . Practicing the church's time sets us at odds with the world's time."

Tools of Transformation: Daily Life and the Ordinary

Dallas Willard points out that "transformation is actually carried out in our real life, where we dwell with God and our neighbors. . . . First, we must accept the circumstances we constantly find ourselves in as the place of God's kingdom and blessing. God has yet to bless anyone except where they actually are."[17]

Our transformation happens in living out our daily life, wherever God has placed us, in the "small moments of today."[18] If your community is struggling with seeing value in the routine of life, with finding contentment in where God has placed us, consider having your church read or do a book study on *Liturgy of the Ordinary* to help you examine how the everyday and ordinary can be sacred. This may be particularly helpful for groups in certain life stages—for example, new parents or adults caring for aging parents.

Such a study helps us reject the lie our culture tells us that we have to be extraordinary to matter. It builds protective factors against the allure of grievance narratives and outrage, which we often seek to make us feel like we're doing something that matters, that it makes a difference (which, as we've already explored—99.9 percent of your social media posts do not make a difference—is a false comfort). Seeing the sacred in the ordinary can help us let go of the unhealthier and false ways in which we find "meaning." Tish Harrison Warren observes that "We tend to want a Christian life with the dull bits cut out. Yet God made us to spend our days in rest, work, and play, taking care of our bodies, our families, our neighborhoods, our homes. What if all these boring parts matter to God? What if days passed in ways that feel small and insignificant to us are weighty with meaning and part of the abundant life that God has for us?"[19]

Tools of Transformation: Breaking Our Addiction and Making Space for Awe

We also need transcendence in our faith, a spiritual connection that takes us out of our physical reality and our human experience and inexplicably allows us to sense the presence of God.

The concept of transcendence is a known phenomenon that has been studied by philosophers and psychologists. They consider it to be a part of the sublime category of emotion, and they even try to break down the various types of emotions that make up the sublime and measure the strength in which humans respond to various types of stimulus.[20] All of this actually seems to take the wonder out of it. And yet, for all of the categorization and attempts at understanding how spirituality and transcendence work, it is one part of neuroscience that scientists still find "a vexing mystery." One scientist noted in a 2023 article, "the highest level of consciousness, the primal human experience, is so unique, so hard to describe, so different from experiences with the world outside our bodies that we may never be able to fully capture consciousness with brain research."[21] Good; I'm glad some things are mysterious.

Finding moments and spaces to experience God seem harder to find.

One school of thought may be that our brains are literally being rewired with more usage of technology. Neuroscientists can see differences in the brains of today's children as compared to the brain scans of children from ten and twenty years ago.[22] Though adults have less neuroplasticity than children, our brains are being rewired too. German researchers found that individuals with smartphone addiction showed "lower gray matter volume"[23] in "regions of the brain associated with hearing, memory, emotions, speech, decision-making and self-control."[24] This change is similar to what is observed in people with substance addictions.

I probably do not even need to give you a study to show that our attention spans are shorter than they used to be. (How many times have you been interrupted or interrupted yourself to check your phone while you read this chapter?) Our attention span has decreased. By one measure, it has dropped 67 percent in twenty years.[25]

All of this interruption, by the way, stresses us out. It increases cortisol, blood pressure, and anxiety—which is fine in small amounts. If we're preparing for a big speech or test, a bit of cortisol helps us focus. But constant cortisol can lead to long-term negative health impacts.

It is difficult to experience transcendence in the midst of constant noise. Even when we block out that noise, our brains have been rewired to be in constant movement. Our inability to sit still in the quiet, to simply be, prevents us from experiencing aspects of God's pursuit of us.

Laying aside Every Weight

If our entertainment, screens, and busyness are interfering with our ability to commune with God, we need to remove the hinderances, set boundaries with the things that cause us the greatest distractions, and restore natural rhythms of work and rest. It may seem draconian to put in place boundaries for yourself and your family, but I am convinced that not doing it is stealing our joy.

In his book *The Tech-Wise Family*, Andy Crouch lays out a compelling case that our most important work—becoming human beings of wisdom and courage and encouraging others (like our children) to be as well—is greatly impeded by the distractions of our world.[26]

Technology is a tool. It cannot build character; it cannot form us. And if it is getting in the way of connecting with God, we need to be willing to make changes to our daily habits.

In a more recent book, Crouch further explores the damage technology has done to our ability to relate to one another. Though he is not writing about extremism, he captures many of the same societal ailments that create vulnerabilities to extremism—loneliness and alienation; a desire for recognition. The crux of his thesis is that we were created to love with all our hearts, souls, minds, and strength. This is what human flourishing looks like. This is what gives us meaning and purpose. "What happens when nothing in our lives develops those capacities? With what, exactly, will we love?"[27]

If we cultivate healthy boundaries with technology, we have the space to do the work of being a human: developing wisdom, character, and courage, and cultivating relationships and rightly ordered love of the Lord and our neighbor.

Disenchantment

There are other reasons we struggle with finding transcendence. For us, as great-grandchildren of the Enlightenment and creatures of a Western world that worships science, it is culturally normal to be cynical, or at least skeptical, of the supernatural. Mike Cosper explores this and several other factors leaving us disenchanted in his book *Recapturing the Wonder*.

He suggests that part of that cultural bent toward science and knowable, provable truth has led some of our faith traditions to "think knowledge of the Bible is all that matters, so we fail to attend to our character, our soul, and our relationships. Our way of living the Christian life leaves all of these things unchanged."[28] In this error, knowledge becomes the sole pathway of discipleship, but ignores practicing the *way* of Jesus.

So how do we re-embrace the transcendence of our faith? Cosper suggests practicing attention and presence by pausing, being silent, and being still. Finding times and spaces to have solitude. Embracing our human limitations—accepting that God is a mystery and we will not fully understand everything, including our suffering. Rejoicing in the abundance we have been given and pushing back against our culture of scarcity and consumerism by feasting and giving generously. And embracing our radical dependency on God. Cosper offers a number of recommendations in his book, which I strongly encourage you to read, and I suggest that you invite your church into some of these practices.

Beholding Awe

There has been a surge of studies on the power of awe.[29] One study defines awe as "an emotional response to perceptually vast stimuli that transcend current frames of reference."[30] I translate that as an emotion that stops us in our tracks (good for helping us pause and be present!). The actual set of emotions we may experience are complex. Awe is a mix of wonder, marvel, curiosity, contemplation, joy, delight, gratitude, fear, reverence, and respect.

Experiences of awe offer tremendous emotional and health benefits. Awe reduces stress.[31] People with dispositions to experience "higher" awe are happier than those with lower tendencies of experiencing awe.[32] Awe increases generosity, ethical decision making, willingness to volunteer,[33] and tolerance of others' norm violations.[34] It also decreases entitlement.[35]

One study summarized the benefits of awe like this: "Awe leads to increased humility, a diminished sense of self, an increased awareness of how one is embedded in social networks, and an awareness of shared humanity with others."[36]

And, critically for our purposes, awe has also been shown to decrease the factors that lead to polarization and extremism. For example, it reduces dogmatism about the viewpoints we hold and reduces our negative views about those with differing viewpoints.[37]

We believe that the fear of the Lord is the beginning of wisdom. I wonder if in seeing something that causes us to pause and marvel, it serves as a reminder of how big, grand, fearful, and awesome God is. Create space to allow for awe in your life.

One last thought: I wonder if practicing these disciplines— particularly presence, silence, joy, and awe—could undo the damage to our brains caused by our addiction to technology? Does returning to "ancient paths"—practicing the fear of the Lord—also physically heal our brains? Is this part of what happens when we "renew our minds"?

OVERCOMMUNICATE WHERE OUR HOPE IS FOUND

Modern studies of leadership have emphasized the importance of overcommunicating your vision and goals. Best-selling author and expert in organizational health Patrick Lencioni breaks down four disciplines for leaders to create a healthy organization. Three of the four have to do with clarity. He is specifically speaking about leaders setting out clear guidance for an organization: Why do we exist? How do we behave? What do we do? How will we succeed? What is most important right now? Who must do what? In doing so, they are creating clarity for their team (step 2). Then step 3 is to overcommunicate clarity. Through repetition, simplicity, multiple mediums, and cascading messages they constantly communicate what they've defined in step

2. Step 4 is to reinforce their clarity—making sure all aspects of the organization's functions align with their clarity.[38]

It's easy in our world of knowledge acceleration, epistemological crises, and constant change to lose sight of this principle. The most important thing we can do within our community is to speak with clarity about the living hope we have in Jesus (1 Peter 1:3). The writer of Hebrews calls it "a sure and steadfast anchor of the soul" and tells us to "hold fast to the hope set before us" (Hebrews 6:19, 18).

This is our clarity—a heavenly orientation means we place our hope in Christ.

The reason we can be steady in this dark age of chaos, the reason we can be the nonanxious presence, is not due to any strategies promising earthly gain. We do not anchor our hope in the next election, a politician, a religious leader, better education, training in civility and tolerance, or plans for depolarization, deradicalization, and peace. Anything on this earth in which we place our hope will fail us.

No, we anchor our hope in Christ alone. We anchor our hope in knowing how the story ends: God wins and we, his people, get to enjoy that victory. We anchor our hope in God's presence with us now—the rest, the peace, the strength to endure this earth's pain.

We need to repeat it, tell stories, use simplicity, and use multiple mediums and cascading messages that point people to the hope that is theirs in Jesus. Over time, with the repetition of the gospel message and the Spirit's help, our heart will align with our intellectual understanding. Earthly fear will not hold such a grip over our behavior and attitudes. We will be freed up to rest in our Savior and rejoice in the coming fulfillment of "an inheritance that is imperishable, undefiled, and unfading, kept in heaven for [us]" (1 Peter 1:4).

As we pursue peace in our churches, let us do so not out of fear of extremism but out of our pursuit and delight in God. In one of King David's psalms, he writes that we should not worry about those who persecute us and those who seem to succeed in their evil. Instead, he calls us to "trust in the Lord and do good," to dwell in the place where God has placed us and "take delight in the Lord, and he will give you the desires of your heart" (Psalm 37:3–4 NIV)

To delight is to take joy, to feast, to have extreme satisfaction and take great pleasure in.

We take delight in our children, our new romantic partner, and hopefully the spouse of our youth. This type of love is what we're called to have for the Lord.

And notice that when you delight in God, He promises to give you the desires of your heart. We are told elsewhere in Scripture that in pursuing and loving God, he molds and forms our heart, so that when we delight in Him, he purifies our desires. I think there is a good argument to be made, particularly given the context in which David starts—people attacking us and causing harm—that this reference to desires is aligned with those core needs of identity, belonging, and security.

Putting on the mind of Christ and becoming formed into his image means delighting in God as Christ delighted in the Father and Spirit. It is not just the head knowledge (the right thinking about theology), it's not just right practices (following the means of Jesus, putting away sin, and being obedient to his commands), and it's not just spiritual disciplines that help us commune with God. Being Christ-like should ultimately be exhibited in the way we love God and love others—with delight.

ELEVEN

FROM POLARIZATION TO PEACE

Healing Our Communities

OUR CONTEMPT IS KILLING US

Something is very wrong in our country. We have more attacks, more deaths, more injuries, and more trauma each year than the year prior.

No place is safe. Universities, high schools, and middle schools. Even elementary schools and preschools. Public and private schools. A sorority house, a yoga class, Walmart, the office. Concerts, movie theaters, bowling alleys, food festivals, nightclubs. Hospitals, subways, grocery stores, malls, hotels, bars, restaurants, banks. Synagogues, churches, mosques, Sikh temples.

Every part of the public square has become the scene of an attack of mass violence.

Long after the satellite trucks go home; the offerings of thoughts, prayers, and flowers at the vigil fade; and the vitriolic yelling at each other for defending the Second Amendment or needing more gun restrictions or more mental health or implementing red flag laws have, once again, moved off of our social media feeds, the devastated families, friends, and communities struggle to find ways to survive each day, let alone rebuild. The trauma and wounds have generational impact.

Ten months after the horrific massacre at an elementary school in Uvalde, Texas, a mom who lost her child that tragic day responded

197

to the Nashville shooting at Covenant School by saying that she had completely changed her mind about having more children: "I will not bring them into this cruel, evil world."[1] She is only thirty years old.

The woeful inadequacy of my vocabulary begins to show. Devastated. Heartbroken. Undone. Wretched. Gutted.

None of these do justice to describe the horror of the loss of a child, let alone the children left in the wake, who must process what happened and live with the consequences the rest of their lives.

At night, when I can let my guard down, I feel the full weight of our failure. Of my failure. We supported a system that spent trillions of dollars; passed rafts of legislation; drafted numerous strategies, policies, and regulations; and ran unknown numbers of investigations and intelligence operations, all to protect us from Al-Qaeda, when the threats are coming from *within*. From *us*. We failed. I failed.

And when I say the threat was coming from *us*, I don't just mean the shooters or the extremists. I mean all of us.

A democratic republic puts the power in the hands of the people. That means we all have blood on our hands. We are all complicit in allowing our children to be mercilessly targeted. This is the result of society's criminal negligence.

It does not have to be this way. We, the people, can change this trajectory.

It begins perhaps not where you think. Not with new strategies and laws, more money, better intelligence, and more effective protective measures. It begins with fixing our own hearts. We must stop hating our neighbor. We must stop trying to "own" each other. We must stop participating in contempt for our fellow Americans who we have disagreements with on how to keep our kids safe. We must stop buying the lies the infotainment sector is selling. The "other" side is not posing an existential threat to our existence or to the health, safety, or future of our families. But our participation in this contempt cycle is.

I'm not asking Americans to stop having opinions about policy in this country. I am asking us to grow up and learn how to disagree the way adults do. These are our kids who we are putting at risk because of our inability to have mature, adult conversations.

My generation grew up listening to our parents, friends, and peers invested in amplifying grievances, under the guise of entertainment, and (almost gleefully) growing the partisan divide. The next generation bore witness to (and experienced the results of) cemented gridlock and performative politics doling out sweeping generalizations that pushed us further apart and gathered us into tribes.

And, sadly, this generation is learning from their parents and grandparents and influencers across the social landscape that it is okay in the "new normal" to hate "the other side," to cast aside charity and embrace the post-truth era, and to lean in to anger and disgust by dehumanizing others. We are shouting past one another. And when the shouting does not work, what comes next? As the old cliche says, our children are watching, but what are they seeing from those in authority? What will they be mimicking or potentially taking to further extremes?

Contempt leads us to violence. I'm not making an emotional or spiritual plea. I'm telling you that the data demonstrates this. Contempt is anger mixed with disgust.[2] It says you are worthless. You are disgusting. You are worthy of my scorn. It often manifests in sarcastic tweets against the other side asserting that "the reason this tragedy happened is because of your side." Contempt dehumanizes the opponent, who are our fellow citizens and human beings. They feel it and return in kind. Contempt upon contempt upon contempt—spiraling downward. The cycle doesn't stop.

This is no different from what extremist ideologues do to create moral justification for violence. It is the reason why we have so many vulnerable, radicalizing, and radicalized people today compared to fifteen years ago. While we might not make the plan for violence or pick up the gun, we are participating in a cycle that lays the ground-work for the next act of violence. And while many are raging against the lack of accountability, those who weigh in on every issue, vigor-ously shaking the hornets' nest, are most often not held accountable for stirring up the vulnerable, who hear the disgust and act upon it.

Our angry words are causing the other side to dig in and not hear us. Lots of studies have been done on this going back six decades. When we slander the other side, it actually causes them to intensify their oppo-sition to us. This is known as the boomerang effect. One study showed that "If people change their views at all, the odds are more than three-to-one that they will become more extreme in their original position."[3]

Have you ever seen someone change their mind based on an angry, sarcastic, or demeaning tweet? "Gee, you're right, I am a baby killer because I support the Second Amendment." If you actually want to see progress—laws changed, kids protected—then recognize that insult-ing the other side (including the social media version of it) will have the opposite effect.

When we are yelling, we cannot listen and reason. How are we going to find the path forward if we are so blindingly angry at the "other"?

How do we make progress? We start with not presuming the worst of our opponents and acknowledging that we all have the same goal: we want the violence to stop. What we disagree on is *how*. Yes, we can cherry-pick (or nut-pick, as some prefer to call it) examples on the extremes that perhaps don't share this goal, but they are not representative of the other side. Acknowledge that the vast majority of the other side are not so easily swept up into a catch-all generalization, and more importantly, they aren't heartless monsters obsessed with taking away our rights or forcing their will on America. We cannot allow the few but loud voices on the fringe to win by demonizing the majority in the other party.

It's tempting, when our children are threatened, to take our horror and anger out on an easier target. The contempt gives us a false sense of power, as if we contributed to fixing the problem. It takes maturity and courage to lay down our defense mechanisms and begin to work on true solutions to protect our children and our society.

Anyone who agrees that we don't want our children slaughtered in the next mass attack, they are our allies, not our enemies. We can roll up our sleeves and find common ground.

We will *never* make progress any other way. How do I know? Take one example of mass attacks—school shootings—at high, middle, and elementary schools. As of December 2023, there have been 392 school shootings since Columbine in 1999. In that time, 203 children, educators, and others were killed, another 437 have been injured. These are lives lost or forever altered, and those numbers do not begin to cover the thousands of friends and family and communities destroyed in the wake. The even more stunning number is that more than *359,000 students* have *experienced* gun violence at school.[4]

If you are one of those fortunate to have never experienced gun violence, you are increasingly likely to be only once or twice removed from a family, friend, or coworker who has. And the situation is getting worse. Except for 2020 (when school was virtual for many), the number of school shootings has been increasing since 2018; 2022 was the highest year on record with forty-six school shootings.

We must try something different. And the more we fight each other, the worse the violence is becoming. We can keep taking to our social media feeds to post the next "gotcha" meme, or we can actually do something to protect our children.

PREVENTION IS A COMMUNITY-BASED MISSION

The mornings were early, and though I tried, I rarely beat my boss, Joe, in. Sensitive compartmented information facilities—known as SCIFs—were jammed into the 120-year-old Eisenhower Executive Office Building, overdue for renovations, which meant that I had to walk through his office to get to mine. He'd been there for at least an hour already, sitting at the conference table in his office, with a yellow highlighter and a ruler, going line by line through the terrorist threat matrix. On paper, our job was to coordinate domestic counterterrorism policy across government agencies on behalf of the president. But the first four hours of our day weren't about policymaking or briefing memos. In those early days, coordinating federal agencies' responses to homeland threats fell to us: the Domestic Counterterrorism Directorate at the White House. I was a junior policy staffer on a small team made up mostly of field operators from the alphabet soup of security agencies, including FBI, CIA, Secret Service, and DOD Special Forces.

The Department of Homeland Security (DHS) and the Terrorist Threat Integration Center (TTIC), established in 2003, were still getting their feet underneath them. The 9/11 Commission report wasn't out yet, but discussions on how to "break down the wall" between intelligence and law enforcement were ongoing. The TTIC would eventually become the National Counterterrorism Center (NCTC) and take over our function (it is generally believed that it is best not to have operations run out of the White House), but for a small period in between the wake of the attacks of September 11, 2001, and the establishment of formalized multiagency institutions like NCTC, such coordination was run out of the White House Situation Room.

We would sit around Joe's conference table every morning reviewing each new piece of intel that had come in and preparing questions we were going to ask the agencies of the national security apparatus at the seven a.m. secure video teleconference (known as a SVTC and pronounced sivitz, like *civic* with a *z* at the end) which we co-chaired with the National Security Council's Office of Combatting Terrorism. Around that time of day, the president's daily briefing in the Oval Office would be ending, and we would often be passed notes by the homeland security advisor, Fran Townsend: the president wants an update on the plan to address this threat by this afternoon.

We were looking for the dots on the map that, if connected, might indicate the planning of a complex, coordinated attack. These were attacks that took months to years to plan and involved multiple people and lots of logistics. Those dots might be communications, funding, training, operative travel, rumors of plans, bomb-making material, dry runs, and command and control.

Consequently, the early days of preventing terrorist attacks were the mission of intelligence, military, and law enforcement communities.

As I explained in chapter 3, my belief is that these tools are necessary but not sufficient for today's threat, both because we too narrowly define prevention and because the predominant threat has drastically changed from that of a complex coordinated attack.

A core part of DHS's work is to empower, equip, and enable others to do the "securing." This is particularly true in the area known as "preparedness." The National Preparedness Goal is composed of five mission areas: prevention, protection, mitigation, response, and recovery.

There was a debate in the lead-up to the establishment of DHS as to whether we should adopt the model of many of our international allies and establish an interior ministry (not to be confused with our Department of the Interior) to directly manage all aspects of security. The idea was passed over due to principles of federalism and the Tenth Amendment, which allows the states to regulate for the health, safety, and welfare of its citizens—also known as police powers.

Consequently, when you call 911 for help with a medical emergency or break-in, the first responders are your local fire, EMS, and law enforcement. If an emergency becomes of such size and scope that it overwhelms local first responders, most communities have mutual aid compacts in place that allow them to call neighboring counties or

cities to assist. If they need even more support, the state is called in
to assist. Sometimes states leverage mutual aid compacts with other
states to assist when their resources are exhausted. And finally, in
certain large-scale emergencies the Federal Emergency Management
Agency (FEMA) provides support—usually through the coordination
of resources (people, supplies, money) across the spectrum of emergency support functions. (Somewhere along the way, the American
public got confused and seem to think every emergency is managed
out of Washington. Best practices of emergency management call for
on-site management of a disaster.)

Since its creation in 2003, DHS has initiated numerous programs
and activities to provide support to state, local, tribal, and territorial governments and nonprofit and private sector partners across the
National Preparedness System. FEMA, the primary lead for mitigation, response, and recovery missions, has worked to hone doctrine,
policy, concepts of operation, and training since the 1980s. The Cybersecurity and Infrastructure Security Agency (CISA), which leads the
protection mission, has been at it for fifteen years.

Until 2019, when DHS released its first strategy for counterterrorism, not only was there no office at DHS responsible for systematically
building prevention capability across the country, but prevention was
also largely seen as a narrow set of capabilities for disrupting an attack
and defeating (or arresting) terrorists.[5]

The new prevention strategy recognized that the best way to
prevent terrorism and extremism is to prevent people from radicalizing
and moving toward violence in the first place. While there had been
some earlier efforts in the late 2000s and early 2010s to prevent radicalization, they were led by law enforcement and largely focused on
countering ideology, which not only proved to be ineffective but also
led to a backlash from communities that felt targeted by law enforcement based on their race, religion, or nationality.

The 2019 strategy moved to a public-health approach to prevention. In the medical context, primary prevention approaches, such as healthy nutrition and vaccinations, aim to prevent illness or disease before it occurs. Secondary prevention involves screening for early onset of disease, while tertiary prevention involves treating or managing the disease.

We can apply this approach to the extremism space. Primary prevention focuses on building community resilience and mitigating risk factors by building protective factors and inoculating the community against conspiracy theories and propaganda used by extremists. Secondary prevention involves detecting and intervening with individuals who are in the process of radicalizing and/or at risk of mobilization to violence. Tertiary prevention occurs within the criminal justice context, developing threat management plans as alternatives to prosecution or incarceration, and for use during community reentry after serving a prison sentence.

These are the nuts and bolts of the prevention capability I believe we need to build out in our communities.

The Government's Responsibilities

In 2019, we revamped an office, now called the Center for Prevention Programs and Partnerships (CP3), to be the prevention complement to FEMA (response and recovery) and CISA (protection). CP3 empowers, enables, and equips communities, cities, and states to develop the capabilities they need to end targeted violence and terrorism. Just as your first responders come from your local community, so will first preventers be locally based.

Governors Should Lead

Each state and each community within a state plays a role in building out prevention capability. Ideally, governors would direct the establishment of a robust, multidisciplinary prevention system, much in the same way that we have layered response capabilities. Several states and cities have launched prevention efforts over the past few years. The National Governors Association's Center for Best Practices released the *Governor's Roadmap to: Preventing Targeted Violence* to assist governors and homeland security advisors in establishing violence prevention capabilities.[6]

One of the key findings of early pilot efforts is that it may be easier to start at the state level to ensure that rural communities and smaller municipalities, which likely lack the resources to provide all the capabilities in a prevention architecture, can be covered with prevention resources. Further, states usually manage the wraparound services that are key to successful interventions.[7] Cities and counties will have local resources to incorporate into the potential suite of prevention services, but ideally, prevention efforts are organized at the state level.

Invest in Prevention's Front-Line Workers

Multiple experts advised that the biggest gap in our capability is trained front-line personnel, primarily licensed clinical professionals, as well as educators.[8] We need graduate schools to incorporate prevention training—particularly on how to identify and intervene with individuals who are radicalizing or are extremists—into their curriculums for social work, education, behavioral health, mental health, public health, and psychology. We need professional associations to develop mid-career training and certifications. One bright spot advancing this important work is the Prevention Practitioners Network—a national network for practitioners providing direct prevention and intervention services.[9] This effort will help professionalize and self-govern the discipline as it matures.

Be Agile, Embrace Innovation, and Develop a Continuous Learning Culture with Transparency and Higher Risk Tolerance

The prevention discipline should maintain its continuous learning culture and be transparent as we innovate and adapt to emerging threats. Governments, especially politicians, tend to be risk averse. However, risk is innate to innovation, and innovation is necessary to effectively counter extremism. Like any experiment, interventions and prevention work have suffered failures. These failures have bred lessons learned, and those of us working in this space are doing our due diligence to ensure that these lessons learned are built into future endeavors.[10] With that said, there is still much to learn.

Congress, the executive branch, state governments, foundations, and other private funders must be aware of a significant obstacle in proving the efficacy of prevention work: you cannot prove a negative. While we can leverage funding to examine success rates of intervention and prevention programming to some extent, it is all but impossible to report how many people were successfully dissuaded from adopting extremist beliefs, becoming radicalized, and committing violent acts. Those conducting work in this space, as well as the entities that fund them, need to be open to innovation, iteration, and transparency regarding what works and what doesn't. Lives are at risk, and the necessary innovation cannot wait, regardless of the risk that comes along with it.

Congress and State Legislatures Should Authorize Prevention and Rapidly Scale Prevention Resources

It is not my intent to bore you with bureaucratic details about laws and budgets. So allow me to put it rather bluntly. Regardless of politicians' rhetoric about needing to "do something" to stop the spread of violence, in the six years I have been advocating for building out prevention capability, I can count on one hand the number of politicians who were willing to put the money where their mouth is.

Several think tanks have been advocating for even longer. They estimated how much the US should be spending on what was then called countering violent extremism. Here are some of the recommendations that were collated in the report on prevention RAND produced for DHS:[11]

- In 2016, DHS's Homeland Security Advisory Council recommended that the CP3 Grant program increased from $10 million to $100 million.
- During the same time frame, the Washington Institute for Near East Policy labeled activities in this area "drastically underfunded across the board."
- The CSIS Commission on Countering Violent Extremism cited "a dearth of resources [as] a major barrier to galvanizing a CVE movement and scaling up promising initiatives" and endorsed the earlier recommendation to increase DHS partnerships–focused funding to $100 million but went further, recommending total funding for CVE across the domestic and international spaces of $1 billion.
- In 2018, RAND compared US spending to other European countries. They used two methodologies. RAND's recommendation was based on a comparison with the European countries:
  - The spending-per-incident value comparison—the mean result suggested that the US should spend approximately $142 million annually.
  - The spending-per-million-population ranged from approximately $360,000 (Canada) to a high of $1.7 million (Germany). Using these numbers results in US estimates ranging from approximately $100 million to $500 million, with the mean result of approximately $290 million.

These estimates occurred before we saw the drastic uptick in domestic violent extremism in 2019, and before the COVID-19 pandemic, January 6, and other factors increased polarization and uncertainty.

Since then, our allies have increased their funding to combat extremism at home. Over the period from 2021 to 2024, the German government committed a total of over €1 billion (about US$1.1 billion) to fight racism and right-wing extremism.[12] The United States has about four times the population of Germany.[13] In 2022, Australia announced a doubling of their funding of violent extremism programs—spending about around US$85 million. Some of the new funding includes US$17.4 million to expand intervention programs in regional areas, US$9.8 million to rehabilitate extremists in custody, and US$5.7 million for new research.[14] The United States has thirteen times the population of Australia.[15] If we use these new numbers as our scale, then based on the United States population,[16] we should be spending about $1.1 billion a year on domestic prevention programming.

More recently, the Atlantic Council in the summer of 2023 recommended that the US federal government should provide *$20 billion* to states and communities to build up successful prevention capabilities.[17]

During my tenure, we were able to secure a significant increase in funding, thanks to one of those few congressmen I mentioned, former representative Tom Malinowski, who did the behind-the-scenes work to get it into the budget. It was impressive from a bureaucratic standpoint—but the numbers are not. CP3 currently receives $10 million to operate and administers $20 million in grants for state and local governments and nonprofits. *A total of 30 million dollars is spent in the United States* on domestic prevention programming through CP3 and other agencies,[18] an amount that has been relatively flat since 2020. And recently House Republicans have been trying to cut this small amount of funding.

We are not funding prevention at the scale it needs to be funded at in order to be effective and save lives. If the school shootings and mass attacks were being planned and conducted by ISIS or a cartel, I believe we would easily be spending billions. I fear we have become numb to these attacks and believe the rhetoric that there is "nothing that we can do"[19] or that the *only* solution is more gun control.

Pass Extreme Risk Protection Orders in All States and Set Up Robust Systems for Implementing Them

Extreme Risk Protection Orders (ERPOs), also known as Severe Threat Order of Protection (STOP) or red flag laws, are temporary measures designed to de-escalate emergency situations by removing access to guns. ERPOs must be approved by a judge. Some states allow individuals to file them directly, in which case it usually must be requested by a family or household member. But some states may require you to involve a law enforcement officer to file the request. The "temporary" part could mean two weeks or up to a year, and the orders can be renewed.

The data tell us that most mass attackers leak their plans in advance of carrying out an attack or bystanders knew something was wrong.[20] Without the prevention systems discussed above or ERPOs, law enforcement is often unable to do anything but a "knock and talk." In the aftermath of an attack, law enforcement often validates that the individual showed concerning signs but that there was no legal mechanism for them to act because no crime had been committed. This was true of the El Paso Walmart attacker, the Marjory Stoneman Douglas High School shooter, the Nashville Christmas bomber, and the shooter at the Indianapolis FedEx facility, to name only a few.

If Tennessee had an ERPO mechanism, the shooter responsible for killing three children and three adults at the Covenant School in Nashville, who was reportedly under emotional duress for months prior to the attack, could have been prevented from obtaining weapons.[21]

A number of conservatives, including legal scholars, have endorsed the concept.[22] They do not believe it violates the Second Amendment. It also has strong public support; in 2019 "77% of Americans supported family-initiated ERPOs."[23] And a poll in 2022 measured support at 81 percent.[24] Florida's red flag law was passed after the Parkland High School tragedy by the very conservative governor Rick Scott and is actively using the law.[25]

Implementation is not a given. A year before a shooter attacked a grocery store in Buffalo, New York, motivated by white supremacist ideology, he had been ordered to have a psychiatric evaluation and spent a day and a half in a psychiatric hospital.[26] New York has an ERPO law, had the family or the law enforcement officers filed for an ERPO, the shooter would at least have had more difficulty finding a weapon, and it would have increased the likelihood of law enforcement being tipped off that something might have changed in his risk assessment.

Illinois also has an ERPO law. The shooter at the Independence Day Parade in Highland Park, Illionois, had previously attempted suicide and had police engagements at his home when he threatened to kill people at his house. No ERPO was filed.[27]

Implementation is always the hardest part of competent governing. When new laws are passed, executive branch officials have to determine who is going to be responsible for setting up new programs and people have to be trained on the new law, and all of that takes money. In the case of Illinois, it was reported that the state had not provided education or training to law enforcement or the public on how to use the ERPO law.

Our Responsibilities as Citizens

Stop the Gun Idolization and Glorification Culture and Have Adult Conversations to Reform Gun Laws

I am not an expert in the Second Amendment or gun laws. There are many amazing people and organizations that are studying how we can reduce gun violence. I know enough about public policy to tell you it's complex and there is no one-size-fits-all solution. Yes, we need ERPOs, waiting periods for purchases, increased mental and behavioral health resources, physical protective measures at locations that are frequently targeted, prevention programs that allow us to intervene before someone crosses a criminal threshold, and law enforcement presence on school campuses. All of it. A politician who tells you that only one thing is needed is dishonest or incompetent. It's hard to tell these days, as incompetence is growing.

I can tell you from working with law enforcement my entire career that most of the people in that profession are strong supporters of the Second Amendment—*and* would like to see more restrictions on guns. Most of those I know would like the assault weapons ban to be restored. Their biggest challenge in preventing attacks is the proliferation of guns in the country. We have more guns than people in the United States.[28]

When I heard my friends in law enforcement soberly explain their positions, it changed my position on gun control. I tend to defer to the people who swore an oath to protect my community and would be the first in to save my kids if, God forbid, a school shooting were to occur.

I'm not a constitutional scholar; I'm not going to lay out all of the arguments for how and why to do more with gun reforms. But I will tell you that I think it matters.

I am a public policy professional, and I have seen that legislatures often pass bills in the heat of the moment. Bad laws will not solve things. And bad laws will likely be overturned and lead to a backlash. Good laws need to be developed based on data and facts. I appreciate what former governor Doug Ducey did in developing Arizona's plan to enhance the safety of their schools. They studied every significant school shooting since Columbine and incorporated security measures based on those findings.

I am an expert in extremism. And the right's obsession with guns has gone off the deep end in the last decade. As with everything we've looked at, the silent majority of gun owners are responsible in exercising their gun rights. They are not obsessed. But a loud and outrageous minority on the right have taken a right to bear arms for the sake of self-defense and conflated it with freedom of religious expression. I don't know what else to think when we see AR-15 lapel pins instead of American flags on US congresspeople,[29] a proliferation of Christmas cards with every family member bearing automatic rifles,[30] or a campaign ad that shows the candidate, a former Navy SEAL, in tactical gear and "hunting RINOs"—the acronym for *Republicans in name only*—suggesting the candidate is going to shoot his political opponents.

Why does it matter? Because this escalating obsession is leading to historic highs in gun sales, which have been marketed by "conspiracy-theory-fueled political partisanship."[31] And a small percentage carry that obsession out to a violent end.

A former gun executive's twelve-year-old son was assaulted by an armed man in tactical gear during a protest after George Floyd's death. It prompted the executive, Ryan Busse, to leave the gun industry and write a book about their marketing tactics. In an article for the *Atlantic* he highlights tactics that are more than just conspiracy theories—they are directly related to domestic violent extremists.

Palmetto State Armory advertised their AK-47-style pistol decorated in the "Big Igloo Aloha" pattern, a reference to the Boogaloo Bois—a violent extremist group.[32]

Bushmaster launched its "Man Card" advertising campaign in 2010. Here's how the former executive described it:

> "*The Bushmaster Man Card declares and confirms that you are a Man's Man, the last of a dying breed, with all the rights and privileges duly afforded," the ad copy read. If you're hearing there, in "dying breed," an anticipatory echo of the "Great Replacement" theory that inspired the alleged killer in May [2022]'s mass*

*shooting in Buffalo, New York, you're not mistaken: The conclu-
sion that this type of marketing has contributed to creating today's
radical violent extremists is inescapable. . . . One of the guns used
by the Buffalo shooter was a Bushmaster XM-15.*[33]

Busse asserts that many of the gun companies are now pitching to
violent extremists, often using social media posts with symbols that the
extremist would recognize but might be lost on the average person. They
market to them because it sells. They wouldn't do it otherwise. Busse
concludes that "it undeniably created a culture of extremism that encouraged a new type of 'tactical' mass shooter. America is seeing the deadly
results of the violence incubated by these dark advertising fantasies."[34]

If you are a responsible gun owner, you have a responsibility to
push back on gun-fetish culture. When people who do not own guns
do it, they are dismissed as "woke" and unconstitutional. But if the
overwhelming majority of responsible gun owners were to push back
on the NRA, performative politicians, and gun manufacturers, it may
have a chance at bringing us back from the ever-darkening spiral of
gun violence we're enduring on a daily basis.

Use Your Vote and Your Voice to Advocate for Changes

Targeted violence and terrorism have not only rattled the sense of security we expect to feel in our Republic, but they also inflict lasting harm
upon everyone directly and indirectly impacted. Too many families
have buried loved ones. Too many first responders have arrived at scenes
of unimaginable devastation and are forced to live with those images
for the rest of their lives. The National Center for PTSD at the US
Department of Veterans Affairs estimates that 28 percent of people who
witness terrorism, targeted violence, and other mass shootings develop
post-traumatic stress disorder, while another third will have acute stress
disorders that require lengthy and sometimes intensive treatments.[35]

We are very early in the process of maturing prevention. I believe that this is at least a decade-long investment in building to a baseline level of capability across the country. But it is one that will eventually provide significant returns on investment, reducing costs associated with attacks and law enforcement activities and, more important, saving lives and restoring peace of mind to communities that are too frequently targeted by violence.

As a democratic republic, change happens when the people tell their government to change. Pick one or all of these topics and make a call, send an email, or visit in person your representatives in your city council, state legislature and the Congress, your mayor, governor, and president. Our representatives are acting unserious because the exhausted middle have checked out and an extreme and loud minority is dominating the conversation. We need responsible citizens modeling constructive disagreement (without contempt!) and allowing the competition of ideas to return to our country.

Educate Yourself on Primary Prevention: Building Protective Factors to Mitigate Vulnerabilities

As we have explored, numerous societal factors contribute to our vulnerability. Isolation, uncertainty, anxiety, outrage, and contempt are common features in our media. Polarization creates an ever-hardening us/them context and the mainstreaming of extremism. We have also explored that while there is no single driver of radicalization, certain factors have demonstrated stronger prevalence in studies of mass attackers and extremists,[36] including being disrespected, having psychological distress, experiencing a recent crisis, witnessing verbal statements in support of violent extremism, and feeling like a helpless victim.[37]

Further, certain cognitive susceptibility factors in someone's background (specifically, chronic stress, obsessive thinking, and isolation) and *then* having a crisis (specifically, interrupting the pursuit of a life goal) created one of the shortest paths to exposure to extremism.

There is no standardized definition for *resilience* or *protective factors*. I'm using these terms to refer to the existence of personality traits, experiences, attitudes, behaviors, intentions, or life situations that provide a buffer to other risk factors or that reduce risk factors. It is quite easy to be inadvertently exposed to extremist ideology online. We cannot prevent crises or the life events that might lead to psychological distress or experiences of disrespect and humiliation. Therefore, the goal in primary prevention is to build up protective factors that can reduce the impact of those risks when they occur.

A recent study out of the Centre for Research and Evidence on Security Threats (CREST) surveyed fifty-one papers published between 1998 and 2021 that contained findings about protective factors.[38] They found that most studies focused on risk factors, thus there is a limited understanding of what protects against radicalization or involvement in extremism—or, perhaps more precisely, which factors have a greater impact. The protective factors listed below are collated from the CREST survey as well as guides that have been produced for the general public. If you are a prevention practitioner or researcher, I suggest reviewing the research report directly as there will be complexities and nuances that will be relevant to you.[39] As new evidence becomes available that updates these protective factors, we will post it on PathBacktoPeace.org.

Individual Protective Factors—Psychological, Sociodemographic, Religious

- Self-control of attitude, intention, and behavior
- Empathy
- Conflict coping skills
- Positive coping mechanisms

- A sense of humor
- Openness to experience
- Higher levels of educational attainment,[40] especially in subjects that focus on complex ideas over black-and-white thinking
- Having a nuanced understanding of religion and ideology
- Religious commitment, depth, and scope of knowledge (protective against radicalization)
- Exposure to nonviolent belief systems and narratives
- A secure job
- Involvement in extracurricular activities

Family

- Strong attachments—a supportive family or healthy social support system
- Raised with a "positive parenting" style[41]
- Parental involvement in child's life
- Having a nonviolent family
- Having experienced the incarceration of family members
- Being married

Peers

- Friendships outside of immediate social groups (implying diversity of friendships)
- Associating with nonviolent peers
- Having more social contacts
- Having access to supportive social relationships
- Societal inclusion and integration

Society

- Strong ties to the community and a sense of social cohesion
- Access to resources to address trauma and mental health issues

- A diversity of nonviolent outlets for addressing grievances
- The ability to pursue nonviolent, legally, and socially sanctioned methods of conflict resolution

Now, as you read those, you probably immediately think, *Well, these aren't security functions.* And I agree with you! These items fall under the roles of parents, educators, friends, clergy, and community leaders.

You might also think, *Gee, if we could solve these issues, it would help a number of other challenges facing our youth and other vulnerable people.* You would be correct! There is evidence that someone vulnerable to extremism is also susceptible to a number of other ills: gang recruitment, recruitment into human trafficking, alcohol or drug abuse, self-harm, suicide, and violent extremism. Primary prevention activities will build resilience to a number of harms.

You might also notice that some of these factors are things that cannot be changed. Our environment or experiences of childhood, for example. But we have agency over other factors and can make changes in those areas in our own lives or encourage others to. Certain changes may require the assistance of a counselor or proactively placing yourself in situations where you can strengthen a weakness. For example, if you or a loved one do not handle conflict well, you could read a book, visit with a counselor, or join a support group to learn better ways to resolve conflict.

The goal in primary prevention is to build up resilience that can reduce the impact of risk factors when they occur. Building resilience takes time, and ideally, it begins when we are children. So in this regard, adults seeking to build peace in their communities should invest in building resilience in the children and adolescents in their communities.

To Build Community Resilience, Invest in the Youth of Your Community
The adolescent experience is ripe for exploitation across the factors we discussed earlier: needs, narratives, and networks. Tweens and teens are in the process of identity formation, which involves seeking belonging and significance.[42] And this transition is made significantly harder by a peer-oriented culture (as opposed to the child-adult attachment culture that was the norm in child development until the 1950s).[43]

A decade into the prevalence of social media and smart phone, we can see the significant damage that has been caused.[44] Jonathan Haidt has asserted that the mental illness crisis in generation Z (teens and young adults) is not just correlated to social media, but in examining the more than one hundred studies on the question, it is clear that on the whole, they show "strong and clear evidence of causation."[45] Social media is one of the major causes of the epidemic.

The surgeon general's office released an advisory in May 2023 urging caution in providing adolescents and children access to social media. Acknowledging that more research is needed, they warned, "the current body of evidence indicates . . . that social media can also have a profound risk of harm to the mental health and well-being of children and adolescents."[46] The job of a parent, caregiver, teacher, or youth mentor has never been more difficult.

As a parent of generation alpha kids and a counterterrorism professional, I read Greg Lukianoff and Jonathan Haidt's *The Coddling of the American Mind* in horror. Their hypothesis is that our youth have adopted three great untruths:

1. *Fragility*: what doesn't kill you makes you weaker
2. *Emotional reasoning*: always trust your feelings
3. *Us versus them*: life is a battle between good people and evil people[47]

Hopefully, by this point in the book you can intuitively see why I would be horrified. All three of these myths create vulnerability to extremism. Let me connect the dots:

Untruth: I am fragile

Consequences of Untruths: Overprotection and lack of experience with risk and life stressors at a young age has led to teens and adults with extremely high anxiety and desires for third parties (like college administrators) to "protect them," resulting in increased grievances and feeling that their identity is being threatened.

Extremism Risk Factors: "Grievances and feelings of victimization can contribute to a young person's vulnerability to radicalization."[48] Feeling like a "helpless victim" is one of the highest-ranking risk factors.[49]

Untruth: Trust your feelings

Consequences of Untruths: "Emotional reasoning is the cognitive distortion" that occurs when a "reactive emotional state" is accepted as reality "without investigating what is true."[50] Such cognitive distortions include catastrophizing, labeling, blaming, overgeneralizing, and dichotomous thinking.[51] This has led to catastrophizing speech as "violence." Once "violence" is redefined as words that offend you, using physical forms of violence is interpreted as self-defense.[52]

Extremism Risk Factors: Creates the moral justification for "hostile action," including violent hostile action.

Untruth: Us versus them

Consequences of Untruths: A belief that "I am good, and people who disagree with me are evil." Increases dehumanization of others. Induces mass "othering" through cancel culture.

Extremism Risk Factors:
- "Othering"
- Black-and-white thinking
- Lack of nuance
- Lack of conflict resolution skills
- Lack of empathy

The "us versus them" framing designates the out-group as evil and less than human. "Fragility" creates a sense of being a helpless victim and makes it easier for grievances to be manufactured and fixated on. And "trust your feelings" provides a moral justification for hostile action. My out-group (which is evil) poses a threat to me (because I'm fragile), and they've already attacked us violently (with words), therefore I most use hostile action (physical violence) to protect my success or survival.

Are you concerned yet?! As an expert in extremism, *I am!* It's one of the more compelling explanations I have seen as to why we have had such a spike in mass attacks and school shootings in recent years by older teens and young men—along with the rise of social media leading to a narcissism epidemic.[53]

One of Lukianoff and Haidt's observations that interested me the most as a parent was their assertion that paranoid parenting styles and reductions in free play (without parents hovering over them) has led to an expectation of "safetyism." Because Generation Z was not given the opportunity to fight with their friends without an adult intervening or get lost on their bike and have to figure out how to get home, they missed out on opportunities to build core resilience skills at a young age. Those skills require experiential repetition, and they build on each other. Here's how they explain it:

> *Experience is so essential for wiring a large brain that the "first draft" of the brain includes a strong motivation to practice behaviors that will give the brain the right kind of feedback to optimize itself for success in the environment that happens to surround it. [This applies to language, physical skills, and social skills.] . . . The brain is "expecting" the child to engage in thousands of hours of play—including thousands of falls, scrapes, conflicts, insults, alliances, betrayals, status competitions, and acts of exclusion— in order to develop. Children who are deprived of play are less likely to develop into physically and socially competent teens and adults.*[54]

They show that the lack of play impacts their ability to cooperate and manage conflict—the basic skills we need in democracies.[55] There is even a growing body of evidence that links "play deprivation to later anxiety and depression."[56]

If you want to build resilience to extremism, start young. We need to give children plenty of non-technology free play. (Free play is chosen and directed by the participants. Music lessons and organized sports are not free play!) And we need to be calling out these myths for what they are: lies that are harming our kids and damaging society. Lukianoff and Haidt make a series of other recommendations for how we can repair some of this damage. If you are a parent or educator, or otherwise regularly in a position to influence youth, I highly recommend reading their book.

Inoculation: Talk to Your Loved Ones about Extremism

One of the more promising findings in recent years is that we can build immunity to conspiracy theories and extremist ideologies much like we vaccinate against disease.[57] While we cannot argue someone out of their ideology once they are radicalized, if we introduce a person to the manipulation techniques used and small amounts of the ideology framed in a negative way, it reduces the likelihood they will support the extremist ideology if they are ever exposed to it "in the wild" in the future. This is also called pre-bunking.[58]

The opposite instinct has been cultivated by traditional media standards in the past. Traditional news organizations had journalistic standards that precluded them from airing or printing stories about conspiracy theories or extremist ideology. In the past, giving something airtime was to breathe life into it and offer it a platform of legitimacy. With the atomization of news and social media, we no longer have gatekeepers to our news. The public will see extremist ideology and conspiracy theories at some point; it's only a matter of time. Thus, we need a new approach. We need to introduce the concepts before they hear them in the wild.

Inoculation works at any age. So if you have a family member or friend prone to conspiracy theories, you could try this technique with them. But it is especially important for parents, caregivers, and youth workers to engage with the kids in their lives about extremism. It's not unlike other guidance parents and caregivers are given about sex, drugs, and vaping. They will hear about it at some point, so we'd rather they hear it from us. Talk early and often, in an age-appropriate and developmentally appropriate way about hate and extremism. For specific recommendations on how to speak to tweens and teens about extremism, see appendix 1 and visit PathBacktoPeace.org for the latest research.

Secondary Prevention: "Building Earlier Off-Ramps" and Equipping the Community to Detect Radicalization

Secondary prevention involves detecting and intervening with individuals who are in the process of radicalizing and/or at risk of mobilization to violence. We are able to do this because researchers at the US Secret Service National Threat Assessment Center (NTAC)[59] and elsewhere have studied individuals who carried out acts of mass violence and found that regardless of ideology or motivation—whether the attacks were acts of workplace violence, domestic violence, school-based violence, or terrorism—similar themes are evident among the perpetrators.[60] This allows us to design threat assessment and management capabilities that are based on behavior.

Threat assessment leverages a deep evidence base to identify concerning behaviors and assess the level of risk an individual may pose. Based on that assessment, the team will recommend strategies for managing the risk and de-escalating the concerning behavior.[61]

The goal of these efforts is to disrupt the radicalization process and, for those who have radicalized, attempt to help them find nonviolent ways to address their grievances or problems before they cross a criminal threshold. These engagements are happening before the threat rises to a level requiring law enforcement. Dynamic factors of risk can change quickly, thus it is important for law enforcement to be a part of the team or to be consulted at intervals. They are best positioned to know when the tools of law enforcement are necessary. However, I believe they should not *lead* threat assessment and management. Recent evidence has shown that interventions led by law enforcement are less effective than those led by others, and that heavy-handed law enforcement efforts can actually deepen radicalization.[62] For these reasons, I'm a strong advocate for threat assessment teams led by members of a multidisciplinary team who are not law enforcement personnel.

The factors that drive individuals to radicalize and mobilize to violence are almost consistently observed by those who know the individuals best. Multiple studies have demonstrated that families, friends, and other bystanders who are concerned for the well-being of these individuals are critical to prevention, as they are often the ones who will recognize behavioral changes over time that may be indicative of radicalization and mobilization to violence.

You can help protect your community by familiarizing yourself with these evidence-based behavioral indicators and risk factors of radicalization, found in appendix 2, and the mobilization to violence indicators, found in appendix 3.

Cynthia Miller-Idriss, a scholar and expert on youth extremism and radicalization and director of the Polarization and Extremism Research and Innovation Lab (PERIL) at American University, found that in as little as *seven minutes*, parents and caregivers can improve their ability to detect potential radicalization and intervene.[63] PERIL developed a guide to assist parents and caregivers recognize the warning signs of youth radicalization and understand the drivers and grievances that create susceptibility to extremist rhetoric and intervene more effectively.[64]

When I spoke with Miller-Idriss, she emphasized how critical it is that we "build earlier off-ramps." Parents and caregivers are most likely to be the first to detect the behavioral changes indicative of radicalization. While parents and the network of adults who engage with youth alone can't solve our country's violent extremism challenge, they can play a crucial part in building societal resilience to radicalization and detecting and disrupting radicalization early.

Visit PathBacktoPeace.org to access links to the PERIL guide and other resources designed to help parents, caregivers, and adults who engage with youth. All of these are free online and take only a few minutes to review.

The field of violence prevention is strengthening but still immature. We desperately need more mental and behavioral health providers in this country in general, but especially those with training in violence prevention and extremism disengagement. We also need better longitudinal studies,[65] and the field needs to do a better job of raising community awareness and helping busy citizens prioritize the key things we need to do to build resilience.

Despite these limitations, we can all be taking steps—even small ones—that will build resilience in our communities.

TWELVE

HELPING THE RADICALIZED
No One Is beyond Hope

F amilies with loved ones who are radicalized have compared the
situation to a substance addiction or being in a cult. Depending on their loved one's level of involvement in extremism, it can
turn the family's world upside down. It may even feel like a death: the
person you knew and loved is no longer there. If you find yourself in
this situation, I am so sorry. I know it is painful. While this experience may feel shocking, you are not alone. There are many families
wrestling with this right now. Resist the urge to withdraw from your
community, because you will need their support.

If you are friends with someone who has a radicalized loved one,
they need your support. Some people may experience deep shame from
having a loved one go off the deep end to traffic in hate, particularly
if it is contradictory to the family's values or religion. They may try to
withdraw because of this shame. Your presence is important. They need
reassurance that they are loved and supported. There may be practical
ways you can help them, too, but most likely they just need your presence. You cannot fix the situation, and attempts to do so will likely
backfire. But you can encourage them to seek out support from some of
the resources given in this chapter and at PathBacktoPeace.org.

HOW TO HELP THE RADICALIZED

All of the previous caveats still apply: Radicalization is not a linear process; an individual may meet the definition at one point and then jump back to an earlier stage in the process. While we are using these categories to help us think through what actions we can take to intervene, we should recall that it can be very difficult to know if someone is radicalized. Most radicalized individuals never cross the line into criminal behavior. So take a deep breath. Most likely your loved one, given time and some help, can move to a healthier frame of mind.

So how do we know if someone is radicalized? You might not be able to fully know for sure. You can attempt to engage them in conversation and find out what's going on in their life. This process involves practicing active listening, being curious, and asking open-ended, respectful questions to gain an understanding of their grievances, fears, frustrations.

Many of us in the conservative or Christian community who have loved ones who participate daily in the outrage infotainment complex are already concerned that they perceive an existential threat and have observed rhetoric that crosses into the lower end of the spectrum.

At this point, we have had enough engagements with our loved ones to know we cannot argue them out of their ideology. And the truth is, our loved one may or may not engage with us on this topic. It is common for people to withdraw as they become more radicalized. We may even have a hunch, especially if we know their backstory, as to the underlying drivers that led them to be susceptible to extremist ideology.

So what do we do? How do we know when we need to get help?

Before we explore disengagement and deradicalization, let me state the most important part up front: *If you have evidence or concerns that your loved one is planning an act of violence or other criminal activity, call local law enforcement.* Not sure? Go to appendix 3 and review the signs and indicators of someone mobilizing to violence. If you feel as if something is off, it is better to err on the side of intervening with law enforcement. It may feel like a betrayal to your loved one, but statistically, they are unlikely to survive an attack. Loving them means stopping them from doing harm to others and themself. Likewise, *if your loved one is considering self-harm, call 988, the Suicide and Crisis Lifeline, or a trusted mental health counselor.* The best way to reduce mass violence and deaths of despair in our country is for those of us close to the person of concern to reach out for help.

If your loved one is in crisis or experiencing emotional duress and you are concerned that they might hurt themself or others, check to see whether your state has an extreme risk protection order (ERPO) law, also known as a red flag law.[1] You should consider invoking it whether or not your loved one has access to weapons or has talked about them. The trigger should not be whether they already have weapons but rather if, in their duress, you have sensed or they have indicated that they are considering suicide or violence toward others, including mass attacks or domestic violence. Every state's process for invoking these laws will be different, and, based on recent attacks, it is clear we need more robust processes for implementing these authorities.

You may do an initial evaluation and decide that your concerns do not rise to the level of petitioning for an ERPO or law enforcement action. If later, however, your loved one experiences a crisis—loss of a loved one, loss of a job, removal from school, financial crisis, public humiliation, or other traumatic event—you may need to reevaluate their risk. Leverage the resources of trained professionals to help you navigate the crisis. Often, if supported with proper mental health care, no further action is necessary.

How to Engage Your Loved One about Your Concerns

Assuming that your concerns do not rise to the level of petitioning for an ERPO or law enforcement action at the moment, then what do you do? Let's look at how you might handle a few broad categories. In all cases, your primary goals are to get your loved one help if you can and maintain a relationship with them in the process.

When you do engage with them, here are some recommendations to keep in mind:[2]

- Be calm and approach them out of love. If you are angry or more interested in "proving" you are right, it will make the situation worse.
- Be curious, ask open-ended questions, and demonstrate that you are listening. No lectures.
- If your loved one says something offensive, don't shut down the conversation. You can be honest that you disagree with them, but do it respectfully.
- Don't be dismissive or judgmental or mock or ridicule a person for their beliefs.
- Do not try to take on the ideology; you will not talk them out of their beliefs.
- Find ways to empathize with the grievances that are legitimate without validating their extremist "solution."
- Reassure the individual that you love and care for them.

For additional suggestions on how to talk to tweens, teens, adults, and older adults who you are concerned may be radicalizing, see appendix 1.

Setting boundaries will look different in each circumstance. In general, you should ensure that you are not enabling or rewarding their extremist behavior. Unless it is for your family's health and safety, try to avoid cutting off contact with the person of concern. With teens, do not threaten to kick them out of the house unless they leave their extremist group. As we explored in earlier chapters, relational loss can deepen radicalization.

And if your loved one rejects you—they move out of the house or won't return calls or texts—make an effort to stay in touch from time to time by sharing family news or news about friends. You're looking to keep the door open so that the message that they are loved, that you miss them, that they are welcome anytime will hopefully someday get through to them.

Your role requires patience, offering continued reassurances of your love and care for the person of concern, and seeking help for your loved one when they will receive it. You should not attempt to try to "save" the person yourself.

This is a long road. Ensure you have support for yourself. At a minimum, be sure you are practicing good self-care (exercise, healthy diet, good sleep, and finding time to relax, laugh, and enjoy life). You should also consider attending a support group if there is one in your area or operating online and perhaps seeing a mental health counselor to help you process what you are going through.

PEOPLE *CAN* CHANGE: WHAT TO EXPECT WITH DISENGAGEMENT AND DERADICALIZATION PROGRAMS

At Moonshot, when we present on our methodologies for intervention we start with this basic premise: people can change. We have evidence from researchers, practitioners, and Moonshot's own practice of online intervention. A note of caution, however: the process of change takes time, and our loved ones have to be open to it. There are no quick fixes here.

A recent study by RAND Corporation interviewed former extremists and their families and friends to analyze their experiences of deradicalization.[3] They noted that there was no standard model for exiting extremism, but two experiences stood out for their prevalence and relative success.

First, people left extremists groups because they were disillusioned or burned out. Often they become disappointed that the group or movement was not as advertised. Sometimes the disillusionment is about the leader of the group; other times it is the result of observations of hypocrisy or being tired of infighting within the group. And sometimes disillusionment and burnout come from realizing high costs: lost jobs and lost relationships. This is why holding people accountable for their behavior and setting boundaries are important. Feeling the consequences of their behavior is one of the ways people are motivated to make a change.

The second reason people left was intervention by an individual or group. The interventions were conducted by "acquaintances, life partners, other former radicals, friends, journalists, children, other family members, religious authorities, current radicals, therapists, and school officials."[4] The interventions that most often failed involved family members or punitive interventions by law enforcement. These instances led to *increased* extremism.

There is still much for us to learn, but I felt it important to share these findings as both an encouragement and a warning. Sometimes we need to let time take its course and let people experience the consequences of their behavior. People often become disillusioned and seek to depart on their own. Some who have successfully exited point to "unplanned exposures to diversity, kindness, and religious education" as helping move them in the direction of disengaging.[5] This is why we want to keep lines of communication open, continue to treat our loved ones with kindness, and remind them they have a safe place to return to.

Likewise, despite your heart's best intention, family members may not be the best suited for a formal intervention. It is wiser to seek professional assistance to determine the best course of action for your loved one.

When they are ready to exit, look for programs that use licensed clinical providers, such as mental health counselors, social workers, psychologists, and psychiatrists, who have been trained on the basics of extremism or are involved in the Prevention Practitioners Network. There are a few reputable programs that involve former extremists serving as peer mentors to those seeking to exit and other trained professionals. It is important that such programs incorporate social workers, behavioral health professionals, psychologists, psychiatrists, law enforcement, probation officers, and faith and community leaders, to work alongside the peer mentor to meet the needs of the person attempting to exit. The research currently suggests that these efforts are best done one-on-one—not in a group setting—because everyone's pathway into and out of extremism is different. Good programs will recognize each individual's unique experiences in extremism and reasons for exiting. As with radicalization, so with exiting—there is not necessarily a linear path, and it is a process. But in the case of exiting, the process is often slow. We cannot force the change in behavior, networks, ideology, and identity. People have to want to change.

When choosing a program, be careful to work with individuals or organizations that abide by ethical standards and professional best practices. For examples, see Moonshot's referral practice standards or Life After Hate's framework for intervention best practices.[6]

The initial goal is to help the person of concern disengage from extremism. Deradicalization may or may not happen. You may not be able to change their mind and disavow their conspiracy theory or ideology. Disengagement, however, is about external behaviors, taking actions to move away from the networks and narratives that fuel the extremism and finding ways to address the underlying core needs through more positive means.

Exit programs first seek to build trust with the individual and create awareness of the possibility that they can change and their life can go on without the extremist group or ideology. This process may be very difficult for some. In disengaging, they are leaving behind a network that served as their community, a place where they found belonging and significance. Others may already be disillusioned with their extremist group or ideology by the time they are willing to work with an exit program, which makes departing a bit simpler.

Programs have to be careful to not push the exiting individual too quickly and unintentionally trigger defense mechanisms that could lead to a return to extremism. Over time, programs will help the exiting individual gain awareness of their problematic beliefs and behaviors. In an ideal situation the individual is able to take responsibility for their actions and seek to make amends with anyone who was harmed by their extremism.

Finally, in an ideal situation, a well-developed program will assist the exiting person with developing protective factors along the Substance Abuse and Mental Health Services Administration (SAMHSA) eight dimensions of wellness: social, environmental, physical, emotional, spiritual, occupational, intellectual, and financial.[7]

———————

The state of research on how best to help people change is nascent. Inevitably, by the time you pick up this book, we will have new and better research that further refines how to help individuals exit extremism. Consequently, what I share here are broad brushstrokes to orient you. If you find yourself in need of these services, go to the recommended resources section of PathBacktoPeace.org for the latest information about disengagement and deradicalization and for links to services near you.

CONCLUSION

SEEKING THE PEACE OF THE CITY

The hope of the gospel does not mean denying evil but expecting its defeat.
It does not mean pretending away grief or neglecting lament but craning our
necks to glimpse the horizon of a new day.
—JEN POLLOCK MICHEL[1]

We have gone deep into understanding extremism; radicalization processes; how our needs, narratives, and networks can create vulnerability; and how to build protective factors in ourselves and within our communities. We used fancy terms and looked at decades of research on extremism.

But if you walk away remembering only one thing, let it be this: people can change, which means our society can change, and you are equipped to help them change by *practicing* love. Not the feeling, but the *action* of love.

This is backed by brain science, social science, and the practical experience of those who have clawed their way back from extremism.

I'm not suggesting we hold hands and sing "Kumbaya." This isn't the Beatles' song "All You Need Is Love." I wish it were that simple.

The love we need to practice is radical, disciplined, other-centered, and self-sacrificing. It offers accountability, kindness, compassion, patience, and mercy. Practicing it is gritty—we do it well some days and fail miserably others. It works slowly, but its influence is deep.

It's also not new. But we've forgotten it. It has its roots in ancient texts. While a significant portion of the back half of the book was focused exclusively on people who profess to be Christians, this call to love is universal wisdom. Most major religions in the world practice a form of this radical love.

Hatred can be overcome only by love.
—MAHATMA GANDHI,[2] HINDU

Hate is not conquered by hate; hate is conquered by love.
This is a law eternal.
—GAUTAMA BUDDHA,[3] BUDDHIST

And the servants of the Most Merciful are those who walk
upon the earth easily, and when the ignorant address them
[harshly], they say [words of] peace.
—QURAN 25:63, MUSLIM

You shall love your neighbor as yourself.
—LEVITICUS 19:18, JEWISH TORAH, CHRISTIAN OLD TESTAMENT

The whole world is sustained by love.
—MIDRASH TANCHUMA, JEWISH

Love is the only force capable of transforming
an enemy into a friend.
—MARTIN LUTHER KING JR.[4]

What we should not do is wait for our power-driven politicians, the profit-driven infotainment industry, and, sadly, many pastors and seminarians and parishioners to stop marketing fear and contempt. They're not likely to change anytime soon.

But we *can* change—one person, one relationship at a time.

Not everyone is equipped to do the work of deradicalization. It is not safe or wise for some to engage directly with their "enemies." But everyone can practice the action of love in their daily life. Everyone can cultivate a culture that considers others as no better than ourselves. Everyone can draw a bigger circle, even in the face of confrontation. Love, without expecting reciprocation, has the power to stop people in their tracks.

Thus, regardless of your religious background and beliefs, I hope you walk away from this book with a commitment to put away the contempt, the hate, the "othering" that empowers extremism. Commit to practicing kindness and love with those in your community. Commit to building bridges to people who have had different experiences and people who think differently than you. Commit to humility and curiosity. And when they return your kindness with anger and hate, commit to a gentle answer that turns away wrath. This is how we de-escalate extremism and radicalization. And this is how we rebuild our communities.

———

My fellow sisters and brothers in Christ, our responsibility to pursue reconciliation and speaking the truth in love is both a joyful and heavy calling. Most Christians have seen remarkable transformations occur in their own lives and in the lives of others. We may have even seen an entire church or community transformed through repentance and forgiveness. But it has been a long time since we've seen large-scale transformations. It seems an almost insurmountable task.

I have hope that through the ministry of Christ's love, we can bring healing to our relationships, our families, and our communities.

It's not too late for us. But this is a long journey, a multigenerational rebuilding project. And there are no guarantees.

Mark Sayers closed his book on leading in ministry during this liminal age with this encouragement: "Crisis always precedes renewal."[5] There is truth to that—a pattern in history, nature, and God's design. I pray for that. And until the Lord demonstrates otherwise, I agree that we should labor on that basis.

But I also think we need to be prepared if none of it works. What if polarization and extremism grow? What if mass shootings, terrorism, and political violence become our norm?

What if your friends embrace the deceitful calls of being prepared for the "spiritual battle" by taking up arms and calling for "revolution"? What if the soft civil war continues with both sides verbally harassing the other and using the instruments of civil authority to oppress and harm the minority in counties, cities, states, and the federal government?

What if pastors are jailed for teaching an orthodox view of Scripture? What if your children or grandchildren are unable to practice the Christian faith in public because America becomes more like China? What if America fails? What if the American church fails?

I'm not playing the what-if game to cause fear. I'm suggesting that we need to consider our response if the worst-case scenario happens. As people of faith, we will increasingly be the minority and, at times, be targets of ridicule or persecution. We can grieve this change. We can be grateful of the legacy of faith in our country (and acknowledge its many failures, too), but the goal isn't to preserve the past. We need to wrestle and come to terms with the potential that the American church may not be restored. There are no guarantees in this world. Our faith does not promise us power, control, health, or wealth—it promises us the cross.

Our calling is a way of mystery and unknowns. It is a good thing to wrestle with this. We have a model in Jacob (Genesis 32:24–31).

God can handle our wrestling. And at some point, we also must let go and accept it.

We do not know what God's plan is for this swath of land in North America that currently is governed by a democratic republic form of government named the United States of America. We do not know if God will renew His church in our country or if He will remove our lampstand (Revelation 2:5).

Writing about the moral convulsions cycle we are presently enduring, David Brooks reflected:

> *One question has haunted me while researching this essay: Are we living through a pivot or a decline? During past moral convulsions, Americans rose to the challenge. They built new cultures and institutions, initiated new reforms—and a renewed nation went on to its next stage of greatness. I've spent my career rebutting the idea that America is in decline, but the events of these past six years, and especially of 2020, have made clear that we live in a broken nation. The cancer of distrust has spread to every vital organ.*
>
> *Renewal is hard to imagine. Destruction is everywhere, and construction difficult to see. The problem goes beyond Donald Trump. The stench of national decline is in the air. A political, social, and moral order is dissolving. America will only remain whole if we can build a new order in its place.*[6]

We can find comfort that we are in the company of a great cloud of witnesses who have gone before us. We read with more seriousness the stories of the apostles, the early church, the faithful believers persecuted by the church powerful in the Middle Ages and Reformation period, and those believers living now in China, Iran, Syria, and other countries where terrorist groups and the state persecute Christians.

And we look to the Lord Jesus Himself, who endured the ultimate worst-case scenario for us. He was rejected by his community, abandoned by his friends, scorned and mocked by the religious and civil authorities of his day. And after being tortured nearly to the point of death, he was hung on a cross for more mockery and pain in the midst of a supernatural darkness that took over the land, a darkness that harkens back to the pre-Genesis state of the cosmos when "the earth was without form and void, and darkness was over the face of the deep" (Genesis 1:2). A darkness of chaos and disorder.

Because Jesus endured the great darkness, the chaos, the uncertainty, the evil, and our sin, we get to receive the great light Isaiah foretold (9:2).

——————

Our calling is not a new one for believers. The prophet Jeremiah wrote a letter to the surviving remnant of Jews in Babylon to encourage them. False prophets had come among the exiles and told them they would be going home soon. Jeremiah wrote to the exiles to correct this deception, telling them to build homes, plant gardens, and have children. And he tells them to "seek the welfare of the city where I have sent you into exile, and pray to the Lord on its behalf, for in its welfare you will find your welfare" (Jeremiah 29:7).

Babylon serves as an archetype of the world system in the Bible. God is calling the Israelites to pray for the city, which is ruled by an ungodly system, and seek its welfare. God was also calling on them to pray for the very people who had destroyed their home, had possibly killed family and friends, and were now their captors. They were the epitome of an enemy. And they had already demonstrated an existential threat to Judah. Yet God does not direct them to take revenge, but to turn the other cheek. It is a glimpse of the Kingdom of God that

Jesus will usher in. Seeking the welfare of the city is a way to love our neighbor—even those who hate us.

By the way, the word translated *welfare* in Jeremiah 29:7 is the Hebrew word *shalom*. The most frequent translation for *shalom* is "peace."

This is our calling—to be peacemakers. We are faithful, even when we do not know what God will do with our efforts. We trust Him. Abide in Him. Rest in Him. Find our shalom in Him. We dig deep roots, cultivate a flourishing garden, and seek the welfare of our neighborhood, our workplace, our community, our city.

And when we do that, we guide our communities to the path of peace.

ACKNOWLEDGMENTS

This book would not be possible but for the extremism research community, prevention practitioners, law enforcement, and policymakers who are dedicating their lives to preventing violence. While we certainly have much still to discover, your work is saving lives today and I'm so grateful. Thank you to everyone whose work is cited and for the many, many more people who contribute to the field. I'm particularly grateful for the encouragement, experience, and insights from J.M. Berger, Kathleen Belew, Nate Blumenthal, Colin Clarke, Sathianathan Clarke, John Cohen, Catrina Doxsee, Ross Frenett, Daveed Gartenstein-Ross, Paul Gill, Ryan Greer, Bruce Hoffman, Seamus Hughes, Seth Jones, Mark Juergensmeyer, Arie Kruglanski, Matt Leavitt, Josh Margolin, Mary McCord, Cynthia Miller-Idriss, Ali Noorani, Arie Perliger, John Picarelli, Vidhya Ramalingam, Nicholas Rasmussen, Oren Segal, George Selim, Erroll Southers, Brette Steele, Jessica Stern, Jacob Ware, Sammie Wicks, Sara Winegar Budge, and the brilliant people at Moonshot.

I believe the solution to our community's extremism problem is rooted in the church's return to its first love: Jesus. The ideas and suggestions laid out in part 2 of the book come from the great cloud of witnesses with whom I've had the privilege of doing life. These include, first and foremost, my mom and dad, and my grams and grandmother—their deep love for Scripture, persistent prayer, and faithful witness has blessed me with a rich spiritual heritage. And also the many faithful people I've journeyed with in churches, small groups, Bible studies, RUF, and mission trips—it is a blessing to say there are too many of you to list here. Thank you for your friendship and encouragement.

I'm also indebted to a number of pastors and Bible teachers who helped think through the application of extremism research in the context of a biblical worldview, in addition to the sermons and books referenced in the notes. A special thank-you to Brad Edwards, Michael Graham, Bryce and Ashley Hales, Luke and Janet Miedema, Russell Moore, Napp Nazworth, Carmen LaBerge, Katye Riselli, and Jared Stacy. Thank you for your courage and faithful witness.

The years in the Trump administration were among the most difficult I've experienced professionally, spiritually, and personally. When I ponder my own protective factors—why I did not succumb to group-think or the pressure to compromise my values—I believe it was God's grace and a whole host of people who helped me along the way: Morgan, Paige, Christina, Tori, Kat, and Katye. Each of you played such a formative role in helping me become who I am. I'm grateful for the decades-long deep bonds of friendship.

My women's small group mentioned in the intro—Shireen, Rithy, Wendy, Liz, Tafanie, and Kat—helped me as I was returning to my faith, never stopped praying for me, and encouraged me to speak out.

Early in my career, my mentors, General John A. Gordon and Col. Joe Rozek, modeled how to be a good public servant, how to faithfully carry out your responsibilities, take care of your people, respectfully question leadership, and operate with integrity in difficult circumstances. Thank you.

I'm also grateful for the many other colleagues I served with during the George W. Bush administration. Having grounding in what a "normal" functioning government looked like was critical for navigating the Trump years.

While the circumstances of the Trump administration were difficult, working with the women and men of DHS is one of the highlights of my career. Many career civil servants took a chance on me
and helped me carry out my responsibilities. There is no way I can list
everyone (and if I did, I might make your work more difficult), but
know it was such a privilege to serve with you. Thank you for what you
do to keep us safe. To the CTTP and CP3 teams especially, thank you
for your dedication and professionalism. It was the honor of a lifetime
to serve with you.

I'm so profoundly grateful for the colleagues who became friends,
held me accountable, and helped me navigate very difficult situations. Briana, Russ, John, Nate, Hillary, Casie, Andy, Tom W., Olivia,
Kirsten, Jennifer, Patty, Connie, Drennan, Sue—thank you for keeping me sane.

To the Cabal (you know who you are)—thank you for welcoming me, encouraging me, and providing a safe space to vent and work
through the challenges of leading as a woman in national security.

There were also political appointees who joined the administration to serve with similar motives as mine. When we would find one
another, it was like a breath of sanity while everyone around you was
drowning in madness. General Kelly, Kirstjen, Elaine, Claire, John,
Chris, Miles, Kristen, Matt, Dan, Tom B., Tom P., Jameson, Lauren,
Sam, Meghann, Valerie, Adam, Hannah, Emily, Evan, Regan, and
Zach—and I'm sure I'm missing some—thank you for your service
and your friendship.

These past few years have been quite the adventure. I have been
beyond blessed with new friendships and partnerships that helped
me navigate the new world I found myself in. I'm so grateful for the
Defending Democracy Together crew—Bill Kristol, Tim Miller, Sarah
Longwell, Meaghan, Ben, and Barry—who helped me find my voice
and realize I wasn't alone. And I'm so, so grateful to Ross and Vidhya

for giving me the opportunity to join Moonshot and the encouragement and space to write. And to the entire Moonshot team—it is an honor to be your colleague and work with you on the mission to reduce violence in our communities.

This book would not exist but for three people: my editor, Daisy Hutton, who sought me out after reading an interview I gave to Politico and planted the seed for *Kingdom of Rage*; my husband, Gil; and my dear friend and gifted author, Katye Riselli, who persuaded me to take on the challenge.

Daisy—it feels like I spent much of the last two years questioning my judgment in taking this project on, but your confidence in the message and in me, and your kindness to me, kept me going. I'm so thankful for your insights, critiques, and editing skills—you could see the gems in the midst of my *many* words. You have my deepest admiration and gratitude.

I'm grateful to my agents Keith Urbahn and Matt Carlini at Javelin for holding my hand as we crafted the book proposal. And I'm so thankful for the team at Hachette and Worthy Books—from the graphic designers to the marketing team, and especially for Marissa Arrigoni—guiding me through all of the details of the post-writing steps of publishing a book. Thank you to my research assistants, Grace Crowder and Sofia Alvarado, for expertise and research help, and to my assistants, Andrea and Liz, for helping me with the juggle. And a special thank you to Luke Miedema, Brad Edwards, Katye, and Gil for being my sounding boards and reviewing chapter drafts.

I'm grateful for all the people I formally and informally interviewed as I was working through everything from how to write a book, to the framing of the book, to the key questions I was trying to understand around our community's challenges—thank you for sharing your stories.

I wrote and edited a good portion of the book in the mountains of Colorado. It was a year of respite and renewal. Our family was so grateful for the hospitality, kindness, and encouragement we received from the Grace Church and the Waldorf School communities. A special thank you to Robynn for her friendship and support.

Mom, Dad, Gil, Katye, and Katherine—thank you for covering me in prayer these last three years. Each of you has endured me "processing" and talked me off of several ledges. I would not have finished without you. Thank you. I love you.

Mom—thank you for the many visits to help with the kids and make sure we were fed so I could write.

My darlings, Josh and Maddie—thank you for going on this adventure with me! Thank you for your patience, for doing extra chores around the house when I was writing, and for being so incredibly encouraging. I'm so blessed to be your mom! I love you.

My beloved Gil, my rock—thank you for your steadfast strength, encouragement, and love, and for the myriad practical ways you kept our family steady in the seasons of writing. I thank God for you. Joy the journey.

My precious Savior—there were moments in writing where a discovery or connection would just blow me away and I *knew* you were in the midst of it. There were many more moments of struggle, frustration, and doubt—You were there too. Thank you for your sufficient grace, for your strength being carried out in my weakness. Soli Deo Gloria.

APPENDIX 1

HOW TO TALK TO LOVED ONES ABOUT EXTREMISM AND WHAT TO DO IF YOU THINK A LOVED ONE IS RADICALIZING

BUILDING PROTECTIVE FACTORS IN OUR KIDS

Our goals are to protect our children and to teach them how they can help their friends. More often than not, it is a peer who will notice, before an adult, that something is wrong and that a friend needs help before self-harm or harm of others occurs.

What to Say to Tweens (Ages 8–12)

If you can, it is really important to begin framing these conversations when kids are tweens—in an age-appropriate way, of course. If your kids spend anytime online, even if you have things "locked down," they are likely to encounter extremist content or ideology perhaps without even realizing it. And if they don't, their friends will. So starting at this age is important. They're more open to learning from you, and starting younger allows you to create a rhythm of familiarity for these conversations to continue into the teen years.

As with other challenging topics, you want to invite your child to come to you with any questions. That means that when they come to you with questions, you must set aside time to answer or collaboratively discover the answer together. Psychologists who specialize in tween and teen behavior will tell you that it's important to not react to the questions, however wild they may be. Michelle Icard says we should practice "Botox Brow"[1] because their brains are rewiring and their prefrontal cortex is not fully developed. If they perceive any reaction, they will shut down. So practice being nonreactive when they come to you with a question. The goal is to have open lines of communication into the teen years, so that they are more likely to share with you when they need adult help, perhaps for themselves or for a friend.

Your goals at this age are to help kids recognize and reject hateful content and rhetoric, such as racist, sexist, homophobic, antisemitic, or antireligious, or general justifications of violence. That includes training them to recognize when they're being bullied online, and what to do about it. If your school doesn't offer it, look into digital literacy and cyber civics programs available online.

You can find links to parent resource guides produced by the Anti-Defamation League, ScreenHate.org, and PERIL at PathBacktoPeace.org.

What to Say to Teens

If you were able to start these discussions when your kids were in their tweens, then keep going and build on past conversations. If you were not able to start early, there's no time like the present.

With teens, in addition to helping your kids develop an awareness of various extremist ideologies, you also want to discover what they are seeing and hearing. Be curious, ask open-ended questions, and listen. Talking while doing another activity like driving or cleaning the kitchen can help reduce the pressure.

Exposure to extremist content is inevitable, unfortunately. The extreme has gone mainstream, and extremist youth culture is very good at infiltrating the mainstream youth culture. The goal is to build awareness of how bad actors exploit and manipulate through propaganda and disinformation.

Ask what they are doing online, what they're learning, and which platforms they spend time on. Ask about what videos, music, or memes they've enjoyed lately—extremist propaganda is often hidden in humor and shared without individuals fully understanding the meaning behind it.

Educate yourself about your child's point of view or ideology so that you can explore it further in future conversations. Discuss the news and educate your kids on how propaganda and disinformation are used to manipulate people.

Don't panic if your child has stumbled upon or is exploring content you think qualifies as extremist (remember Botox Brow!). First, it is nearly impossible for exposure not to occur if they are spending any time online. Ask questions and keep the conversation open. Don't express judgment, but you can share your concerns about how they might be spending their time. The most important thing is to maintain a relationship. Even if you are offended or scared by what your teen is expressing, don't react. Instead, educate yourself and get help if you need it.

Training Teens on Warning Signs and When to Get Help

Unfortunately, many recent mass attacks (e.g., Buffalo, Uvalde) have come from teens and young adults. So in addition to talking about extremism itself, we also need to talk with our kids about warning signs they may detect in a friend or acquaintance (see the lists in appendixes 2 and 3). You want your child to tell you (or a teacher, coach, or guidance counselor) if a friend or acquaintance is talking about violence, or if they just think someone they know needs help.

It may help to let your child know that their generation is dealing with challenges that we did not. We are still trying to figure out the best way to help. More kids are anxious and depressed than ever before, and unfortunately we have an epidemic of mostly older boys and young men who see violence as an answer to their pain and grievances. Encourage your child to speak up if they have concerns about a friend.

We also want to reassure our teens that the overwhelming majority of people do not radicalize, and even fewer will do something violent. But we all can do more to reduce hate and violence.

Staying Up-to-date on Extremist Narratives

Conspiracy theories, extremist groups, ideologies, recruitment tactics and preferred platforms all change pretty quickly. Groups often disband and re-form under different names. I recommend that you find some trusted resources and check them a couple of times a year to keep up-to-date with current conspiracy theories and extremist narratives. Visit PathBacktoPeace.org for a list of suggested websites and guides.

In 2023, the most prevalent violent extremist ideologies that we see youth attracted to are variations of white supremacist extremism, antisemitism, incel, and violent nihilism. Learn the basics about those ideologies; you can go back to chapter 4 for a refresher or visit websites that keep up-to-date on current developments. Current extremist topics, phrases, or attitudes of concern may include:

- *White supremacist extremism:* great replacement, white genocide, racial realism, scientific racism—arguments that genetics, evolution, or psychology supports racist stereotypes, blaming immigrants for societal problems.
- *Antisemitism:* references to "global elites," George Soros, other tropes and symbols. See ADL's Hate Symbols database.[2]
- *Incel:* male supremacy or misogynistic, derogatory attitudes toward women, expressing a desire for societal chaos, societal collapse, or violent nihilism.
- *Violent nihilism:* discussing "societal chaos" or "societal collapse"; a desire to "burn it all down" or statements like

"there is no political solution." This has become more common among mass attackers in recent years.

Safeguarding Online

There are any number of online harms that we parents have to stay on top of (e.g., sexting, sextortion, cyberbullying, and sex trafficking recruitment). The recommendations for safeguarding your child from extremism will be similar to protecting them from those harms. And the level of safeguarding you apply will be dependent on the child's age and your family's approach to tech usage generally.

If you are talking with your tween and teen about extremism and how they may stumble upon things online, you can ask them to share with you when they think they've seen something.

Depending on how you set up your home Wi-Fi and your child's devices, you can block certain sites that are known as havens for extremism—for example, 4Chan, Gab, 8Kun, Kiwi Farms, Incels.co, etc.[3]

Some sites have limited moderation, relying on users to report violations, which allows extremists to spread content and recruit more easily. Unless there is a compelling reason why your child needs to access them, I would steer clear: Minds, BitChute, RiotChat, Rocket Chat, Odysee/Lbry, Parler, MeWe, Live, Rumble, and Patriots.win.[4]

Extremists often use encrypted or anonymized apps and services. If your child has one on their device, find out why.

Extremists exploit mainstream sites, too. Don't forget to keep the conversation going with your kids.

WHAT TO DO IF YOU THINK A LOVED ONE IS RADICALIZING

Extremism in Youth (under the Age of Eighteen)

If you have concerns that your child, your grandchild, or a youth with whom you have a strong relationship may be radicalizing, the first step is to educate yourself and curate a team of people to help you assess what is going on in their life. Please don't ignore your concerns. If something in your gut is telling you something's wrong, check it out.

Don't assume this is normal teenage stuff that they will grow out of or that they'll get over it. Don't assume your kid "could never do that." Life for a teenager today is exponentially more difficult than when we were teens. Adolescents have natural vulnerabilities that are exacerbated by social media. Extremists prey on those vulnerabilities and entice kids with "solutions" of violence at a scale we never experienced. The median age of a school shooter is sixteen.[5] The youngest school shooters have been six years old; two of them were intentional shootings.[6] Don't ignore your gut.

Review the warning signs lists in appendixes 2 and 3 and make a list of the things you are observing. Then look for an opportunity to engage with the child of concern, asking innocent questions, such as "Oh, I'm not familiar with that. What does that mean?" You may get a direct answer and learn it is benign and nothing to be concerned about. But if their answer is an eye roll, it's hard to know if that's just a teen being a teen or a teen trying to hide something. You'll probably need to dig deeper.

Hate morphs at the speed of the internet. With your list of observations in mind, take a look at the think tanks and nonprofits that publish information online to keep up-to-date on the latest iterations of conspiracy theories, memes, recruitment tactics, and extremist ideologies. I recommend ScreenHate.org, which is specifically tailored for what to look for and how to talk with youth on these topics. ADL also has an up-to-date hate symbols database, which may be helpful if you are in the investigatory stage of trying to determine what exactly your child has been exposed to.[7] My website PathBacktoPeace.org also tracks and updates this information on a routine basis.

With this information in hand, ask to meet with adults who know your child: coaches, teachers, other family members, and community leaders. Have they noticed any recent behavioral changes or behaviors of concern? Are they aware of anything happening in your child's life that might be causing difficulties, such as bullying, relational difficulties, failing a class, or having difficulty with a particular teacher?

If after these conversations you continue to be concerned that your child is exhibiting signs of radicalization, ask their school if they have access to a threat assessment team or individual threat assessment professionals who have specialized training to assess how much risk an individual may pose. These services may also be offered by your city or state. If such an assessment occurs, the team or professional should make a recommendation on a process to manage the risk moving forward.

If a threat assessment through the school or government is not possible, look for a mental health professional, preferably one who has training in violence prevention. The same group that created Screen-Hate.org, coordinates the Prevention Practitioners Network. There is a directory you can use to look up a licensed provider near you. Even if there is not someone nearby, you may be able to do virtual counseling sessions. To find the directory and even more resources, download the ResilienceNet app by One World Strong.[8]

If at all possible, I suggest connecting with one of these professionals before you approach your child or consider the below actions to restrict their activities.

If the loved one is your child and under the age of eighteen, you have more control, legally speaking. You can require that they attend mental or behavioral health counseling. You can grant permission to the school or a counselor to engage with the child. You can even grant permission to law enforcement to speak with the child and search the home for concerning materials or weapons.

You can also set parameters on where they go and with whom they spend time. You could consider restricting tech usage, including blocking certain websites or removing phones and computers altogether—or at least removing them from their room. (Keeping technology in common spaces reduces risk of exposure to extremism. It also has the side benefit of keeping kids healthier.)

As a parent of a teenager, I am well aware that taking too hard a line with our teens on any topic, but particularly access to technology, can backfire significantly. The boundaries we can set with a twelve-year-old are different from what we can do with a seventeen-year-old. With a twelve-year-old, I would lean toward a stronger stance of cutting access to technology. At that age, we have more control over their activities, where they are spending time, and with whom, and we have time and space to rebuild the relationship. At seventeen, that will likely be impossible to enforce and may do harm to your relationship.

The process of adolescence creates natural vulnerabilities. Teens are in the midst of trying to find their identity and prove their significance. Withdrawal and isolation are sometimes part of the normal development process. Teens desire respect and want to be treated as adults, even as they are willing to engage in risky behavior that makes parents uncomfortable about giving them such freedom. If we set limits that are too strong or, worse, belittle our teens in the process of setting limits, this can be a source of humiliation and could create more of an opening or drive for extremist ideology.

Our most important asset is our relationship with our child. That attachment offers the strongest protective factor. Do what you can to preserve it. If your relationship is damaged, consider eliciting the aid of an adult you trust and your child feels comfortable confiding in. This can often be a coach, a teacher of their favorite subject, an aunt or uncle, or an adult cousin or sibling.

EXTREMISM IN ADULTS

If your loved one is over the age of eighteen, your tools are more limited and your ability to persuade becomes more important. At PathBacktoPeace.org, I've listed a few national organizations that work with families of loved ones engaged in extremism. Depending on the severity of the case, you might consider reaching out to one of them so they can help you think through how to approach your loved one with your concerns.

No doubt, your loved one has already brought some form of pain or tension to the family or friendship. I recommend engaging with a licensed professional counselor to help you set boundaries and ensure you and everyone else in the household are getting the care they need. If it is physically and psychologically safe for you to do so, your goal is to maintain an empathetic relationship with healthy boundaries with the person of concern. This has a twofold purpose: People who have successfully disengaged from extremism credit accountability and love as the keys that helped them have the courage to disengage. And by staying in touch, you may be able to detect if there has been a shift in their behavior that warrants additional intervention.

To the extent possible, reaffirm your love and care for the individual. Let them know you are there for them when they are ready to talk.

EXTREMISM IN AGING ADULTS

Friends have called me with concerns about an aging family member, usually a father or uncle, who has developed deeper antigovernment sentiment in the last few years. Typically, these individuals have spent inordinate amounts of time, often isolated in retirement, listening to outrage factories or reposting disrespectful memes on Facebook. They tend to be very concerned with the "moral decline" of the country and deeply saddened and maybe even offended that we cannot go back to simpler times. Discussions with them (or a glance at their Facebook page) resembles talk of "grave concerns" with sweeping generalized claims (or partisan memes) mixed with trendy or trite platitudes and out-of-context biblical truths (or random posts of Scripture references, sometimes served up as passive-aggression).

While we have had an uptick in violent acts by people in their sixties and seventies, they tend to not be politically motivated. (I find these acts very concerning and puzzling, but they seem to be associated with carrying out revenge for personal grievance.)

Before I proceed, please hear this caveat: context matters a lot. We should not assume that just because they are older, they are incapable of harming others. We should absolutely look at the list in appendixes 2 and 3 and get help for our loved one if we are seeing signs of ideation of violence or preparation for violence.

Aging and certain diseases can lead to risk factors. For example, increased aggression and anger are normal for individuals with dementia or some measure of clinical depression. Usually these are offset by lack of mobility or the cognitive deficiencies that prevent forming a coherent plan, but we should not assume.

In my friends' cases, we came to the conclusion that while the behavior was concerning, it did not rise to the level of staging a family intervention or calling law enforcement. One friend's father's mobility was severely restricted, which would have made it difficult to plan or carry out an act of violence. In both cases, the persons of concern were married and the spouses were a calming voice in their lives. There were no recent crises, personal humiliations, or rejections. Neither had access to high-powered weaponry. Those factors could change, of course, and my friends might need to be prepared to intervene if the loss of a spouse or some type of personal humiliation leads to more concerning behavior.

My hypothesis is that the concerning behavior of the seventy-plus age group might be explained by the fact that they are the first generation to age into their golden years with access to 24/7 outrage infotainment and social media. As people age, it is normal to be frustrated with our decline; physically and mentally we cannot do what we used to be able to do with ease. The loss of social interaction, particularly after retirement, and loss of agency due to health challenges, combined with pain or chronic pain that makes us irritable—all of which are fairly common as we age—can lead to depression, anxiety, and anger. This makes aging individuals a prime target for the outrage infotainment complex.

Further, we have a growing aging population. People are living longer, and baby boomers started to retire in 2011, a process that appears to have accelerated due to the pandemic.[9] In 1980, 11 percent of the population was sixty-five or older. It is now 17 percent and on a trajectory to reach 23 percent over the next 10 years.[10] That's one in five Americans. By 2034, there will be more adults over the age of sixty-five than children under eighteen in the US.[11] Why do demographic trends matter? As markets have done for seventy years now, the infotainment industry will continue to cater to the boomers, because there is money to be made there. We should expect the outrage industry to continue to stoke grievances of our parents and grandparents.

The other reason we see more elderly people in the population voicing their frustration and anger is they now have a way to amplify their voice: social media. And isolation behind a keyboard often enables them to put forward ideas without the social filter they may have in the direct personal company of others or in social settings that dictate some measure of decorum and purposefully moderated (or spouse-generated) self-control.

So what should we do? As with most things, people older than us, especially our parents, don't usually want or heed the advice of their children. They are not likely to respond well to chiding them for their inappropriate behavior or "othering" statements online. If there is someone their age your loved one of concern would listen to—perhaps a spouse, sibling, or friend—they would be more likely to effect change than a younger person could. Take that person to lunch, share your concerns, and see if they would be willing to talk to your loved one. (They should follow the guidance on how to talk with a loved one about extremism.)

If you have influence over what your parents are watching and consuming, consider offering entertainment alternatives to cable news and opinion shows. (If they live with you and you pay the cable bill, keep that in mind.) Encouraging our retired family members to continue to serve in the community, if they are physically able, is a great way to reduce isolation and exposure to outrage. Plus, as we discussed earlier, proximity to those who are different from us humanizes people and reduces the likelihood extremist messages will work. If you notice a change in behavior—like an increase in negative posts or an increase in anger—set aside time to check in and see what else might be going on. Please, for their safety and that of others, don't avoid these tough conversations.

Most importantly, maintain a relationship and reassure them you love them. People with strong attachments are less likely to commit acts of violence.

I'll return to my caveat: we should not assume that just because they are older, they are incapable of harming others. Though the vast majority of mass shootings and terrorist attacks are perpetrated by older teens and adults in their twenties and thirties, there have been tragic exceptions to the trend. The Nashville Christmas bombing, in which thankfully no one was injured or killed but the bomber himself, was carried out by a sixty-three-year-old. The Las Vegas Music Festival shooter was sixty-four; he is responsible for the deadliest mass shooting in US history. An eighty-seven-year-old living in a senior apartment complex shot from a second-floor balcony into a common area. He killed one and injured two others before killing himself.[12] And in January 2023, there were two mass shootings in California within two days, carried out by a seventy-two-year-old and sixty-six-year-old.

Older attackers tend to be more isolated and less likely to leak details of their attacks.[13] They do not seek fame as younger attackers often do but are more often motived by interpersonal conflict or legal or financial crises. You should absolutely look at the lists that follow in appendixes 2 and 3 and get help for your loved one if you are seeing signs of ideation of violence or preparation for violence.

APPENDIX 2

RISK FACTORS FOR RADICALIZATION

As we explored in chapter 7, researchers have identified more than a hundred risk factors for extremism.[1] The top factors we examined are re-listed at the top of the list below; the remaining factors (8–15) are pulled from the 2021 National Counterterrorism Center's "US Violent Extremist Mobilization Indicators" booklet.[2]

The presence of a risk factor does not necessarily mean that someone is radicalizing or that an individual will use violence. One could have several of these risk factors and never radicalize or seek violence. When threat assessments are conducted, such factors are considered in determining the level of risk someone may pose. Consequently, if you are concerned about recent changes in someone's behavior and you are aware that they have one of these risk factors in their background, it suggests you should request help sooner.

1. Being disrespected or humiliated
2. Psychological distress
3. A recent crisis
4. Witnessing verbal statements in support of violent extremism
5. Feeling like a helpless victim
6. Nonviolent offending
7. Being a victim of violence as a child

8. Family, significant other, and/or peers espousing or supporting a violent extremist ideology

9. History of encouraging violence by dehumanizing people who are not in the same identity group or who are ideological opponents

10. History of notable noncompliance with restrictions, boundaries, or laws

11. History of stalking, harassing, threatening, or menacing behavior

12. History of violence (not necessarily related to terrorism), unstable mental state resulting in threat to self or others, or past exposure to violence and/or a traumatic event

13. Negative response to or failure to cope with existing, new, or changing personal circumstances, including personal relationships, family dynamics, employment, and/or substance abuse or dependence

14. Presence of real or perceived injustice or a feeling of being wronged (grievances); may be broad or specific to a person, group, or event

15. Previous travel or exposure to a conflict zone or an area of high political or social violence, including personal or noncombatant travel

For both behavioral indicators and risk factors, listen to your gut. If you feel something is off, it is better to ask from help. Visit Path-BacktoPeace.org to review one of the guides or access the prevention practitioners directory to find someone. All you may need is a quick consult to reassure you that everything is fine. But if something more is going on, a mental or behavioral health professional can walk you through what to do.

APPENDIX 3

INDICATORS OF MOBILIZATION TO VIOLENCE

B elow are indicators of mobilization to violence. These are pulled directly from the 2021 National Counterterrorism Center's "US Violent Extremist Mobilization Indicators" booklet, which you can access online and download for yourself.[1] These indicators are likely to be updated in the coming years as more research becomes available; always check websites to see the latest recommendations.

Much like the warnings in appendix 2, the behaviors you are looking for are things that are out of the norm for the individual of concern. The guide identifies three behavioral stages (motivation, preparation, and mobilization) and five indicator types (financial, ideology, intent, relationships, tactics, and travel).

MOTIVATION INDICATORS

"Physical or virtual actions that build, solidify, or communicate violent ideological beliefs; these indicators do not necessarily suggest an impending attack or violent extremist travel."[2] Motivation indicators warrant getting help. Depending on your state or city's prevention resources, this could be from a threat assessment and management team, a qualified mental and behavioral health professional, or law enforcement.

1. Professing intent to harm law enforcement if law enforcement takes action or statement of intent to harm others (typically ideological opponents) if confronted

2. Expressing desire or willingness to die for a violent extremist ideology

3. Threatening specific violence against a particular physical target, especially in response to current news reporting on political and legislative issues or other flashpoint events that speak to one's ideological concerns

4. Threatening violence toward specific individuals, including civilian, government, law enforcement, or military personnel

5. Producing, promoting, or extensively consuming violent extremist content online or in person, including violent extremist videos, narratives, media, and messaging for suspected criminal purposes

6. Posing with weapons and imagery associated with violent extremism in photos or videos, especially if paired with threats or expressed interest in carrying out violence against an ideological target for suspected criminal purposes

7. Expressing acceptance of violence as a necessary means to achieve ideological goals (for example, communicating a desire for revenge against ideological opponents) and saying that nonviolent means are ineffective or unavailable

8. Attempting to radicalize others—especially family members and peers—to violence

9. Praising, or researching to emulate, past successful or attempted attacks or attackers

10. Increasing or extreme adherence to conspiracy theories as a justification of violence against ideological targets

11. Engaging in outbursts or fights with or condemning behavior of family, peers, community, or authority figures while advocating violent extremist ideology

12. Adopting more than one violent extremist ideology

13. Rejecting nonviolent voices in favor of violent extremist ideologues

14. Changing vocabulary, style of speech, or behavior to reflect a hardened point of view or new sense of purpose associated with violent extremist causes, particularly after a catalyzing event

15. Isolating oneself from family and peers, particularly if citing violent extremist doctrine or ideology

PREPARATION INDICATORS

"Physical or virtual actions suggesting an attack or violent extremist travel may occur in the near term (weeks before an attack or violent extremist travel)."[3] Preparation indicators should also lead to quick consultation with law enforcement.

1. Communicating intent to engage in violence or a direct threat with justification for action, particularly if presented as necessary or inevitable, in person or online

2. Unusual building or testing of explosives, especially if tailored to a specific target

3. Planning or preparing to travel abroad to join violent extremist organizations, seek training, or engage in a conflict zone

4. Planning or preparing to travel within the United States to participate in violent extremist activity

5. Seeking or claiming religious, political, or ideological justification or validation for a planned violent act

6. Unusual purchase of military-style tactical equipment (for example, body armor or personal protective equipment) in a manner that raises suspicion of planning violence

7. Breaking away from a larger group or creating a more exclusive or operationally secure group to discuss or plan specific violent activity

8. Surveilling potential attack targets

9. Increased use of physical concealment tactics (for example, countersurveillance techniques, disposable phone) in support of planning a specific act of violence

10. Increased use of online concealment tactics (for example, deleting, hiding, or manipulating social media or other online accounts to misrepresent location or hide group membership, contacts, or activities) in support of planning a specific act of violence

11. Communicating directly with or seeking to develop a relationship with violent extremists, or being contacted directly by them, for suspected criminal purposes

12. Unusual efforts to obtain explosive precursors, especially illegally or surreptitiously

13. Acquisition of weapons or ammunition for suspected criminal purposes

14. Change in or initiation of physical or weapons training for suspected criminal purposes

15. Planning or pursuing suspicious travel activity (for example, unusual purchase of one-way tickets, false excuses for international travel, fraudulent passport application) in a manner that raises suspicion of potential violence

16. Sending or receiving unexplained financial resources or equipment to/from violent extremists

17. Creating, joining, or implying membership/ association—in person or online—with violent extremists for the purpose of furthering violent activity

18. Conducting research for target or tactic selection for violent acts (for example, acquiring blueprints, maps, schematics, or technical specifications)

19. Pursuing or exploiting jobs or personnel who provide sensitive access to enable violent acts (for example, critical infrastructure, the intelligence community, law enforcement, military)

20. Attempting to seek technical expertise (for example, in aviation, biology, chemistry, electronics) to enable planned violence

MOBILIZATION INDICATORS

"Physical or virtual actions suggesting an attack or violent extremist travel may be imminent (days/hours before an attack or violent extremist travel)."[4] If you observe mobilization indicators, this warrants immediate action. *Call 911.* Document as much as you can. Also, please be careful. A number of mass attacks have started with the attacker harming or killing family or roommates at home before traveling to their target for additional killing.

1. Traveling, within the United States or abroad, to carry out or participate in violent extremist activity

2. Engaging in a threatening interaction or violently refusing to comply with law enforcement based on violent extremist ideology

3. Disseminating one's own martyrdom or last will video or statement (for example, a pre-attack manifesto or final statement)

4. Conducting a dry run of an attack or assault or attempting to gain proximity or access to targets

5. Identifying—in person or online—specific details of an intended violent activity, including target(s), time frames, and participant roles

6. Disposing of meaningful personal assets or belongings in an unusual manner, particularly with a sense of urgency or without regard for personal financial gain

7. Unusual goodbyes or post-death instructions

NOTES

For more information and links to updated research and resources referenced in the book, visit PathBacktoPeace.org.

INTRODUCTION

1. Jonathan D. Karl, "The Man Who Made January 6 Possible," *The Atlantic*, November 9, 2021, https://www.theatlantic.com/ideas/archive/2021/11/trump -johnny-mcentee-january-6-betrayal/620646.

2. "Executive Order on Protecting American Monuments, Memorials, and Statues and Combating Recent Criminal Violence," June 26, 2020, https:// trumpwhitehouse.archives.gov/presidential-actions/executive-order-protecting -american-monuments-memorials-statues-combating-recent-criminal-violence.

3. Patrick Tucker, "DHS's Portland Stunt Could Undermine the Agency for Years, Former Officials Warn," *Defense One*, July 2020, https://www.defenseone.com /policy/2020/07/dhss-portland-stunt-could-undermine-agency-years-former -officials-warn/167048.

4. For example, David French, Russell Moore, Beth Moore, etc.

CHAPTER ONE: WHAT HAPPENED?

1. Chris Cameron, "These Are the People Who Died in Connection with the Capitol Riot," *New York Times*, January 5, 2022, https://www.nytimes.com /2022/01/05/us/politics/jan-6-capitol-deaths.html.

2. "As Partisan Hostility Grows, Signs of Frustration with the Two-Party System," Pew Research Center, August 2022, https://www.pewresearch.org/politics /2022/08/09/as-partisan-hostility-grows-signs-of-frustration-with-the-two -party-system. See also Geoffrey Skelley and Holly Fuong, "3 in 10 Americans Named Political Polarization as a Top Issue Facing the Country," Five Thirty- Eight, June 14, 2022, https://fivethirtyeight.com/features/3-in-10-americans -named-political-polarization-as-a-top-issue-facing-the-country.

3. For example, Gallup surveys negative emotions annually. Stress increased 5 points in 2020; anger increased 2 points (Julie Ray, "2020 Sets Records for

Negative Emotions," Gallup, July 20, 2021, https://news.gallup.com/poll /352205/2020-sets-records-negative-emotions.aspx). See also the 2021 CNN poll on anger: Chris Cillizza, "We're All Just So Damn Angry," CNN Politics, September 10, 2021, https://www.cnn.com/2021/09/10/politics/anger-american -electorate-cnn-poll/index.html. See also Sarah Lyall, "A Nation on Hold Wants to Speak with a Manager," *New York Times*, January 1, 2022, https:// www.nytimes.com/2022/01/01/business/customer-service-pandemic-rage.html.

4. CDC Data for 2020 indicates a 30 percent increase in homicides over 2019, the highest ever increase recorded. The 2021 data, which was not completely analyzed yet, indicates the further increases in homicide. "New CDC/NCHS Data Confirm Largest One-Year Increase in U.S. Homicide Rate in 2020," October 6, 2021, https://www.cdc.gov/nchs/pressroom/nchs_press_releases /2021/202110.htm. For current data visit https://www.cdc.gov/nchs/nvss/vsrr /mortality-dashboard.html.

5. Ben Collins and Ryan J. Reilly, "After Mar-a-Lago Search, Users on Pro-Trump Forums Agitate for 'Civil War'—Including a Jan. 6 Rioter," NBC News, August 9, 2022, https://www.nbcnews.com/politics/justice-department/mar -lago-search-users-trump-forums-agitate-civil-war-jan-6-rioter-rcna42148.

6. Alan Feuer, "As Right-Wing Rhetoric Escalates, So Do Threats and Violence," *New York Times*, August 13, 2022, https://www.nytimes.com/2022/08/13 /nyregion/right-wing-rhetoric-threats-violence.html.

7. Dan Balz, Scott Clement, and Emily Guskin, "Republicans and Democrats Divided over Jan. 6 Insurrection and Trump's Culpability, Post-UMD Poll Finds," *Washington Post*, January 1, 2022, https://www.washingtonpost.com /politics/2022/01/01/post-poll-january-6.

8. "Threats to American Democracy ahead of an Unprecedented Presidential Election," PRRI, October 25, 2023, https://www.prri.org/research/threats-to -american-democracy-ahead-of-an-unprecedented-presidential-election.

9. G. J. Wintemute, S. L. Robinson, A. Crawford, et al., "Views of Democracy and Society and Support for Political Violence in the USA: Findings from a Nationally Representative Survey," *Injury Epidemiology* 10, no. 45 (2023), https://doi.org/10.1186/s40621-023-00456-3.

10. Wintemute, Robinson, Crawford, et al., "Views of Democracy and Society and Support for Political Violence in the USA."

11. Wintemute, Robinson, Crawford, et al., "Views of Democracy and Society and Support for Political Violence in the USA."

12. Some in the Christian pacifist tradition argue that just war and self-defense are not legitimate reasons for violence. For more, see Preston M. Sprinkle and Greg Boyd, *Nonviolence: The Revolutionary Way of Jesus* (Colorado Springs: David C. Cook, 2021).

13. There are three major branches of Christianity: Eastern Orthodox, Roman Catholic, and Protestant. All three embrace the centrality of Jesus Christ to

their faith but vary in their understanding of salvation, worship practices, sacraments, and governance.

14. Tim Keller describes the gospel as "Through the person and work of Jesus Christ, God fully accomplishes salvation for us, rescuing us from judgment for sin into fellowship with him, and then restores the creation in which we can enjoy our new life together with him forever." Because salvation in Christianity is completely reliant on God's work, Jesus' death and resurrection on the cross, and an individual's acceptance or belief of his gift of grace, there is no outward action or test we humans can apply to another human to *know* that they are in fact a believer. There is guidance to us in the New Testament that we will know a true believer by their "fruit," and there are tests in the Old and New Testament for how to know a true versus a false prophet, but ultimately it is God who is judge and only God can see the heart. (1 Samuel 16:7; Matthew 7:15–20.)

15. Within Protestantism there are more than a dozen denominational families, many of which have numerous denominations. For example, there are more than twenty Baptist denominations. There are also independent nondenominational Protestant churches. The evangelical churches primarily come from the Protestant branch of the church.

16. "Among Protestants, Born-Again or Evangelical Christians Continue to Outnumber Non-Evangelicals," Pew Research Center's Religion & Public Life Project, December 8, 2021, https://www.pewresearch.org/religion/2021/12/14/about-three-in-ten-u-s-adults-are-now-religiously-unaffiliated/pf_12-14-21_npors_0_2.

17. "What Is an Evangelical?" National Association of Evangelicals, https://www.nae.org/what-is-an-evangelical. For research purposes, NAE and LifeWay Research assess strong agreement with the following four points to evaluate if someone is an evangelical by *belief*: the Bible is the highest authority, it is important to encourage non-Christians to trust Jesus as their savior, Jesus' death removed the penalty of sin, and trust in Jesus alone brings salvation.

18. Catherine Brekus, *Sarah Osborn's World: The Rise of Evangelical Christianity in Early America*, New Directions in Narrative History (New Haven, CT: Yale University Press, 2013).

19. Timothy Keller, "How Do Christians Fit into the Two-Party System? They Don't." *New York Times*, September 29, 2018, https://www.nytimes.com/2018/09/29/opinion/sunday/christians-politics-belief.html.

20. Eighty-eight percent of white evangelical protestants identify as Republicans or lean Republican. See "America's Changing Religious Landscape," Pew Research Center, May 12, 2015, https://www.pewresearch.org/religion/religious-landscape-study/religious-tradition/evangelical-protestant/party-affiliation.

CHAPTER TWO: THE PATH TO EXTREMISM

1. J.M. Berger, *Extremism* (Boston: MIT Press, 2018), 113.

2. David Fromkin, "The Strategy of Terrorism," *Foreign Affairs*, July 1975, https://www.foreignaffairs.com/articles/1975-07-01/strategy-terrorism.

3. For example, Joseph Kahn and Tim Weiner, "World Leaders Rethinking
   Strategy on Aid to Poor," *New York Times*, March 18, 2002, https://www
   .nytimes.com/2002/03/18/world/world-leaders-rethinking-strategy-on-aid
   -to-poor.html. Alberto Abadie wrote that "the notion that poverty generates
   terrorism is consistent with the results of most of the literature on the
   economics of conflicts. In particular, the results in Alberto Alesina et al.
   (1996) suggest that poor economic conditions increase the probability of
   political coups. Paul Collier and Anke Hoeffer (2004) show that economic
   variables are powerful predictors of civil wars, while political variables have
   low explanatory power. Edward Miguel et al. (2004) show that, for a sample
   of African countries, negative exogenous shocks in economic growth increase
   the likelihood of civil conflict. Because terrorism is a manifestation of political
   conflict, these results seem to indicate that poverty and adverse economic
   conditions may play an important role explaining terrorism." Alberto Abadie,
   "Poverty, Political Freedom, and the Roots of Terrorism," *American Economic
   Review* 96, no. 2 (May 2006): 50–56, https://economics.mit.edu/files/11865.

4. For example, according to Brian Katulis and Peter Juul, the US spent $2 trillion
   in the first twenty years post 9/11, on direct war costs and reconstruction,
   humanitarian aid, and building up local security forces (Brian Katulis and
   Peter Juul, "The Lessons Learned for U.S. National Security Policy in the 20
   Years since 9/11," Center for American Progress, September 10, 2021, https://
   www.americanprogress.org/article/lessons-learned-u-s-national-security-policy
   -20-years-since-911). See ForeignAssistance.gov for annual breakdown of
   assistance by country and sector.

5. For example, Alan B. Krueger and Jitka Malečková, "Education, Poverty, and
   Terrorism: Is There a Causal Connection?" *Journal of Economic Perspectives*
   17, no. 4 (Fall 2003): 119–144; and Abadie, "Poverty, Political Freedom, and
   the Roots of Terrorism." Studies of ISIS foreign fighters (people from outside
   of Iraq and Syria) found that "countries with higher economic prosperity and
   lower inequality were more likely" to have residents travel to Syria. See Berger,
   Extremism, 114. See also Diego Gambetta and Steffens Hertog, "Uncivil
   Engineers: The Surprising Link between Education and Jihad," *Foreign Affairs*,
   March 2016, https://www.foreignaffairs.com/articles/2016-03-10/uncivil
   -engineers. Variations of these studies have been repeated dozens of times over
   the past twenty years, confirming that radicalization and extremism cannot be
   simplistically explained by external structural factors or religion.

6. Berger, *Extremism*, 115.

7. Berger, *Extremism*, 2.

8. The Overton Window of Political Possibility was created in the mid-1990s by
   Joseph P. Overton. For more on the Overton Window, see Nathan Russell,
   "An Introduction to the Overton Window of Political Possibilities," Mackinac
   Center for Public Policy, January 4, 2006, https://www.mackinac.org/7504.

9. Berger, *Extremism*, 44.

10. Berger, *Extremism*, 24.

11. Berger, *Extremism*, 25.

12. Gazi Islam, "Social Identity Theory," in *Encyclopedia of Critical Psychology* (New York: Springer-Verlag, 2014), 1781–1783, https://link.springer.com/referencewo rkentry/10.1007/978-1-4614-5583-7_289.

13. Islam, "Social Identity Theory."

14. Berger, *Extremism*, 25.

15. Berger, *Extremism*, 75–76.

16. Berger, *Extremism*, 26.

17. Berger, *Extremism*, 57.

18. Berger, *Extremism*, 57.

19. Berger, *Extremism*, 57.

20. Haroro J. Ingram, "Deciphering the Siren Call of Militant Islamist Propaganda: Meaning, Credibility, and Behavioural Change," International Centre for Counter-Terrorism—The Hague, September 2016, https://www.jstor .org/stable/resrep29420.

21. Berger, *Extremism*, 82–83.

22. Berger, *Extremism*, 99–100.

23. Noémie Bouhana, "The Moral Ecology of Extremism: A Systemic Perspective," Commission for Countering Extremism, July 31, 2019, https://www.gov .uk/government/publications/the-moral-ecology-of-extremism-a-systemic -perspective.

24. Berger, *Extremism*, 121–122.

25. Berger, *Extremism*, 62.

26. Berger, *Extremism*, 63.

27. Bruce Hoffman, *Inside Terrorism*, 3rd ed. (New York: Columbia University Press, 2017), 307–308. See also Alex P. Schmid, "Radicalisation, De-Radicalisation, Counter-Radicalisation: A Conceptual Discussion and Literature Review," International Centre for Counter-Terrorism—The Hague, March 2013, http://icct.nl/app/uploads/2013/03/ICCT-Schmid-Radicalisation -De-Radicalisation-Counter-Radicalisation-March-2013_2.pdf, 22.

28. Jeff Victoroff, "The Mind of the Terrorist: A Review and Critique of Psychological Approaches," *Journal of Conflict Resolution* 49, no. 1 (2005): 3–42, http://www.jstor.org/stable/30045097.

29. David Webber and Arie W. Kruglanski, "The Social Psychological Makings of a Terrorist," *Current Opinion in Psychology* 19 (February 2018): 131–134. HTTPS://DOI.ORG/10.1016/J.COPSYC.2017.03.024; Schmid, "Radicalisation, De-Radicalisation, Counter-Radicalisation," 22.

30. Webber and Kruglanski, "The Social Psychological Makings of a Terrorist."

31. Orlandrew E. Danzell and Lisandra M. Maisonet Montañez, "Understanding the Lone Wolf Terror Phenomena: Assessing Current Profiles," *Behavioral*

Sciences of Terrorism and Political Aggression 8, no. 2 (2016): 135–159, https://doi.org/10.1080/19434472.2015.1070189.

32. Berger, *Extremism*, 124–125.

33. Fathali M. Moghaddam, "The Staircase to Terrorism: A Psychological Exploration." *American Psychologist* 60, no. 2 (2005): 161–169, https://doi.org/10.1037/0003-066X.60.2.161.

34. Caitlin Clemmow et al., "Vulnerability to Radicalisation in a General Population: A Psychometric Network Approach," *Psychology, Crime, and Law*, 29, no. 4 (2023): 408–436, DOI: 10.1080/1068316X.2022.2027944.

35. Clemmow et al., "Vulnerability to Radicalisation in a General Population."

36. Michael A. Hogg and Joseph A. Wagoner, "Uncertainty–Identity Theory," in *The International Encyclopedia of Intercultural Communication*, 1–9, 2017, https://doi.org/10.1002/9781118783665.ieicc0177. See also Michael A. Hogg, "From Uncertainty to Extremism: Social Categorization and Identity Processes," *Current Directions in Psychological Science* 23, no. 5 (2014): 338–342, https://doi.org/10.1177/0963721414540168.

37. Webber and Kruglanski, "The Social Psychological Makings of a Terrorist."

38. Webber and Kruglanski, "The Social Psychological Makings of a Terrorist."

39. Webber and Kruglanski, "The Social Psychological Makings of a Terrorist."

40. Jyette Klausen. "A Behavioral Study of the Radicalization Trajectories of American 'Homegrown' Al Qaeda-Inspired Terrorist Offenders," Office of Justice Programs, US Department of Justice, 2016, https://www.ojp.gov/pdffiles1/nij/grants/250417.pdf.

41. Christopher Wray, "Worldwide Threats to the Homeland," Federal Bureau of Investigation, September 17, 2020, https://www.fbi.gov/news/testimony/worldwide-threats-to-the-homeland-091720. See also Brandi Buchman, "Greatest Threat to US: Radicals Moving Quickly 'From Flash to Bang,'" FBI Chief Tells Congress," Courthouse News Service, September 17, 2020, https://www.courthousenews.com/fbi-head-tells-house-of-daunting-window-from-flash-to-bang.

42. A University of California Davis mega survey of nearly nine thousand people conducted in May 2022 found that 56 percent of Republicans agreed with the statement: "The traditional American way of life is disappearing so fast that we may have to use force to save it." In a 2019 Pew Research Center study, 81 percent of white Republicans identify as Christians. Thus 56 percent of those 81 percent self-identifying Christian Republicans equates to 45 percent of Christian Republicans asserting a justification for violence. See Garen J. Wintemute et al., "Views of American Democracy and Society and Support for Political Violence: First Report from a Nationwide Population-Representative Survey" (preprint), July 2022, https://doi.org/10.1101/2022.07.15.2227769 3; "In U.S., Decline of Christianity Continues at Rapid Pace," Pew Research Center, October 17, 2019, https://www.pewresearch.org/religion/2019/10/17/in-u-s-decline-of-christianity-continues-at-rapid-pace.

CHAPTER THREE: TOO CLOSE TO HOME

1. For the Biden administration, see FBI director Christopher Wray's September
    2021 testimony, asserting that domestic violent extremists and homegrown
    violent extremists (HVE) "together form the most significant terrorism danger
    to our country." (See note 8 in this chapter for more about HVEs.) Christopher
    Wray, "Threats to the Homeland: Evaluating the Landscape 20 Years after
    9/11," statement before the Senate Homeland Security and Governmental
    Affairs Committee, Washington, DC, September 21, 2021, https://www.fbi
    .gov/news/testimony/threats-to-the-homeland-evaluating-the-landscape-20
    -years-after-911-wray-092121. For the Trump administration, in addition to
    my congressional testimony and other civil servant counterterrorism officials,
    see DHS acting secretary Chad Wolf's foreword in the 2020 Annual DHS
    Homeland Threat Assessment. Wolf noted his particular concern about "white
    supremacist violent extremists who have been exceptionally lethal in their
    abhorrent, targeted attacks in recent years." https://www.dhs.gov/sites/default
    /files/publications/2020_10_06_homeland-threat-assessment.pdf.

2. Terrorism is just one of form of hostile action that extremist groups may
    undertake. While there is a danger in an overly narrow focus on one tactic,
    the bulk of government resources focus on preventing, protecting against, and
    responding to acts of terrorism. It is also where the preponderance of research
    and data collection have historically focused. Consequently, when trying to
    provide a comparison of extremist groups and movements, the data tend to
    be centered around acts, or attempted acts, of terrorism. Not all violence is
    terrorism or violent extremism. Self-defense is not terrorism. Militaries that
    abide by the Geneva Convention do not use terrorism in warfare. And though
    many illegitimate states practice terroristic tactics against their own people,
    often in a systematic way, the better word for that is *oppression*. Berger also
    considers oppression a form of extremist hostile action.

3. Bruce Hoffman, *Inside Terrorism*, 3rd ed. (New York: Columbia University
    Press, 2017), 43.

4. J.M. Berger, *Extremism* (Boston: MIT Press, 2018), 103.

5. Ironically, the concept of terroristic acts were originated by state or religious powers
    to "consolidate power" and "establish order." Hoffman, *Inside Terrorism*, 3.

6. The FBI defines *international terrorism* as "violent, criminal acts committed by
    individuals and/or groups who are inspired by, or associated with, designated
    foreign terrorist organizations or nations (state-sponsored)." "Terrorism," FBI,
    https://www.fbi.gov/investigate/terrorism.

7. "Timeline: The Rise, Spread, and Fall of the Islamic State," *Wilson Center*,
    October 2019, https://www.wilsoncenter.org/article/timeline-the-rise-spread
    -and-fall-the-islamic-state.

8. The San Bernardino and Orlando attackers are examples of what the
    government calls a Homegrown Violent Extremist or HVE. An HVE is
    a person of any citizenship who lives or operates primarily in the United

States or its territories, and who advocates, engages in, or is preparing to engage in or support terrorist activities in furtherance of a foreign terrorist organization's objectives, but who is acting independently of foreign terrorist direction. In short, an HVE is inspired by but not directed by a foreign terrorist organization. Because HVEs are acting to further the goals of a foreign terrorist organization, they are considered foreign intelligence threats under the authorities of the intelligence community and domestic public safety entities. But because they are located within the territories of the United States—certain counterterrorism tools (e.g., the military) cannot be used, and other tools have more stringent legal requirements. For more, see "Homegrown Violent Extremism Mobilization Indicators." NCTC, FBI, and DHS, January 2019, https://www.dni.gov/files/NCTC/documents/news_documents/NCTC-FBI -DHS-HVE-Mobilization-Indicators-Booklet-2019.pdf.

9. Hoffman, *Inside Terrorism*, 43.

10. The white power movement adopted leaderless resistance at the 1983 Aryan Nations World Congress gathering in Hayden Lake, Idaho. Kathleen Belew, *Bring the War Home: The White Power Movement and Paramilitary America* (Cambridge, MA: Harvard University Press, 2018), 105.

11. Bennett Clifford, "Racially/Ethnically Motivated Violent Extremist (RMVE) Attack Planning and United States Federal Response, 2014–2019," George Washington University Program on Extremism, May 2021, https://extremism .gwu.edu/sites/g/files/zaxdzs2191/f/RMVE%20Attack%20Planning%20and %20United%20States%20Federal%20Response.pdf.

12. "Strategic Intelligence Assessment and Data on Domestic Terrorism," Federal Bureau of Investigation and Department of Homeland Security, October 2022, https://www.dni.gov/files/NCTC/documents/news_documents/2022_10_FBI -DHS_Strategic_Intelligence_Assessment_and_Data_on_Domestic_Terrorism .pdf; "Domestic Violent Extremism Poses Heightened Threat in 2021," Office of the Director of National Intelligence, March 2021, https://www.dni.gov /files/ODNI/documents/assessments/UnclassSummaryofDVEAssessment -17MAR21.pdf.

13. "Strategic Intelligence Assessment and Data on Domestic Terrorism."

14. See Miller-Idriss's commentary on contested labels. Cynthia Miller-Idriss, *Hate in the Homeland: The New Global Far Right* (Princeton, NJ: Princeton University Press, 2020), 15–16.

15. Mark Juergensmeyer, *Terror in the Mind of God: The Global Rise of Religious Violence*, 4th ed. (Berkeley: University of California Press, 2017), 13.

16. Berger, *Extremism*, 33.

17. Hoffman, *Inside Terrorism*, 90.

18. Hoffman, *Inside Terrorism*, 91.

19. Hoffman, *Inside Terrorism*, 86.

20. Juergensmeyer, *Terror in the Mind of God*, 5.

21. Hoffman, *Inside Terrorism*, 88.

22. Samuel P. Huffington, *Who Are We? The Challenges to America's National Identity* (New York: Simon & Schuster, 2004), 62.

23. Monica Duffy Toft, Daniel Philpott, and Timothy Samuel Shah, *God's Century: Resurgent Religion and Global Politics* (New York: W. W. Norton, 2011), 13.

24. Paul David Miller, *The Religion of American Greatness: What's Wrong with Christian Nationalism* (Downers Grove, IL: InterVarsity Press, 2022), 30–31.

25. Miller, *The Religion of American Greatness*, 36.

26. "How France's 'Great Replacement' Theory Conquered the Global Far Right," France 24, November 8, 2021, https://www.france24.com/en/europe/20211108 -how-the-french-great-replacement-theory-conquered-the-far-right.

27. Adolf Hitler, *Mein Kampf,* annotated translation (Boston: Reynal & Hitchcock, by arrangement with Houghton Mifflin Company, 1939), vol. 1, chap. 11, "Nation and Race."

28. "Hate beyond Borders: The Internationalization of White Supremacy," Anti-Defamation League, September 17, 2019, https://www.adl.org/resources/report /hate-beyond-borders-internationalization-white-supremacy.

29. The concept of white genocide has a much longer history; and the phrase was popularized in the 1970s–1990s by *The Turner Diaries* novel and white supremacist, David Lane. For more, see: Bridge Initiative. "Factsheet: Great Replacement/White Genocide Conspiracy Theory." https://bridge.georgetown .edu/research/factsheet-great-replacement-white-genocide-conspiracy-theory/.

30. For example, Tal Axelrod and Kendall Ross, "Ramaswamy Defends Debunked Conspiracy Theories He Shared at Republican Debate," ABC News, December 7, 2023, https://abcnews.go.com/Politics/ramaswamy-defends-debunked -conspiracy-theories-shared-republican-debate/story?id=105464858; "Laura Ingraham: Vote Republican or You Will Be Replaced by Immigrants," Media Matters for America, October 16, 2018, https://www.mediamatters.org /laura-ingraham/laura-ingraham-vote-republican-or-you-will-be-replaced -immigrants; "Fox Host Jeanine Pirro Pushes White Supremacist 'Great Replacement' Conspiracy Theory," Media Matters for America, August 29, 2019, https://www.mediamatters.org/jeanine-pirro/fox-host-jeanine-pirro -pushes-white-supremacist-great-replacement-conspiracy-theory.

31. Matt Gaetz (@RepMattGaetz), "There is an attempted cultural genocide going on in America right now. It calls for patriots to stand up and say that America is a great country worthy of our pride and our defense," X (formerly Twitter), July 12, 2020, https://twitter.com/RepMattGaetz/status/1282320656500174848, showing a clip of the Matt Gaetz interview on *Justice with Judge Jeanine*, July 11, 2020.

32. Trip Gabriel, "Trump Escalates Anti-Immigrant Rhetoric with 'Poisoning the Blood' Comment," *New York Times*, October 6, 2023, https://www.nytimes .com/2023/10/05/us/politics/trump-immigration-rhetoric.html.

33. Hitler, *Mein Kampf*, 396.

34. (1) October 27, 2018: Tree of Life Synagogue shooting in Pittsburgh, Pennsylvania, killed eleven and injured six; (2) April 27, 2019: Chabad of Poway Synagogue, Poway, California, killed one and injured three; (3) August 3, 2019: Walmart, El Paso, Texas, killed twenty-three and injured twenty-two; (4) Tops Friendly Market, Buffalo, New York, killed ten and injured three.

35. Catrina Doxsee et al., "Pushed to Extremes: Domestic Terrorism amid Polarization and Protest," Center for Strategic and International Studies, May 17, 2022, https://www.csis.org/analysis/pushed-extremes-domestic-terrorism -amid-polarization-and-protest.

36. The federal government does use this category, and criminal acts associated with these movements would likely not be considered domestic violent extremism. Thus we have no data associated with arrests, deaths, attacks, or plots. Researchers such as CSIS and J.M. Berger track it and classify it generally as far-left extremism. Class-based ideologies, such as communism, can "take on an extremist dimension, as in the case of Marxist or Maoist terrorism, which (in principle, at least) seek to eliminate the existence of an upper class" (Berger). Within the US this type of extremism may be affiliated with anarchist or antifa activists. Activities tend to be less extremist hostile action and more civil disobedience, such as disrupting access to infrastructure or offices, which may cause economic loss but not necessarily property destruction—as we saw in the Occupy Wall Street movement. The 1999 "Battle for Seattle" during the World Trade Organization Conference is another example that did lead to vandalism and property destruction. See Berger, Extremism, 38.

37. Catrina Doxsee et al., "Methodology and Codebook for Pushed to Extremes: Domestic Terrorism amid Polarization and Protest," Center for Strategic and International Studies, May 17, 2022, https://www.csis.org/analysis/pushed -extremes-domestic-terrorism-amid-polarization-and-protest.

38. There were forty-three attacks categorized as perpetrators by the violent far right in 1995. Seth G. Jones, Catrina Doxsee, and Nicholas Harrington, "The Escalating Terrorism Problem in the United States," Center for Strategic and International Studies, June 17, 2020, https://www.csis.org/analysis/escalating -terrorism-problem-united-states.

39. Brian A. Jackson et al., "Practical Terrorism Prevention: Reexamnining U.S. National Approaches to Addressing the Threat of Ideologically Motivated Violence," Homeland Security Operational Analysis Center operated by the RAND Corporation, 2019, https://www.rand.org/pubs/research_reports / RR2647.html.

40. "Worldwide Threats to the Homeland," Federal Bureau of Investigation, September 17, 2020, https://www.fbi.gov/news/testimony/worldwide-threats-to -the-homeland-091720.

41. Michael D. Shear, Adam Goldman, and Emily Cochrane, "Congressman Steve Scalise Gravely Wounded in Alexandria Baseball Field Ambush," *New York*

Times, June 14, 2017, https://www.nytimes.com/2017/06/14/us/steve-scalise-congress-shot-alexandria-virginia.html.

42. Catrina Doxsee et al., "Pushed to Extremes: Domestic Terrorism amid Polarization and Protest," Center for Strategic and International Studies, May 17, 2022, https://www.csis.org/analysis/pushed-extremes-domestic-terrorism-amid-polarization-and-protest.

43. CSIS review of 219 attacks categorized as left wing, from 1994 to 2020. Seth G. Jones, Catrina Doxsee, and Nicholas Harrington, "The Tactics and Targets of Domestic Terrorists," Center for Strategic & International Studies, July 2020, https://www.csis.org/analysis/tactics-and-targets-domestic-terrorists.

44. For example, "Anarchist/Left-Wing Violent Extremism in America: Trends in Radicalization, Recruitment, and Mobilization," George Washington University Program on Extremism and National Counterterrorism, Innovation, Technology, and Education Center, November 2021, https://extremism.gwu.edu/sites/g/files/zaxdzs2191/f/Anarchist%20-%20Left-Wing%20Violent%20Extremism%20in%20America.pdf; Seth G. Jones, Catrina Doxsee, and Nicholas Harrington, "The Escalating Terrorism Problem in the United States," Center for Strategic and International Studies, June 2020, https://www.csis.org/analysis/escalating-terrorism-problem-united-states; Kataryzna Jasko et al., "A Comparison of Political Violence by Left-Wing, Right-Wing, and Islamist Extremists in the United States and the World," July 2022, https://doi.org/10.1073/pnas.2122593119.

45. Jones et al., "The Escalating Terrorism Problem in the United States."

46. Doxsee et al., "Pushed to Extremes: Domestic Terrorism amid Polarization and Protest."

CHAPTER FOUR: EXPLOITING THE CROSS

1. John Dickson, *Bullies and Saints: An Honest Look at the Good and Evil of Christian History* (Grand Rapids, MI: Zondervan Reflective, 2021), 6.

2. Dickson, *Bullies and Saints*, 6.

3. Dickson, *Bullies and Saints*, 6.

4. Dickson, *Bullies and Saints*, 6.

5. Dickson, *Bullies and Saints*, 91.

6. Dickson, *Bullies and Saints*, 3.

7. Jonathan D. Redding, *One Nation under Graham: Apocalyptic Rhetoric and American Exceptionalism* (Waco, TX: Baylor University Press, 2021), 13.

8. Redding, *One Nation under Graham*.

9. Gazi Islam, "Social Identity Theory," in *Encyclopedia of Critical Psychology*, edited by Thomas Teo (New York: Springer-Verlag, 2014), 1781–1783.

10. "White Supremacy," Glossary of Extremism and Hate, Anti-Defamation League, https://www.adl.org/resources/glossary-terms/white-supremacy.

11. Juan F. Perea, "Policing the Boundaries of the White Republic: From Slave Codes to Mass Deportations," in *A Field Guide to White Supremacy*, edited by Kathleen Belew, and Ramón A. Gutiérrez (Berkeley: University of California Press, 2021).

12. Perea, "Policing the Boundaries of the White Republic," 68.

13. Andrew Gyory, *Closing the Gate: Race, Politics, and the Chinese Exclusion Act* (Chapel Hill: University of North Carolina Press, 1998).

14. Zach Levitt et al., "'War against the Children,'" *New York Times*, August 30, 2023, https://www.nytimes.com/interactive/2023/08/30/us/native-american -boarding-schools.html.

15. Levitt et al., "'War against the Children.'"

16. Levitt et al., "'War against the Children.'"

17. Kathleen Belew and Ramón A. Gutiérrez, eds., *A Field Guide to White Supremacy* (Berkeley: University of California Press, 2021), xiii.

18. Benjamin Wormald, "Chapter 1: The Changing Religious Composition of the U.S.," in *America's Changing Religious Landscape* (report), Pew Research Center, May 12, 2015. https://www.pewresearch.org/religion/2015/05/12/chapter-1-the -changing-religious-composition-of-the-u-s.

19. "Report on Slavery and Racism in the History of the Southern Baptist Theological Seminary," Southern Baptist Theological Seminary, December 2018, https://sbts-wordpress-uploads.s3.amazonaws.com/sbts/uploads /2018/12/Racism-and-the-Legacy-of-Slavery-Report-v3.pdf. For a deeper explanation of why the so-called curse of Ham is not biblically correct, see Garrett Kell, "Damn the Curse of Ham: How Genesis 9 Got Twisted into Racist Propaganda," Gospel Coalition, January 9, 2021, https://www .thegospelcoalition.org/article/damn-curse-ham.

20. "Report on Slavery and Racism in the History of the Southern Baptist Theological Seminary," 41–42.

21. Arie Perliger, *American Zealots: Inside Right-Wing Domestic Terrorism*, Columbia Studies in Terrorism and Irregular Warfare (New York: Columbia University Press, 2020), 35–36.

22. Perliger, *American Zealots*, 37.

23. *The Birth of a Nation* framed the post–Civil War KKK as heroes protecting white people, particularly white women, from Black aggression. The movie broke ground for its cinematic techniques and was the first movie screened in the White House by President Woodrow Wilson. It was the most profitable movie in the US for twenty-two years. See Perliger, *American Zealots*, 37.

24. Perliger, *American Zealots*, 37.

25. Becky Little, "How Prohibition Fueled the Rise of the Ku Klux Klan," March 27, 2023. https://www.history.com/news/kkk-terror-during-prohibition.

26. David Chalmers, "The Ku Klux Klan in Politics in the 1920's," *Mississippi Quarterly* 18, no. 4 (1965): 234–247, http://www.jstor.org/stable/26473702.

27. Chalmers, "The Ku Klux Klan in Politics in the 1920's."

28. Chalmers, "The Ku Klux Klan in Politics in the 1920's."

29. Chalmers, "The Ku Klux Klan in Politics in the 1920's."

30. Chalmers, "The Ku Klux Klan in Politics in the 1920's."

31. Perliger, *American Zealots*, 39.

32. Perliger, *American Zealots*, 44.

33. Perliger, *American Zealots*, 44.

34. Perliger, *American Zealots*, 40.

35. "Fascism, n.," Oxford English Dictionary, July 2023, https://doi.org/10.1093/OED/5460363500.

36. For more on this explanation, see Ronald J. Granieri, "The Right Needs to Stop Falsely Claiming That the Nazis Were Socialists," *Washington Post*, February 5, 2020, https://www.washingtonpost.com/outlook/2020/02/05/right-needs-stop-falsely-claiming-that-nazis-were-socialists.

37. Perliger, *American Zealots*, 42.

38. Perliger, *American Zealots*, 42.

39. Perliger, *American Zealots*, 43.

40. Jessica Stern, *Terror in the Name of God: Why Religious Militants Kill* (New York: Ecco, 2004), 18.

41. It's understandable that the public is concerned with violent extremism within the ranks of the military and law enforcement. Current and retired military and law enforcement possess knowledge and skills that can be leveraged to cause more death or lead to the likelihood of a more successful attack than an unskilled extremist. If they are currently serving, they have access to weapons and information that civilians do not and can exercise power over others given their position. Such things in the hands of an extremist can lead to catastrophic consequences. That said, we should be cautious in how we characterize this challenge. None of the data suggests the problem is "widespread" or that law enforcement and the military are "hotbeds of extremism."

42. Perliger, *American Zealots*, 43.

43. Kathleen Belew, *Bring the War Home: The White Power Movement and Paramilitary America* (Cambridge, MA: Harvard University Press, 2018), 105, 136–137.

44. Belew, *Bring the War Home*, 105.

45. Belew, *Bring the War Home*, 104–105.

46. Belew, *Bring the War Home*, 105.

47. Belew, *Bring the War Home*, 105.

48. Belew, *Bring the War Home*, 104.

49. Kathleen Belew and Ramón A. Gutiérrez, eds., *A Field Guide to White Supremacy* (Berkeley: University of California Press, 2021), 314. Leaderless

resistance was a tactic used prior to this moment. But was formally adopted at the Aryan World Congress and became the dominant strategy after the 1988 Fort Smith sedition trial.

50. Belew and Gutiérrez, *A Field Guide to White Supremacy*, 297, 301.

51. Pepe the Frog, the Kekistan flag, and Day of the Rope are all associated with the white power and Neo-Nazi movements. "Identifying Far-Right Symbols That Appeared at the U.S. Capitol Riot." *Washington Post*, January 15, 2021, https://www.washingtonpost.com/nation/interactive/2021/far-right-symbols -capitol-riot; Ryan J. Reilly, "Feds Say Jan. 6 Rioter Seen Giving Nazi Salute Praised Hitler, Sent Racist Messages," NBC News, March 1, 2022, https://www .nbcnews.com/politics/justice-department/feds-say-jan-6-rioter-seen-giving-nazi -salute-praised-hitler-sent-raci-rcna17645; Meryl Kornfield, "Alleged Capitol Rioter That Grew 'Hitler' Mustache Still Active in Army," *Washington Post*, March 15, 2021, https://www.washingtonpost.com/nation/2021/03/14/army -nazi-sympathizer-capitol-riot.

52. "Patriot Front," Anti-Defamation League, June 6, 2022, https://www.adl.org /resources/backgrounder/patriot-front.

53. The names of the more violent groups often change frequently based on law enforcement pressure. For example, after a series of arrests in 2020, leadership of the Atomwaffen Division (AWD) claimed it was disbanded. Later in the same year, those leaders formed the National Socialist Order (NSO). In 2021, a separate group of former AWD members announced they were reorganizing AWD, which angered the leaders of the NSO. ADL, "Atomwaffen Division (AWD)/ National Socialist Order (NSO)," https://www.adl.org/resources /backgrounder/atomwaffen-division-awd-national-socialist-order-nso; Counter Extremism Project, "Atomwaffen Division / National Socialist Order / National Socialist Resistance Front," https://www.counterextremism.com/supremacy /atomwaffen-division-national-socialist-order.

54. "Leader of Neo-Nazi Group Sentenced for Plot to Target Journalists and Advocates," US Department of Justice, January 11, 2022, https://www.justice .gov/opa/pr/leader-neo-nazi-group-sentenced-plot-target-journalists-and -advocates; Greg Cergol, "Long Island Ex-Marine Led Neo-Nazi Group, Plotted Rape-Involved Synagogue Attack: Feds," NBC New York, July 28, 2022, https://www.nbcnewyork.com/news/local/crime-and-courts/long-island -ex-marine-led-neo-nazi-group-plotted-rape-involved-synagogue-attack-feds /3800158.

55. "Christian Identity's New Role on the Extreme Right," Middlebury Institute of International Studies at Monterey, August 6, 2021, https://www.middlebury .edu/institute/academics/centers-initiatives/ctec/ctec-publications/christian -identitys-new-role-extreme-right.

56. "Christian Identity's New Role on the Extreme Right."

57. "Anti-Semitism," Merriam-Webster, https://www.merriam-webster.com /dictionary/anti-Semitism.

58. Esther 3:6.

59. Sergio DellaPergola, "World Jewish Population, 2020," In *American Jewish Year Book 2020*, edited by Arnold Dashefsky and Ira M. Sheskin (Cham, Switzerland: Springer, 2022), 120:273–370.

60. There are different definitions for how to count whether someone is Jewish. See Emily Guskin, "How Many Jews Live in the U.S.? That Depends on How You Define 'Jewish,'" *Washington Post*, February 23, 2018, https://www .washingtonpost.com/news/post-nation/wp/2018/02/23/measuring-the-size-of -the-u-s-jewish-population-comes-down-to-identity; "US Jewish Population Estimates 2020," American Jewish Population Project, Brandeis University, https://ajpp.brandeis.edu/us_jewish_population_2020.

61. Bennett Clifford, "Racially/Ethnically Motivated Violent Extremist (RMVE) Attack Planning and United States Federal Response, 2014–2019," Program on Extremism, George Washington University, May 2021, https://extremism .gwu.edu/sites/g/files/zaxdzs5746/files/RMVE%20Attack%20Planning%20and %20United%20States%20Federal%20Response.pdf.

62. Lindsay Whitehurst, "The FBI Director Warns about Threats to Americans from Those Inspired by the Hamas Attack on Israel," AP News, October 31, 2023, https://apnews.com/article/fbi-hamas-attack- isis-bb1ceb7ce51cfc05ed751d2ce7983fcd; "Six Facts about Threats to the Jewish Community," Anti-Defamation League, January 17, 2022, https:// www.adl.org/blog/six-facts-about-threats-to-the-jewish-community.

63. "Audit of Antisemitic Incidents 2022," Anti-Defamation League, March 23, 2023, https://www.adl.org/resources/report/audit-antisemitic-incidents-2022.

64. For a deeper understanding of these myths, see "Antisemitism Uncovered: A Guide to Old Myths in a New Era," Anti-Defamation League, n.d., https:// antisemitism.adl.org.

65. "Myth: Jews Have Too Much Power," Anti-Defamation League, n.d.https:// antisemitism.adl.org/power.

66. Becky Little, "How American Icon Henry Ford Fostered Anti-Semitism," History, June 4, 2021, https://www.history.com/news/henry-ford-antisemitism -worker-treatment.

67. Little, "How American Icon Henry Ford Fostered Anti-Semitism."

68. Little, "How American Icon Henry Ford Fostered Anti-Semitism."

69. Belew, *Bring the War Home*, 7.

70. Belew, *Bring the War Home*, 193.

71. Belew, *Bring the War Home*, 193.

72. "Confidence in Institutions," Gallup, June 22, 2007. https://news.gallup.com /poll/1597/Confidence-Institutions.aspx.

73. Mark Pitcavage, "Tax Protest Movement," Anti-Defamation League, originally published 2001, https://www.adl.org/resources/backgrounders/tax-protest -movement.

74. "Hate Group Expert Daniel Levitas Discusses Posse Comitatus, Christian Identity Movement, and More," *Intelligence Report*, June 15, 1998. https://www .splcenter.org/fighting-hate/intelligence-report/1998/hate-group-expert-daniel -levitas-discusses-posse-comitatus-christian-identity-movement-and.

75. Mark Pitcavage, "Camouflage and Conspiracy: The Militia Movement From Ruby Ridge to Y2K," *American Behavioral Scientist* 44, no. 6 (2001): 957–981, https://doi.org/10.1177/00027640121956610.

76. Belew, *Bring the War Home*, 168.

77. Quote from a Michigan Militia member at their annual Field Day in 2008. Amy Cooter, "Citizen Militias in the U.S. Are Moving toward More Violent Extremism," *Scientific American*, January 1, 2022, https://www .scientificamerican.com/article/citizen-militias-in-the-u-s-are-moving-toward -more-violent-extremism.

78. Cooter, "Citizen Militias in the U.S. Are Moving toward More Violent Extremism."

79. "Fact Sheets on Unlawful Militias for All 50 States Now Available from Georgetown Law Institute for Constitutional Advocacy and Protection," Institute for Constitutional Advocacy and Protection, September 22, 2020, https://www.law.georgetown.edu/icap/our-press-releases/fact-sheets-on -unlawful-militias-for-all-50-states-now-available-from-georgetown-laws -institute-for-constitutional-advocacy-and-protection.

80. "Fact Sheets on Unlawful Militias for All 50 States."

81. "Fact Sheets on Unlawful Militias for All 50 States."

82. Belew, *Bring the War Home*, 193.

83. "NAFTA and 'One World,'" *Washington Post*, August 25, 1993, https://www .washingtonpost.com/archive/opinions/1993/08/25/nafta-and-one-world /96a7b95b-b686-420a-b258-aa634f797687.

84. "Senate: U.S. Made Errors at Ruby Ridge." *Chicago Tribune*, December 21, 1995, https://www.chicagotribune.com/news/ct-xpm-1995-12-22-9512220286 -story.html.

85. Mark Potok, "The Waco Raid at 25: Enough with the Fairy Tale Lies," *Daily Beast*, April 19, 2018, https://www.thedailybeast.com/the-waco-raid-at-25 -enough-with-the-fabulist-lies.

86. Mark Pitcavage, "Surveying the Landscape of the American Far Right," George Washington University's Program on Extremism, August 2019, https:// extremism.gwu.edu/sites/g/files/zaxdzs2191/f/Surveying%20The%20Landscape %20of%20the%20American%20Far%20Right_0.pdf.

87. Jessica Watkins considered herself the commanding officer of the Ohio State Regular Militia, which is a "dues-paying subset" of the Oath Keepers. Hannah K. Sparling and Kevin Grasha, "Ohio Militias: Who Are the Oath Keepers, Ohio State Regular Militia?" *Cincinnati Enquirer*, January 21, 2021, https:// www.cincinnati.com/story/news/2021/01/21/ohio-militias-who-oath-keepers

-ohio-state-regular-militia/4231869001; Cooter, "Citizen Militias in the U.S. Are Moving toward More Violent Extremism"; "Leader of Oath Keepers and 10 Other Individuals Indicted in Federal Court for Seditious Conspiracy and Other Offenses Related to U.S. Capitol Breach," US Department of Justice, January 13, 2022, https://www.justice.gov/opa/pr/leader-oath-keepers-and-10 -other-individuals-indicted-federal-court-seditious-conspiracy-and.

88. Cooter, "Citizen Militias in the U.S. Are Moving toward More Violent Extremism."

89. Nicole Sganga, "Anti-LGBTQ+ Hate Is Driven by Extremist Groups and Targets Drag Shows, Study Finds," CBS News, June 22, 2023, https://www .cbsnews.com/news/anti-lgbtq-hate-extremist-groups-targets-drag-shows-study; Doug Livingston and Will Carless, "Nazi Salutes, Pepper Spray and Pistols: Ohio Drag Event Devolves into an Extremist Melee," *USA Today*, March 14, 2023, https://www.usatoday.com/story/news/nation/2023/03/14/drag -storyelling-in-wadsworth-ohio-devolves-into-extremist-fight/11465959002.

90. For example, see these statements by a US senator, a US congressman, a GOP presidential candidate, and the son of a former president: Marco Rubio, "After todays [*sic*] raid on Mar A Lago what do you think the left plans to use those 87,000 new IRS agents for?" X (formerly Twitter), August 8, 2022, https:// twitter.com/marcorubio/status/1556795448614060035; Nick Koutsobinas, "Rep. Biggs to Newsmax: 'It Can Happen to Anyone,'" Newsmax, March 25, 2023, https://www.newsmax.com/newsmax-tv/andy-biggs-donald-trump -alvin-bragg/2023/03/25/id/1113797; Vivek Ramaswamy, "If They Can Do It to Trump, They Can Do It to You," March 30, 2023, https://www.youtube .com/watch?v=nAFRP-mPj8U; Donald Trump Jr., "If they can do it to him they can do it to you . . . and that's clearly been their plan all along," X (formerly Twitter), April 7, 2023, https://twitter.com/DonaldJTrumpJr/status /1644324288919478273.

CHAPTER FIVE: TODAY'S CHRISTIAN EXTREMISM

1. Mason Youngblood, "Extremist Ideology as a Complex Contagion: The Spread of Far-Right Radicalization in the United States between 2005 and 2017," *Humanities and Social Sciences Communications* 7, no. 49 (2020), https://doi.org /10.1057/s41599-020-00546-3.

2. A. Cherney et al., "The Push and Pull of Radicalization and Extremist Disengagement: The Application of Criminological Theory to Indonesian and Australian Cases of Radicalization," *Journal of Criminology* 54, no. 4 (2021): 407–424, https://doi.org/10.1177/26338076211034893.

3. Youngblood, "Extremist Ideology as a Complex Contagion."

4. Alexis de Tocqueville, *Democracy in America and Two Essays on America* (London: Penguin Books, 2003), 598.

5. R. D. Goodwin et al., "Trends in Anxiety among Adults in the United States, 2008–2018: Rapid Increases among Young Adults," *Journal of Psychiatric*

Research 130 (2020): 441–446. https://doi.org/10.1016/j.jpsychires.2020.08 .014.

6. Dan Witters, "U.S. Depression Rates Reach New Highs," Gallup, May 17, 2023, https://news.gallup.com/poll/505745/depression-rates-reach-new-highs .aspx.

7. "Our Epidemic of Loneliness and Isolation," Surgeon General Advisory, Office of the Surgeon General, May 2023, https://www.hhs.gov/sites/default/files /surgeon-general-social-connection-advisory.pdf.

8. Vivek Murthy, "Letter from the Surgeon General," in "Our Epidemic of Loneliness and Isolation."

9. Stats summarized from "Our Epidemic of Loneliness and Isolation," 12–16.

10. "Our Epidemic of Loneliness and Isolation," 13.

11. Data from the General Social Survey, a project of the independent research organization NORC, University of Chicago, funded by the National Science Foundation, https://gss.norc.org/Get-The-Data, as analyzed in Ryan P. Burge, *The Nones: Where They Came from, Who They Are, and Where They Are Going* (Minneapolis: Fortress Press, 2021), 16.

12. Burge, *The Nones*, 32.

13. Jim Davis, Michael S. Graham, and Ryan P. Burge, *The Great Dechurching: Who's Leaving, Why Are They Going, and What Will It Take to Bring Them Back?* (Grand Rapids, MI: Zondervan, 2023), 3.

14. "Our Epidemic of Loneliness and Isolation,"16.

15. Mark Sayers, *A Non-Anxious Presence: How a Changing and Complex World Will Create a Remnant of Renewed Christian Leaders* (Chicago: Moody, 2022), 21–22.

16. Sayers, *A Non-Anxious Presence*, 23.

17. David Brooks, "America Is Having a Moral Convulsion," *Atlantic*, October 5, 2020, https://www.theatlantic.com/ideas/archive/2020/10/collapsing-levels -trust-are-devastating-america/616581.

18. Brooks, "America Is Having a Moral Convulsion."

19. Ben Sasse, *Them: Why We Hate Each Other and How We Can Heal* (New York: St. Martin's, 2018), 58.

20. Sasse, *Them*, 58.

21. Sasse, *Them*, 59.

22. Sasse, *Them*, 50.

23. Brooks, "America Is Having a Moral Convulsion."

24. Special Counsel Robert S. Mueller, III. "Report On The Investigation Into Russian Interference In The 2016 Presidential Election." U.S. Department of Justice, March 2019. Pg. 4. https://www.justice.gov/archives/sco/file/1373816/ download.

25. "Foreign Threats to the 2020 US Federal Elections," National Intelligence Council, March 10, 2021, https://www.dni.gov/files/ODNI/documents /assessments/ICA-declass-16MAR21.pdf.

26. Special Counsel Robert S. Mueller, III. "Report On The Investigation Into Russian Interference In The 2016 Presidential Election." U.S. Department of Justice, March 2019. Pg. 4. https://www.justice.gov/archives/sco/file/1373816/ download.

27. "We assess that Russian President Putin authorized, and a range of Russian government organizations conducted, influence operations aimed at denigrating President Biden's candidacy and the Democratic Party, supporting former President Trump, undermining public confidence in the electoral process, and exacerbating sociopolitical divisions in the US. . . . Moscow's strategy . . . was its use of proxies linked to Russian intelligence to push influence narratives— including misleading or unsubstantiated allegations against President Biden— to US media organizations, US officials, and prominent US individuals, including some close to former President Trump and his administration." "Foreign Threats to the 2020 US Federal Elections."

28. "Executive Summary," in "Soviet Active Measures in the 'Post–Cold War' Era 1988–1991," Active Measures Working Group, United States Information Agency, June 1992, http://intellit.muskingum.edu/russia_folder/pcw_era/exec _sum.htm.

29. Karen Hao, "Troll Farms Reached 140 Million Americans a Month on Facebook before 2020 Election, Internal Report Shows," *MIT Technology Review*, September 16, 2021, https://www.technologyreview.com/2021/09/16 /1035851/facebook-troll-farms-report-us-2020-election.

30. "Treasury Sanctions Russian Proxy Wagner Group as a Transnational Criminal Organization," US Department of the Treasury, January 26, 2023, https:// home.treasury.gov/news/press-releases/jy1220.

31. Mick Krever and Anna Chernova, "Wagner Chief Admits to Founding Russian Troll Farm Sanctioned for Meddling in US Elections," CNN, February 14, 2023, https://www.cnn.com/2023/02/14/europe/russia-yevgeny-prigozhin -internet-research-agency-intl/index.html.

32. Hao, "Troll Farms Reached 140 Million Americans a Month on Facebook."

33. Hao, "Troll Farms Reached 140 Million Americans a Month on Facebook."

34. Isobel Koshiw, "Putin's Alleged War Crimes: Who Are the Ukrainian Children Being Taken by Russia?" *Guardian*, March 17, 2023, https://www.theguardian .com/world/2023/mar/17/vladimir-putin-war-crimes-icc-arrest-warrant-ukraine -children.

35. Alexandra Sharp, "Gruesome Videos Put Russia's Brutality Back in the Spotlight," *Foreign Policy*, April 12, 2023, https://foreignpolicy.com/2023/04 /12/russia-ukraine-beheading-videos-wagner-group-conscription-war-crimes -putin.

36. "Ukraine: Apparent War Crimes in Russia-Controlled Areas," Human Rights Watch, April 3, 2022, https://www.hrw.org/news/2022/04/03/ukraine-apparent -war-crimes-russia-controlled-areas.

37. Bill Bishop and Robert G. Cushing, *The Big Sort: Why the Clustering of Like-Minded America Is Tearing Us Apart* (Boston: Houghton Mifflin, 2008).

38. Gregor Aisch, Adam Pearce, and Karen Yourish, "The Divide between Red and Blue America Grew Even Deeper in 2016," *New York Times*, November 10, 2016, https://www.nytimes.com/interactive/2016/11/10/us/politics/red-blue -divide-grew-stronger-in-2016.html.

39. Aisch, Pearce, and Yourish, "The Divide between Red and Blue America."

40. Cass R. Sunstein, "The Law of Group Polarization," John M. Olin Program in Law and Economics Working Paper 91, 1999.

41. Sunstein, "The Law of Group Polarization," 3.

42. David French, *Divided We Fall: America's Secession Threat and How to Restore Our Nation* (New York: St. Martin's, 2020), 63.

43. "Our DNA," More in Common, November 18, 2023, https://www .moreincommon.com/about-us/our-dna.

44. Daniel Yudkin, Stephen Hawkins, and Tim Dixon, "The Perception Gap: How False Impressions Are Pulling Americans Apart," Hidden Tribes Project, More in Common, June 2019, https://perceptiongap.us/media/zaslaroc/perception -gap-report-1-0-3.pdf, 17.

45. Yudkin, Hawkins, and Dixon, "The Perception Gap."

46. Yudkin, Hawkins, and Dixon, "The Perception Gap," 28.

47. Yudkin, Hawkins, and Dixon, "The Perception Gap," 20.

48. Madison Park and Kyung Lah, "Berkeley Protests of Yiannopoulos Caused $100,000 in Damage," CNN, February 2, 2017, https://www.cnn.com/2017/02 /01/us/milo-yiannopoulos-berkeley/index.html.

49. Greg Lukianoff and Jonathan Haidt, *The Coddling of the American Mind: How Good Intentions and Bad Ideas Are Setting Up a Generation for Failure* (New York: Penguin, 2019), 81–84.

50. Lukianoff and Haidt, *The Coddling of the American Mind*, 83.

51. Peter Beinart, "A Violent Attack on Free Speech at Middlebury," *Atlantic*, March 6, 2017, https://www.theatlantic.com/politics/archive/2017/03 /middlebury-free-speech-violence/518667.

52. Lukianoff and Haidt, *The Coddling of the American Mind*, 88.

53. Lukianoff and Haidt, *The Coddling of the American Mind*, 97.

54. Lukianoff and Haidt, *The Coddling of the American Mind*, 31.

55. Lukianoff and Haidt, *The Coddling of the American Mind*, 31.

56. Greg Lukianoff and Rikki Schlott, *The Canceling of the American Mind: Cancel Culture Undermines Trust, Destroys Institutions, and Threatens Us All—but There Is a Solution* (New York: Simon & Schuster, 2023), 9.

57. Rod Dreher, *Live Not by Lies: A Manual for Christian Dissidents* (New York: Sentinel, 2020), 9.

58. Dreher, *Live Not by Lies*, 93.

59. Dreher, *Live Not by Lies*, 93.

60. Yascha Mounk, *The Identity Trap: A Story of Ideas and Power in Our Time* (London: Allen Lane, 2023), 9.

61. Mounk, *The Identity Trap*, 18.

62. Mounk, *The Identity Trap*, 29.

63. Mounk, *The Identity Trap*, 183.

64. Mounk, *The Identity Trap*, 16.

65. "84% Say Americans Being Afraid to Exercise Freedom of Speech Is a Serious Problem," Siena College Research Institute, March 21, 2022, https://scri.siena .edu/2022/03/21/84-say-americans-being-afraid-to-exercisefreedom-of-speech -is-a-serious-problem.

66. Emily Ekins, "Poll: 62% of Americans Say They Have Political Views They're Afraid to Share," Cato Institute, July 22, 2020, https://www.cato.org/survey -reports/poll-62-americans-say-they-have-political-views-theyre-afraid-share.

67. Ekins, "Poll: 62% of Americans Say They Have Political Views They're Afraid to Share."

68. Sam Allberry, "How Writing on Transgenderism Changed Me," Gospel Coalition, October 25, 2017, https://www.thegospelcoalition.org/article/how -writing-on-transgender-changed-me/.

69. Sam Levin, "More Than 50% of Trans and Non-Binary Youth in US Considered Suicide This Year, Survey Says," *Guardian*, December 17, 2022, https://www.theguardian.com/us-news/2022/dec/16/us-trans-non-binary-youth -suicide-mental-health.

70. Gabrielle Sorto, "A Teacher Says He Was Fired for Refusing to Use Male Pronouns for a Transgender Student," CNN, October 2, 2019, https://www .cnn.com/2019/10/02/us/virginia-teacher-says-wrongfully-fired-student-wrong -pronouns-trnd/index.html; Caleb Parke, "Christian Doctor of 30 Years Loses Job for Refusing to Use Transgender Patient's Preferred Pronoun," Fox News, October 3, 2019, https://www.foxnews.com/faith-values/christian-doctor -fired-gender-pronoun; Giulia Carbonaro, "Teacher Refusing to Use Student's Chosen Pronouns Jailed for Ignoring Order," *Newsweek*, September 6, 2022, https://www.newsweek.com/teacher-refusing-student-chosen-pronouns-jailed -ignoring-order-1740119; Natasha (no surname), "Three Recent Lawsuits Address Gender Pronouns at Work," *Law and Labor*, December 27, 2020, https://lawandlabor.com/law-news/3-recent-lawsuits-address-gender-pronouns -at-work.

71. "Catastrophizing," *Psychology Today*, n.d., https://www.psychologytoday.com /us/basics/catastrophizing.

72. Timothy Dalrymple, quoted in Michael Graham, "The Six Way Fracturing of Evangelicalism," Mere Orthodoxy, June 7, 2021, https://mereorthodoxy.com/six -way-fracturing-evangelicalism.

73. Graham, "The Six Way Fracturing of Evangelicalism"; Skyler Flowers and Michael Graham, "One Year Later: Reflecting on Evangelicalism's Six-Way Fracturing," Mere Orthodoxy, July 12, 2022, https://mereorthodoxy.com/one -year-later-reflecting-on-evangelicalisms-six-way-fracturing.

74. "New Days, Old Demons with Marc Driscoll," *The Charlie Kirk Show*, August 3, 2023, https://thecharliekirkshow.com/podcasts/the-charlie-kirk-show/new -days-old-demons-with-mark-driscoll.

75. Sarah Pulliam Bailey, "Seeking Power in Jesus' Name: Trump Sparks a Rise of Patriot Churches," *Washington Post*, October 27, 2020, https://www.washingtonpost .com/religion/2020/10/26/trump-christian-nationalism-patriot-church.

76. Marc Ambinder, "The Outrage Industrial Complex," *Atlantic*, February 20, 2009, https://www.theatlantic.com/politics/archive/2009/02/the-outrage -industrial-complex/845.

77. Most pinpoint 2009–2011 as the transition points from PC-based internet engagement to phone-based engagement and the adoption of social media. A 2018 study found that when 25 percent of people in a group adopt a new social norm, it creates a tipping point where the entire group follows suit. According to Pew Research—2008 was when 25 percent of Americans had at least one social media profile. It jumped to 50 percent by 2011. Pew did not begin asking about smartphone ownership until 2011, at which point 35 percent of Americans had a smartphone. The iPhone debuted in 2007. See "Tipping Point for Large-Scale Social Change," *Science Daily*, June 7, 2018, https:// www.sciencedaily.com/releases/2018/06/180607141009.htm; "Social Media Fact Sheet," Pew Research Center, April 7, 2021, https://www.pewresearch.org /internet/fact-sheet/social-media; "Mobile Fact Sheet," Pew Research Center, April 7, 2021, https://www.pewresearch.org/internet/fact-sheet/mobile.

78. Zach Schonfeld, "Republicans Erupt over FBI's Mar-a-Lago Raid," *The Hill*, August 8, 2022, https://thehill.com/policy/national-security/3593543 -republicans-erupt-over-fbis-mar-a-lago-raid.

79. Marco Rubio, "After todays [*sic*] raid on Mar A Lago what do you think the left plans to use those 87,000 new IRS agents for?" X (formerly Twitter), August 8, 2022, https://twitter.com/marcorubio/status/1556795448614060035; Daniel Estrin, Alejandra Marquez Janse, and Amy Isackson, "The IRS Misses Billions in Uncollected Tax Each Year. Here's Why," NPR, April 19, 2022, https://www .npr.org/2022/04/18/1093380881/on-tax-day-the-treasury-department-urges -for-more-funding-to-the-irs.

80. Tucker Carlson, "Tucker Carlson: All Governments Hate Religious People," Fox News, March 2, 2023, https://www.foxnews.com/opinion/tucker-carlson -all-governments-hate-religious-people.

81. This phenomenon occurs on the left as well. Those who consume left-wing infotainment with no alternative perspectives are subject to the same effects of group polarization and likely to embrace extremist framings. But as this book addresses Christian extremism, the focus here is on conservative infotainment.

82. For an example, see the January 10, 2021, sermon from Patriot Knoxville Church: https://www.facebook.com/patriotknoxville/videos/get-ready-for-sunday/381226576511092.

83. Alexandra Hutzler, "Biden Attacks Trump and MAGA Republicans as Threat to American Democracy," ABC News, September 1, 2022, https://abcnews.go.com/Politics/biden-attacks-trump-maga-republicans-threat-american-democracy/story?id=89121094.

84. "Franklin's MAGA Mayoral Candidate Gabrielle Hanson Poses with Self-Proclaimed Neo-Nazi in New Post," News Channel 5 Nashville (WTVF), October 18, 2023, https://www.newschannel5.com/news/newschannel-5-investigates/franklins-maga-mayoral-candidate-gabrielle-hanson-poses-with-self-proclaimed-neo-nazi-in-new-post.

85. Amy Cooter, "Citizen Militias in the U.S. Are Moving toward More Violent Extremism," *Scientific American*, January 1, 2022, https://www.scientificamerican.com/article/citizen-militias-in-the-u-s-are-moving-toward-more-violent-extremism.

86. Geraldine Fagan, "How the Russian Orthodox Church Is Helping Drive Putin's War in Ukraine," *Time*, April 15, 2022, https://time.com/6167332/putin-russian-orthodox-church-war-ukraine; Ben Ryan, "Putin and the Orthodox Church: How His Faith Shapes His Politics," Theos Think Tank, February 16, 2022, https://www.theosthinktank.co.uk/comment/2022/02/16/essay-on-vladimir-putin; Amanda Coakley, "Hungary's Orban Tries to Snatch Mantle of Christian Democracy," *Foreign Policy*, August 3, 2021, https://foreignpolicy.com/2021/08/03/hungary-orban-fidesz-christian-democracy-right; Jacob Todd, "The Two Faces of Orban's Hungary: Christian and Neo-Ottoman," Balkan Insight: Reporting Democracy Project, November 8, 2021, https://balkaninsight.com/2021/11/08/the-two-faces-of-orbans-hungary-christian-and-neo-ottoman.

87. The Conservative Political Action Committee, CPAC, held a conference in Hungary n May 2022, and they invited President Orban to speak at their August 2022 conference in Dallas. David Smith, "Orbán Urges Christian Nationalists in Europe and US to 'Unite Forces' at CPAC," *Guardian*, August 4, 2022, https://www.theguardian.com/world/2022/aug/04/viktor-orban-cpac-speech; "Why Republicans Like Putin," *Dallas News*, March 7, 2017, https://www.dallasnews.com/opinion/commentary/2017/03/07/why-republicans-like-putin; David Leonhardt, "The G.O.P.'s 'Putin Wing,'" *New York Times*, April 7, 2022, https://www.nytimes.com/2022/04/07/briefing/republican-party-putin-wing.html.

CHAPTER SIX: A CORRUPTED FAITH

1. Aleksandr Solzhenitsyn, *The Gulag Archipelago* (New York: Harper Perennial Modern Classics, 2007), part 4, chap. 1, "The Ascent."

2. Paul David Miller, *The Religion of American Greatness: What's Wrong with Christian Nationalism* (Downers Grove, IL: InterVarsity Press, 2022), 18.

3. See chapter 2 in Glen Scrivener, *The Air We Breathe: How We All Came to Believe in Freedom, Kindness, Progress, and Equality* (London: Good Book Company, 2022).

4. Gorski and Perry borrow the deep story concept from sociologist Arlie Russell Hochschild; they are "stories which have been told and retold so many times and across so many generations that they feel natural and true: even and perhaps especially when they are at odds with history." Philip S. Gorski and Samuel L. Perry, *The Flag and the Cross: White Christian Nationalism and the Threat to American Democracy* (New York: Oxford University Press, 2022), 6.

5. Tobin Grant, "Why 1940s America Wasn't as Religious as You Think—the Rise and Fall of American Religion," Religion News Service, December 11, 2014. https://religionnews.com/2014/12/11/1940s-america-wasnt-religious-think-rise-fall-american-religion.

6. Jonathan D. Redding, *One Nation under Graham: Apocalyptic Rhetoric and American Exceptionalism* (Waco, TX: Baylor University Press, 2021), 92.

7. Kristin Kobes Du Mez, *Jesus and John Wayne: How White Evangelicals Corrupted a Faith and Fractured a Nation* (New York: Liveright, 2020), 35.

8. Du Mez, *Jesus and John Wayne*, 35.

9. Redding, *One Nation under Graham*, 97.

10. Redding, *One Nation under Graham*, 36.

11. Redding, *One Nation under Graham*, 56.

12. Paul David Miller, *The Religion of American Greatness: What's Wrong with Christian Nationalism* (Downers Grove, IL: InterVarsity Press, 2022), 128.

13. Miller, *The Religion of American Greatness*, 42.

14. Miller, *The Religion of American Greatness*, 60.

15. Miller, *The Religion of American Greatness*, 60.

16. Miller, *The Religion of American Greatness*, 60.

17. Miller, *The Religion of American Greatness*, 128.

18. For more analysis on Christian Nationalism, see Gorski and Perry, *The Flag and the Cross*, 6; Tim Keller, "A Book Review on the Topic of Christian Nationalism," Life in the Gospel, March 8, 2021, https://quarterly.gospelinlife.com/book-review-on-the-topic-of-christian-nationalism; Miller, *The Religion of American Greatness*; Russell Moore, *Losing Our Religion: An Altar Call for Evangelical America* (New York: Sentinel, 2023); Redding, *One Nation under Graham*; Andrew L. Whitehead, *American Idolatry: How Christian Nationalism Betrays the Gospel and Threatens the Church* (Grand Rapids, MI: Brazos Press, 2023).

19. Russell Moore, *Losing Our Religion*, 117.

20. Miller, *The Religion of American Greatness*, 128.

21. Andrew Torba and Andrew Isker, *Christian Nationalism: A Biblical Guide for Taking Dominion and Discipling Nations* (N.p.: Gab AI, 2022), xxviii.

22. Torba and Isker, *Christian Nationalism*, 3.

23. For more on the Christian Reconstructionist movement, see Ligon Duncan, "A Presbyterian Perspective: The Intellectual and Sociological Origins of the Christian Reconstructionist Movement," 9Marks, April 28, 2023, https://www.9marks.org/article/a-presbyterian-perspective-the-intellectual-and-sociological-origins-of-the-christian-reconstructionist-movement.

24. Stephen Wolfe, *The Case for Christian Nationalism* (Moscow, ID: Canon Press, 2022), 279, 391.

25. For example, on white nationalism and racial overtones, see pages 138–141 and footnote 119. On misogyny, see Wolfe, *The Case for Christian Nationalism*, section starting at 448.

26. Torba and Isker, *Christian Nationalism*, 7.

27. Wolfe, *The Case for Christian Nationalism*, 351.

28. Wolfe, *The Case for Christian Nationalism*, 352.

29. Bonnie Kristian, "Left Behind at the Ballot Box," *Christianity Today*, June 12, 2023, https://christianitytoday.com/ct/2023/july-august/politics-eschatology-vote-second-coming-nationalism.html.

30. Du Mez, *Jesus and John Wayne*, 37–38.

31. Du Mez, *Jesus and John Wayne*, 38.

32. Gorski and Perry, *The Flag and the Cross*, 69.

33. Gorski and Perry, *The Flag and the Cross*, 69–70.

34. Du Mez, *Jesus and John Wayne*, 135.

35. Du Mez, *Jesus and John Wayne*.

36. A group of Bible translation organizations are partnering on the Every Tribe Every Nation project to make God's Word accessible to all people by 2033. See here for more: https://eten.bible/who-we-are/#defining-the-goal.

37. "How Many Languages Are in the World Today?" Ethnologue, n.d., https://www.ethnologue.com/guides/how-many-languages.

38. Russell Moore, "Have Bible Quoters Replaced Bible Readers?" RussellMoore.com, January 16, 2018, https://www.russellmoore.com/2018/01/16/bible-quoters-replaced-bible-readers.

39. Moore, "Have Bible Quoters Replaced Bible Readers?"

40. Mark Galli, "Am I Growing Yet?" *Christianity Today*, October 25, 2007, https://www.christianitytoday.com/ct/2007/octoberweb-only/143-43.0.html.

41. "What *Reveal* Reveals," Christianity Today, February 27, 2008, https://www.christianitytoday.com/ct/2008/march/11.27.html.

42. Galli, "Am I Growing Yet?"

43. Katelyn Beaty, *Celebrities for Jesus: How Personas, Platforms, and Profits Are Hurting the Church* (Grand Rapids, MI: Brazos Press, 2022).

44. Rachel Zimmerman, "How Does Trauma Spill from One Generation to the Next?" *Washington Post*, June 12, 2023, https://www.washingtonpost.com /wellness/2023/06/12/generational-trauma-passed-healing.

45. Anthea D. Butler, *White Evangelical Racism: The Politics of Morality in America* (Chapel Hill: University of North Carolina Press, 2021), 26–27.

46. Jemar Tisby, "Trayvon Martin's Murder and the Death of the Evangelical Racial Reconciliation Movement," Substack, February 26, 2022, https:// jemartisby.substack.com/p/trayvon-martins-murder-and-the-death.

47. Aaron Earls, "Pastors More Reluctant to Preach on Race," *Christianity Today*, January 12, 2021, https://www.christianitytoday.com/news/2021/january /pastors-reluctant-preach-racial-reconciliation-lifeway-surv.html.

48. Benjamin Wallace-Wells, "How a Conservative Activist Invented the Conflict over Critical Race Theory," *New Yorker*, June 18, 2021, https://www.newyorker .com/news/annals-of-inquiry/how-a-conservative-activist-invented-the-conflict -over-critical-race-theory.

49. Tisby, "Trayvon Martin's Murder and the Death of the Evangelical Racial Reconciliation Movement"; George Schroeder, "Seminary Presidents Reaffirm BFM, Declare CRT Incompatible," *Baptist Press*, November 30, 2020, https:// www.baptistpress.com/resource-library/news/seminary-presidents-reaffirm-bfm -declare-crt-incompatible.

50. Jared Stacy, " 'Was Jesus Nice?' Is the Wrong Question," JaredStacy.com, October 11, 2022, https://jaredstacy.com/2022/10/11/asking-was-jesus-nice-is -the-wrong-question.

51. Nijay K. Gupta, "Junia, the Female Apostle Imprisoned for the Gospel," *Christianity Today*, March 23, 2023, https://www.christianitytoday.com/ct /2023/march-web-only/junia-female-apostle-paul-fellow-prisoner-preaching -gospel.html.

52. Peter Smith and Holly Meyer, "#ChurchToo Revelations Growing, Years after Movement Began," AP News, June 12, 2022, https://apnews.com/article /entertainment-health-baptist-religion-c7c5f62a5737b3aee20ceaa3f99ab603.

53. Russell Moore, *Losing Our Religion*, 252–253.

CHAPTER SEVEN: UNTANGLING OUR HOPE AND IDENTITY

1. For the follower of Christ, the key for healthy self-examination is recognizing what we have already obtained. Jesus' righteousness has been gifted to us through faith. We do not deserve it and we did not earn it. This part of salvation is "justification"—God gave us Christ's righteousness, making us *positionally* holy (Rom 5:1; 2 Cor 5:21). So our self-examination is not done for the purpose of figuring how to become good enough to be saved. Self-examination helps us walk out our faith after justification. Once saved, Christians will still struggle with sin. The process of becoming more and more

like Christ—more holy—is lifelong. This part of our salvation process is called sanctification. Where justification is purely God's gift—we do nothing but receive the gift in faith—sanctification is the daily effort of living like Christ through the power of the Holy Spirit.

2. Caitlin Clemmow et al., "The Whole Is Greater Than the Sum of Its Parts: Risk and Protective Profiles for Vulnerability to Radicalization, *Justice Quarterly* (2023), https://doi.org/10.1080/07418825.2023.2171902.

3. Caitlin Clemmow et al., "Vulnerability to Radicalisation in a General Population: A Psychometric Network Approach," *Psychology, Crime, and Law* 29, no. 4 (2023): 408–436, https://www.tandfonline.com/doi/full/10.1080 /1068316X.2022.2027944.

4. Caitlin Clemmow et al., "Vulnerability to Radicalisation in a General Population." There were two additional factors in the top cluster: nonviolent offending and being a victim of violence as a child. As noted below, I believe such factors require the support of counseling and/or behavioral health management, and as such are not ideal for self-examination.

5. Arie W. Kruglanski, Jocelyn J. Bélanger, and Rohan Gunaratna, *The Three Pillars of Radicalization: Needs, Narratives, and Networks* (New York: Oxford University Press, 2019).

6. This new identity is bestowed upon us as a gift, not something we have to earn or even could earn if we tried, which also means we don't have to work to keep it. David Powlison says that we receive it because "Christ bears the curse [we] deserve [and] is fully pleasing to the Father and gives [us] His own perfect goodness." David Powlison, "Idols of the Heart and 'Vanity Fair,'" Christian Counseling and Education Foundation, April 14, 2016, https://www.ccef.org /idols-heart-and-vanity-fair.

7. Tim Keller, "How to Talk about Sin in a Postmodern Age," Gospel Coalition, June 15, 2017, https://www.thegospelcoalition.org/article/how-to-talk-sin-in -postmodern-age.

8. Timothy Keller, *Counterfeit Gods: The Empty Promises of Money, Sex, and Power, and the Only Hope that Matters* (New York: Viking, 2009), 64–65.

9. Kruglanski, Bélanger, and Gunaratna, *The Three Pillars of Radicalization: Needs, Narratives, and Networks.*

10. Michael A. Hogg and Joseph A. Wagoner. "Uncertainty–Identity Theory." In *The International Encyclopedia of Intercultural Communication*, 1–9, 2017. https://doi.org/10.1002/9781118783665.ieicc0177. See also Michael A. Hogg, "From Uncertainty to Extremism: Social Categorization and Identity Processes." *Current Directions in Psychological Science* 23, no. 5 (2014): 338–342, https://doi.org/10.1177/0963721414540168.

11. Timothy Keller, *Every Good Endeavor: Connecting Your Work to God's Work* (New York: Viking, 2012).

12. Alan Noble, *You Are Not Your Own: Belonging to God in an Inhuman World* (Downers Grove, IL: InterVarsity Press, 2021), 5.

13. Also known as our reference group. R. K. Merton and A. S. Kitt, "Contributions to the Theory of Reference Group Behavior," in *Continuities in Social Research*, edited by R. K. Merton and Paul S. Lazarsfeld (New York: Free Press, 1950): 40–105.

14. Kruglanski, Bélanger, and Gunaratna, *The Three Pillars of Radicalization*, 54.

15. Kruglanski, Bélanger, and Gunaratna, *The Three Pillars of Radicalization*, 54.

16. Yuval Levin, *A Time to Build: From Family and Community to Congress and the Campus, How Recommitting to Our Institutions Can Revive the American Dream* (New York: Basic Books, 2020), 34.

17. "In essentials unity; in non-essentials liberty; in all things charity" is a philosophy many in Protestantism aspire to. It was used in a tract on Christian unity written by Rupertus Meldenius, a German Lutheran theologian, during the religious conflict known as the Thirty Years War (1618–1648) (Philip Schaff, *History of the Christian Church* [Grand Rapids, MI: W. M. Eerdmans, 1910], 7: 650–653). For most protestants, the essentials are the things for which, if you believe them, you are considered an orthodox Christian. Most of the diversity in US protestant denominations come from areas I would classify as nonessential tenets of the faith. There are a few denominations that consider themselves to be the only "true" way and some denominations that do not adhere to those orthodox essentials and therefore other protestant denominations consider them to be heretical. But generally, the idea of offering grace to a fellow believer who may interpret or understand the teachings of nonessential doctrine differently from you is a part of the orthodox protestant tradition.

18. Yuval Levin, *A Time to Build: From Family and Community to Congress and the Campus, How Recommitting to Our Institutions Can Revive the American Dream* (New York: Basic Books, 2020).

19. A Reuters investigation found 220 examples of threats and intimidation in a sampling of districts (meaning there were more in the country). Gabriella Borter, Joseph Ax, and Joseph Tanfani, "School Boards Get Death Threats amid Rage over Race, Gender, Mask Policies," Reuters, February 15, 2022, https://www.reuters.com/investigates/special-report/usa-education-threats.

20. Greg Lukianoff and Jonathan Haidt, *The Coddling of the American Mind: How Good Intentions and Bad Ideas Are Setting up a Generation for Failure* (New York: Penguin, 2019), 210.

CHAPTER EIGHT: LIVING IN THE AGE OF OUTRAGE

1. Scott Hensley, "Poll: Americans Say We're Angrier Than a Generation Ago," NPR, June 26, 2019, https://www.npr.org/sections/health-shots/2019/06/26/735757156/poll-americans-say-were-angrier-than-a-generation-ago.

2. Anger belongs to the executive functioning subcategory of propensity. It is not the only risk factors of concern; I am focusing on it due to their prominence in conservative and Christian culture at present. Clemmow et al. demonstrated

when propensity risk factors are "high"—it demonstrates a greater vulnerability to extremism compared to other risk factors. Caitlin Clemmow et al., "The Whole Is Greater Than the Sum of Its Parts: Risk and Protective Profiles for Vulnerability to Radicalization," *Justice Quarterly* (2023), https://doi.org/10.1080/07418825.2023.2171902.

3. Steven Stosny, "The Primacy of Anger Problems," *Psychology Today*, January 18, 2009, https://www.psychologytoday.com/us/blog/evil-deeds/200901/the-primacy-anger-problems.

4. Leon Seltzer, "What Your Anger May Be Hiding," *Psychology Today*, July 11, 2008, https://www.psychologytoday.com/us/blog/evolution-the-self/200807/what-your-anger-may-be-hiding, says Steven Stosny's *Treating Attachment Abuse* (New York: Springer, 1995), "offers a *chemical* explanation of how anger—in the moment at least—can act as a sort of 'psychological salve.' One of the hormones the brain secretes during anger arousal is norepinephrine, experienced by the organism as an analgesic. In effect, whether individuals are confronted with physical or psychological pain (or the *threat* of such pain), the internal activation of the anger response will precipitate the release of a chemical expressly designed to *numb* it."

5. "What Is Anger?" Paul Ekman Group, n.d., https://www.paulekman.com/universal-emotions/what-is-anger.

6. Anger belongs to the executive functioning subcategory of propensity. It is not the only risk factors of concern; I am focusing on it due to its prominence in conservative and Christian culture at present. Clemmow et al. demonstrated that when propensity risk factors are "high," it demonstrates a greater vulnerability to extremism compared to other risk factors. Clemmow et al., "The Whole Is Greater Than the Sum of Its Parts."

7. "What Is Anger?"

8. Anger has a physiological response of agitation as well as a response of our heart and our mind; that is, our beliefs, motives, perceptions, and desires are involved in making that moral judgment. Because it involves our bodies, we can be more prone to anger when we're tired or hungry or experiencing stress. One way to think of it is that in our fatigue, it becomes easier to be displeased and make inaccurate value judgments. David Powlison, *Good and Angry: Redeeming Anger, Irritation, Complaining, and Bitterness* (Greensboro, NC: New Growth Press, 2016), 47–48; Robert D. Jones, *Uprooting Anger: Biblical Help for a Common Problem* (Phillipsburg, NJ: P&R Publications, 2005), 15.

9. See, for example, Galatians 5:19–21.

10. For example, Torba and Isker say that Jesus is "not some hippie Mr. Rogers. . . . He flips over tables in the temple. He scorns the Den of Vipers. He rebukes the Synagogue of Satan." Andrew Torba and Andrew Isker, *Christian Nationalism: A Biblical Guide for Taking Dominion and Discipling Nations* (N.p.: Gab AI, 2022), 5.

11. Jones, *Uprooting Anger*, 27.

12. Jones, *Uprooting Anger*, 28.

13. Jones, *Uprooting Anger*, 29.

14. Torba and Isker, *Christian Nationalism*, 33–35.

15. Leviticus 19:10, 23:22; Jeremiah 7:5–7; Zechariah 7:10; James 1:27.

16. "Yellow Journalism," in "Crucible of Empire: The Spanish-American War," PBS, 1999, https://www.pbs.org/crucible/journalism.html.

17. J. Berger and K. L. Milkman, "What Makes Online Content Viral?" Journal of Marketing Research 49, no. 2 (2012): 192–205, https://doi.org/10.1509/jmr.10.0353.

18. Jeff Horwitz and Deepa Seetharaman, "Facebook Executives Shut Down Efforts to Make the Site Less Divisive," *Wall Street Journal*, May 26, 2020, https://www.wsj.com/articles/facebook-knows-it-encourages-division-top-executives-nixed-solutions-11590507499.

19. Brandy Zadrozny, "'Carol's Journey': What Facebook Knew about How It Radicalized Users," NBC News, October 26, 2021, https://www.nbcnews.com/tech/tech-news/facebook-knew-radicalized-users-rcna3581.

20. Keach Hagey and Jeff Horwitz, "Facebook Tried to Make Its Platform a Healthier Place. It Got Angrier Instead," *Wall Street Journal*, September 15, 2021, https://www.wsj.com/articles/facebook-algorithm-change-zuckerberg-11631654215.

21. D. L. Ascher, "The New Yellow Journalism: Examining the Algorithmic Turn in News Organizations' Social Media Information Practice through the Lens of Cultural Time Orientation," PhD diss., University of California at Los Angeles, 2017, https://escholarship.org/uc/item/5k712905. See also Debra Ellis, "Social Media: The Next Frontier for Yellow Journalism," *Social Media Today*, August 8, 2012, https://www.socialmediatoday.com/content/social-media-next-frontier-yellow-journalism; "Is Social Media the 21st Century's Yellow Journalism?" Sheridan, December 10, 2020, https://www.sheridan.com/journals-on-topic/social-media-yellow-journalism.

22. Arthur C. Brooks, *Love Your Enemies: How Decent People Can Save America from the Culture of Contempt* (New York: Broadside Books, 2019), 10.

23. Brooks, *Love Your Enemies*, 10.

24. Brooks, *Love Your Enemies*.

25. Jeffrey Bilbro, *Reading the Times: A Literary and Theological Inquiry into the News* (Downers Grove, IL: IVP Academic, 2021), 7.

26. Brooks, *Love Your Enemies: How Decent People Can Save America from the Culture of Contempt*.

CHAPTER NINE: OUTLIVING THE STUPOR OF EASE

1. Caitlin Clemmow et al., "Vulnerability to Radicalisation in a General Population: A Psychometric Network Approach," *Psychology, Crime, and Law*

29, no. 4 (2023): 408–436, https://www.tandfonline.com/doi/full/10.1080/1068316X.2022.2027944.

2. While crises are known to be a primary cause for radicalization, and most literature on protective factors to radicalization is based on the concept of building resilience to extremism, more research is needed to better understand what types of resilience promotion would prevent radicalization. Rabya Mughal et al., "Public Mental Health Approaches to Online Radicalisation: An Empty Systematic Review," *International Journal of Environmental Research and Public Health* 20, no. 16 (2023): 6586. https://doi.org/10.3390/ijerph20166586.

3. "Psychological Distress," APA Dictionary of Psychology, updated April 19, 2018, https://dictionary.apa.org/psychological-distress.

4. "What Is Psychological Distress? An Overview," BetterHelp, updated October 18, 2023, https://www.betterhelp.com/advice/grief/what-is-psychological-distress-an-overview.

5. "DHS Resilience Framework: Providing a Roadmap for the Department in Operational Resilience and Readiness," Department of Homeland Security, July 2018, https://www.dhs.gov/publication/dhs-resilience-framework.

6. For example, Mark Travers, "A Psychologist Calls Out the Many Dangers of Helicopter Parenting," *Forbes*, November 30, 2022, https://www.forbes.com/sites/traversmark/2022/11/30/a-psychologist-calls-out-the-many-dangers-of-helicopter-parenting; Nicole B. Perry et al., "Childhood Self-Regulation as a Mechanism through Which Early Overcontrolling Parenting Is Associated with Adjustment in Preadolescence," *Developmental Psychology* 54, no. 8 (2018): 1542–1554.

7. Isaac R. Galatzer-Levy and George A. Bonanno, "Heterogeneous Patterns of Stress over the Four Years of College: Associations with Anxious Attachment and Ego-Resiliency," *Journal of Personality* 81, no. 5 (2013): 476–486, https://doi.org/10.1111/jopy.12010; G. Thompson et al., "The Roles of Attachment and Resilience in Perceived Stress in Medical Students," *Canadian Medical Education Journal* 9, no. 4 (2018): e69–e77.

8. Center on the Developing Child at Harvard University. "Resilience." https://developingchild.harvard.edu/science/key-concepts/resilience/.

9. Psychologist Angela Duckworth is known for her work on grit, which she defines as passion and perseverance for long-term goals. For more, see her TED talk ("Grit: The Power of Passion and Perseverence," Ted Talks Education, April 2013, https://www.ted.com/talks/angela_lee_duckworth_grit_the_power_of_passion_and_perseverance) and her book *Grit: The Power of Passion and Perseverance* (New York: Scribner, 2016).

10. The growth mindset concept was coined by Carol Dweck. For more, see her TEDx Talk ("The Power of Believing That You Can Improve," TEDx Norrkoping, November 2014, https://www.ted.com/speakers/carol_dweck) and her book *Mindset: The New Psychology of Success* (New York: Ballantine Books, 2008).

11. Daniel Howard-Snyder and Daniel J. McKaughan, "Faith and Resilience," *International Journal for Philosophy of Religion* 91 (2022): 205–241, https://doi.org/10.1007/s11153-021-09820-z.

12. Özlem Ögtem-Young, "Faith Resilience: Everyday Experiences," *Societies* 8, no. 1 (2018): 10. https://doi.org/10.3390/soc8010010.

13. David French, *Good Faith* podcast, July 2, 2022.

CHAPTER TEN: FROM RADICALIZATION TO RECONCILIATION

1. Sohrab Ahmari, "Against David French–ism," First Things, May 29, 2019, https://www.firstthings.com/web-exclusives/2019/05/against-david-french-ism.

2. Tim Alberta, "How Politics Poisoned the Evangelical Church," *Atlantic*, May 10, 2022, https://www.theatlantic.com/magazine/archive/2022/06/evangelical-church-pastors-political-radicalization/629631.

3. Data from Barna Surveys, https://www.barna.com/research/pastoral-security-confidence.

4. Kyle Rohane, "Our Pulpits Are Full of Empty Preachers," *Christianity Today*, April 19, 2022, https://www.christianitytoday.com/ct/2022/may-june/great-resignation-pulpits-full-of-empty-preachers.html.

5. "Pastors Share Top Reasons They've Considered Quitting Ministry in the Past Year," Barna, April 27, 2022, https://www.barna.com/research/pastors-quitting-ministry.

6. Michael Graham, "The Six Way Fracturing of Evangelicalism." Mere Orthodoxy, June 7, 2021, https://mereorthodoxy.com/six-way-fracturing-evangelicalism.

7. For more on the drastic changes in churches, see Alberta, "How Politics Poisoned the Evangelical Church."

8. Alberta, "How Politics Poisoned the Evangelical Church."

9. Alberta, "How Politics Poisoned the Evangelical Church."

10. Graham, "The Six Way Fracturing of Evangelicalism."

11. For example, the priest Ezra had not broken faith with God but confessed the community's sin as his own (Ezra 9). Likewise, Daniel prays fervently asking God's forgiveness for his people for sins Daniel did not commit (Daniel 9).

12. James Bryan Smith, "Dallas Willard's 3 Fears about the Spiritual Formation Movement," *Christianity Today*, August 22, 2022, https://www.christianitytoday.com/ct/2022/september/dallas-willard-fears-spiritual-formation-movement.html.

13. "National Survey Finds Just 1 in 3 Americans Would Pass Citizenship Test," Institute for Citizens and Scholars, October 3, 2018, https://citizensandscholars.org/resource/national-survey-finds-just-1-in-3-americans-would-pass-citizenship-test. Lincoln Park Strategies conducted the poll for Citizens and Scholars (formerly the Woodrow Wilson National Fellowship Foundation). It

involved forty-one thousand interviews among adults nationwide. The margin of error is approximately ±1.0 percent.

14. Interview of PhD professor, requesting anonymity, February 6, 2023.

15. I'm grateful to Jared Stacy for giving me the framing of proximity as a resilience factor.

16. Timothy S. Lane and Paul David Tripp, *How People Change*, 2nd ed. (Greensboro, NC: New Growth Press, 2008), 5–6.

17. Dallas Willard, *The Divine Conspiracy: Rediscovering Our Hidden Life in God* (San Francisco: HarperSanFrancisco, 1998), 347–348.

18. Tish Harrison Warren, *Liturgy of the Ordinary: Sacred Practices in Everyday Life* (Downers Grove, IL: InterVarsity Press, 2019), 21.

19. Warren, *Liturgy of the Ordinary*, 22.

20. L. C. Bethelmy and J. A. Corraliza, "Transcendence and Sublime Experience in Nature: Awe and Inspiring Energy," *Frontiers in Psychology* 10 (2019): 509, https://doi.org/10.3389/fpsyg.2019.00509.

21. Alan Lightman, "The Transcendent Brain," *Atlantic*, December 5, 2022, https://www.theatlantic.com/science/archive/2022/12/how-the-human-brain-is-wired-for-beauty/672291.

22. Doreen Gentzler, "Neuroscientist Says All of the time We Spend on Phones Is Changing Our Brains," News4, December 18, 2017, https://www.nbcwashington.com/news/local/neuroscientist-says-all-of-time-we-spend-on-phones-is-changing-our-brains/31508.

23. Juliane Horvath et al., "Structural and Functional Correlates of Smartphone Addiction," *Addictive Behaviors* 105 (2020): 106334, https://doi.org/10.1016/j.addbeh.2020.106334.

24. "How Smartphones Are Changing Our Brains," April 22, 2020, News4JAX, https://www.news4jax.com/tech/2020/04/22/how-smartphones-are-changing-our-brains.

25. Gloria Mark, a research psychologist at UC Irvine, found that the average amount of time her study participants spent focused on any screen in 2004 was around two and a half minutes. By 2019, that was down to forty-seven seconds. Aristos Georgiou, "Our Attention Spans Are Declining, and Technology Is Not Solely to Blame," *Newsweek*, March 13, 2023, https://www.newsweek.com/our-attention-spans-declining-technology-not-solely-blame-1787387.

26. Andy Crouch, *The Tech-Wise Family: Everyday Steps for Putting Technology in Its Proper Place* (Grand Rapids, MI: Baker Books, 2017), 66.

27. Andy Crouch, *The Life We're Looking For: Reclaiming Relationship in a Technological World* (New York: Convergent, 2022), 59.

28. Mike Cosper, *Recapturing the Wonder: Transcendent Faith in a Disenchanted World* (Downers Grove, IL: InterVarsity Press, 2017), 19.

29. Though we probably think of awe as a positive emotion, psychologists differentiate between awe that threatens us—like a natural disaster—and awe

that "possesses the characteristics and functions of positive emotions such as gratitude and joy" (Liu et al., "Awe of Nature and Well-Being: Roles of Nature Connectedness and Powerlessness," *Personality and Individual Differences* 201 [2023]: 111946, https://doi.org/10.1016/j.paid.2022.111946). Negative awe is actually more of a complex emotion—we can be in awe of a hurricane's power and threatened by its impact on our community. The awe I'm speaking of here is positive awe.

30. D. M. Stancato and D. Keltner, "Awe, Ideological Conviction, and Perceptions of Ideological Opponents," *Emotion* 21, no. 1 (2021): 61–72, https://doi.org/10.1037/emo0000665.

31. Liu et al., "Awe of Nature and Well-Being."

32. Liu et al., "Awe of Nature and Well-Being."

33. P. K. Piff et al., "Awe, the Small Self, and Prosocial Behavior," *Journal of Personality and Social Psychology* 108, no. 6 (2015): 883–899, https://doi.org/10.1037/pspi0000018.

34. Liu et al., "Awe of Nature and Well-Being."

35. Piff et al., "Awe, the Small Self, and Prosocial Behavior."

36. Andy Tix, "Awe Experiences Decrease Political Polarization," *Psychology Today*, February 22, 2021, https://www.psychologytoday.com/us/blog/the-pursuit-peace/202102/awe-experiences-decrease-political-polarization.

37. Stancato and Keltner, "Awe, Ideological Conviction, and Perceptions of Ideological Opponents."

38. Patrick Lencioni, "Organizational Health," Table Group, n.d., https://www.tablegroup.com/topics-and-resources/organizational-health.

CHAPTER ELEVEN: FROM POLARIZATION TO PEACE

1. Kimberly Garcia (@kim_amerie), "Believe it or not, all of this gun violence, losing my daughter to gun violence has completely changed my mind about having more children. Im 30 years old & already have my mind set to never having anymore kids. I will not bring them into this cruel, evil world. Isn't that sad?" X (formerly Twitter), March 27, 2023, https://twitter.com/kim_amerie/status/1640429067412316168.

2. Warren D. TenHouten, *Emotion and Reason: Mind, Brain, and the Social Domains of Work and Love* (New York: Routledge, 2013), 18.

3. Arthur C. Brooks, *Love Your Enemies: How Decent People Can Save America from the Culture of Contempt* (New York: Broadside Books, 2019), 190.

4. John Woodrow Cox et al., "More Than 359,000 Students Have Experienced Gun Violence at School since Columbine," *Washington Post*, updated December 6, 2023, https://www.washingtonpost.com/education/interactive/school-shootings-database.

5. There were precursor efforts that were built upon to launch the Office for Targeted Violence and Terrorism Prevention in 2019, including the Office

of Terrorism Prevention Partnerships, established in 2017 and before that, its predecessor, the Office for Community Partnerships was also engaged in countering violent extremism. The original CVE grant program began in 2016—but was never built into the main DHS budget and thus went unfunded in 2017 and 2018.

6. Lauren Stienstra and Carl Amritt, "Governor's Roadmap to: Preventing Targeted Violence," National Governors Association, n.d., https://www.nga.org /preventing-targeted-violence.

7. "Wraparound Basics or What Is Wraparound: An Introduction," National Wraparound Institute, n.d., https://nwi.pdx.edu/wraparound-basics.

8. "Workforce," Substance Abuse and Mental Health Services Administration, updated October 13, 2023, https://www.samhsa.gov/workforce.

9. "Prevention Practitioners Network," McCain Institute, https://www .mccaininstitute.org/programs/preventing-targeted-violence/prevention -practitioners-network.

10. For example, Cynthia Miller-Idriss, "From 9/11 to 1/6: The War on Terror Supercharged the Far Right," *Foreign Affairs*, September–October 2021, https:// www.foreignaffairs.com/articles/united-states/2021-08-24/war-on-terror-911 -jan6.

11. Brian A. Jackson et al., "Practical Terrorism Prevention: Reexamining U.S. National Approaches to Addressing the Threat of Ideologically Motivated Violence," Homeland Security Operational Analysis Center operated by the RAND Corporation, 2019, https://www.rand.org/pubs/research_reports /RR2647.html.

12. "A Clear Signal in the Fight against Right-Wing Extremism and Racism," Bundesregierung, November 25, 2020, https://www.bundesregierung.de/breg -en/service/archive/cabinet-right-wing-extremism-1820094.

13. In 2022, the population was 84.3 million. "Population Increased to 84.3 Million in 2022," Statistishches Bundesamt (Destatis), January 19, 2023, https://www.destatis.de/EN/Press/2023/01/PE23_026_124.html.

14. "Australian Gov't Announces New Funding to Counter Violent Extremism," News.cn, February 2, 2022, https://english.news.cn/asiapacific/20220202 /e83bab56129f404cb102d1c7628d274f/c.html; "Significant New Investment to Counter All Forms of Violent Extremism in Australia," Australian government, February 2, 2022, https://minister.homeaffairs.gov.au/KarenAndrews/Pages /significant-investment-counters-violent-extremism-in-australia.aspx.

15. Australia's population in 2021 as conducted by their census was 25.42 million. "Population," Australian Bureau of Statistics, https://www.abs.gov.au/statistics /people/population.

16. Estimated to be 336 Million people in 2023. "The Demographic Outlook: 2023 to 2053," Congressional Budget Office, January 24, 2023, https://www .cbo.gov/publication/58612.

17. Thomas Warrick and Mick Mulroy, "How to Put out the Fires of Violent Political Extremism," Atlantic Council, August 15, 2023, https://www .atlanticcouncil.org/blogs/new-atlanticist/how-to-put-out-the-fires-of-violent -political-extremism.

18. Administrations will counter that there are other grant pool funds that *could* be used for violent extremism programming. Those grant funds are used by state and local governments for other critical public safety funding, meaning that in order for a state to use those funds for prevention, they would have to defund other law enforcement, public safety, emergency management, or public health programs.

19. Ryan Nobles, Kyle Stewart, Scott Wong, and Rose Horowitch, "Tennessee Rep. Burchett Says of School Shootings: 'We're Not Gonna Fix It,'" NBC News, March 29, 2023, https://www.nbcnews.com/politics/congress/tennessee-rep -burchett-says-school-shootings-re-not-gonna-fix-rcna77185.

20. "Mass Attacks in Public Spaces: 2016–2020," National Threat Assessment Center, United States Secret Service, January 2023, https://www.secretservice .gov/newsroom/reports/threat-assessments/mass-attacks-public-spaces/details-1.

21. Eric Levenson, Melissa Alonso, and Nouran Salahieh, "Covenant School Shooter Was under Care for Emotional Disorder and Hid Guns at Home, Police Say," CNN, March 29, 2023, https://www.cnn.com/2023/03/28/us /covenant-school-shooting-nashville-tennessee-tuesday/index.html.

22. For example, David French and Ben Shapiro. David French, "Pass and Enforce Red Flag Laws. Now," Dispatch, May 25, 2022, https://thedispatch.com /newsletter/frenchpress/pass-and-enforce-red-flag-laws-now; Nick Givas, "Ben Shapiro Says 'Red Flag' Laws Could Bring Massive Gun Grab if Not Done Right," Fox News, August 7, 2019, https://www.foxnews.com/media/ben -shapiro-red-flag-gun-control-shootings.

23. Leigh Paterson, "Poll: Americans, Including Republicans and Gun Owners, Broadly Support Red Flag Laws," NPR, August 20, 2019, https://www.npr .org/2019/08/20/752427922/poll-americans-including-republicans-and-gun -owners-broadly-support-red-flag-law.

24. Sabrina Jacobs et al., "After the Uvalde Shooting, Majority of Voters Support Red Flag Laws and Stricter Gun Control," Data for Progress, June 13, 2022, https://www.dataforprogress.org/blog/2022/6/13/after-the-uvalde-shooting -majority-of-voters-support-red-flag-laws-and-stricter-gun-control.

25. Steve Contorno, Leyla Santiago, and Denise Royal, "Florida's Red Flag Law, Championed by Republicans, Is Taking Guns from Thousands of People," CNN, June 1, 2022, https://www.cnn.com/2022/06/01/politics/florida-red-flag -law/index.html.

26. Becky Sullivan, "The Buffalo Suspect Bought a Rifle Months after Cops Ordered a Psychiatric Evaluation," NPR, May 16, 2022, https://www.npr.org /2022/05/16/1099186443/buffalo-suspect-gun-rifle.

27. John Garcia, "Illinois Red Flag Gun Laws: How the Highland Park Parade Shooter Slipped through the Cracks," ABC7 Eyewitness News, July 6, 2022, https://abc7chicago.com/illinois-red-flag-laws-highland-park-shooter-robert -crimo-state-police/12025001.

28. Thomas Black, "Americans Have More Guns Than Anywhere Else in the World and They Keep Buying More," Bloomberg, May 25, 2022, https://www .bloomberg.com/news/articles/2022-05-25/how-many-guns-in-the-us-buying -spree-bolsters-lead-as-most-armed-country.

29. Anisha Kohli, "Why Some Members of Congress Are Wearing AR-15 Assault Rifle Pins," *Time*, February 7, 2023, https://time.com/6253690/ar-15-pins -congress.

30. Thomas Massie (@RepThomasMassie), Merry Christmas! [Christmas tree emoji] ps. Santa, please bring ammo. [gift-wrapped box emoji]" (with a photo of a family around a Christmas tree holding various guns), X (formerly Twitter), December 4, 2021, https://twitter.com/RepThomasMassie/status /1467197523127422979; Fred Wellman (@FPWellman), "This is the fraud @ AndyOgles that represents the district where 3 Elementary school children and 3 staffers were just slaughtered by a shooter wielding the same weapons as his . . . Christmas photo" (with a photo of a family around a Christmas tree holding various guns), X (formerly Twitter), March 27, 2023, https:// twitter.com/FPWellman/status/1640424058922708992; Lauren Boebert (@ laurenboebert), "The Boeberts have your six, @RepThomasMassie (No spare ammo for you, though)" (with a photo of a family around a Christmas tree holding various guns), X (formerly Twitter), December 7, 2021, https://twitter .com/laurenboebert/status/1468411381653323777.

31. Ryan Busse, "The Gun Industry Created a New Consumer. Now It's Killing Us," *Atlantic*, July 25, 2022, https://www.theatlantic.com/ideas/archive/2022 /07/firearms-industry-marketing-mass-shooter/670621.

32. Busse, "The Gun Industry Created a New Consumer."

33. Busse, "The Gun Industry Created a New Consumer."

34. Busse, "The Gun Industry Created a New Consumer."

35. Amy Novotney, "What Happens to the Survivors," *Monitor on Psychology* 49, no. 8 (2018): 36, https://www.apa.org/monitor/2018/09/survivors.

36. Clemmow et al., "Vulnerability to Radicalisation in a General Population: A Psychometric Network Approach," *Psychology, Crime, and Law* 29 no. 4 (2023): 408–436, https://www.tandfonline.com/doi/full/10.1080/1068316X .2022.2027944.

37. Clemmow et al., "Vulnerability to Radicalisation in a General Population." There were two additional factors in the top cluster: nonviolent offending and being a victim of violence as a child. I believe such factors require the support of counseling and/or behavioral health management, and as such are not ideal for self-examination.

38. Ben Lee and Sarah Marsden, "Protective Factors for Violent Extremism and Terrorism: Rapid Evidence Assessment," Centre for Research and Evidence on Security Threats, June 2022, https://crestresearch.ac.uk/resources/protective-factors.

39. These protective factors have been collated from the Lee and Marsden survey and from public guides: Lee and Marsden "Protective Factors for Violent Extremism and Terrorism"; "Terrorism Prevention: Addressing Early Risk Factors to Build Resilience against Violent Extremism," Joint Counterterrorism Assessment Team, February 8, 2022, https://www.dni.gov/files/NCTC/documents/jcat/firstresponderstoolbox/125s_-_First_Responders_Toolbox_Terrorism_Prevention_Addressing_Early_Risk_Factors_To_Build_Resilience_Against_Violent_Extremism.pdf.

40. This does not suggest that one must graduate from college to have this protective factor. From a brain development standpoint, adolescents are able to begin work on complex problems and develop nuanced arguments. Humanities curriculums in high schools usually address this.

41. This finding did not provide a robust definition for "positive parenting." Psychologists generally view positive parenting as emphasizing a relationship with the child that is warm, loving, and kind; emphasizing your child's strengths (catch them being good); setting clear boundaries and being consistent firm with those boundaries; gentle discipline; and allowing natural consequences (no helicopter parenting!). For more, see "What Is Positive Parenting and How Is It Done?" National Childbirth Trust, https://www.nct.org.uk/life-parent/parenting-styles-and-approaches/what-positive-parenting-and-how-it-done; https://health.ucdavis.edu/children/patient-education/Positive-Parenting.

42. Angela Nienierza et al., "Too Dark to See? Explaining Adolescents' Contact with Online Extremism and Their Ability to Recognize It," *Information, Communication, and Society* 24, no. 9 (2021): 1229–1246, https://doi.org/10.1080/1369118X.2019.1697339.

43. Gordon Neufeld, and Gabor Maté, *Hold on to Your Kids: Why Parents Need to Matter More Than Peers* (New York: Ballantine Books, 2005).

44. Psychologist Jean Twenge pinpointed 2012 as the year when cell phones and social media were not optional for teen socialization but became the norm.

45. Jon Haidt, "Social Media Is a Major Cause of the Mental Illness Epidemic in Teen Girls. Here's the Evidence," Substack, February 22, 2023, https://jonathanhaidt.substack.com/p/social-media-mental-illness-epidemic.

46. "Social Media and Youth Mental Health," Surgeon General Advisory, Office of the Surgeon General, May 2023, https://www.hhs.gov/sites/default/files/sg-youth-mental-health-social-media-advisory.pdf.

47. Greg Lukianoff and Jonathan Haidt, *The Coddling of the American Mind: How Good Intentions and Bad Ideas Are Setting up a Generation for Failure* (New York: Penguin, 2019).

48. "Building Networks and Addressing Harm: A Community Guide to Online Youth Radicalization for Trusted Adults, Mentors, and Community Leaders," Southern Poverty Law Center and Polarization and Extremism Research and Innovation Lab (PERIL), 2022, https://www.splcenter.org/sites/default/files /splc-peril-addressing-harm-community-guide.pdf, iting Heidi Ellis et al., "Trauma, Trust in Government, and Social Connection: How Social Context Shapes Attitudes Related to the Use of Ideologically or Politically Motivated Violence," Studies in Conflict and Terrorism 44, no. 12 (2021): 1050–1067.

49. Clemmow et al., "Vulnerability to Radicalisation in a General Population."

50. Lukianoff and Haidt, *The Coddling of the American Mind*, 35.

51. Lukianoff and Haidt, *The Coddling of the American Mind*, 38, appendix 1.

52. Lukianoff and Haidt, *The Coddling of the American Mind*, chap. 4.

53. See Jean Twenge's work: Generation Me, iGen, and The Narcissism Epidemic. http://www.jeantwenge.com/.

54. Lukianoff and Haidt, *The Coddling of the American Mind*, 182–183.

55. Lukianoff and Haidt, *The Coddling of the American Mind*, 194.

56. Lukianoff and Haidt, *The Coddling of the American Mind*, 183.

57. Kurt Braddock, "Vaccinating against Hate: Using Attitudinal Inoculation to Confer Resistance to Persuasion by Extremist Propaganda," *Terrorism and Political Violence* 34, no. 2 (2022): 240–262, https://doi.org/10.1080/09546553 .2019.1693370.

58. Stephan Lewandowsky and Sander van der Linden, "Countering Misinformation and Fake News through Inoculation and Prebunking," *European Review of Social Psychology* 32, no. 2 (2021): 348–384, https://doi.org /10.1080/10463283.2021.1876983.

59. https://www.secretservice.gov/protection/ntac.

60. For example, Caitlin Clemmow et al., "Disaggregating Lone-Actor Grievance-Fuelled Violence: Comparing Lone-Actor Terrorists and Mass Murderers," *Terrorism and Political Violence* 34, no. 3 (2022): 558–584, https://doi.org /10.1080/09546553.2020.1718661; Nils Böckler et al., "Same but Different? Developmental Pathways to Demonstrative Targeted Attacks—Qualitative Case Analyses of Adolescent and Young Adult Perpetrators of Targeted School Attacks and Jihadi Terrorist Attacks in Germany," *International Journal of Developmental Science* 12, no. 1–2 (2018): 5–24, https://doi.org/10.3233/DEV -180255.

61. For more on threat assessment and management teams, see the fact sheet on the CP3 website (https://www.dhs.gov/publication/threat-assessment -and-management-teams) or visit the website of the Association of Threat Assessment Professionals, which trains and certifies its members in behavioral threat assessments (https://www.atapworldwide.org).

62. Ryan Brown et al., "What Do Former Extremists and Their Families Say about Radicalization and Deradicalization in America?" RAND Corporation, 2021, https://www.rand.org/pubs/research_briefs/RBA1071-1.html.

63. Cynthia Miller-Idriss and Susan Corke, "How Parents Can Learn to Recognize Online Radicalization and Prevent Tragedy—in 7 Minutes," *USA Today*, May 8, 2021, https://www.usatoday.com/story/opinion/2021/05/08/online-radicalization-parents-can-learn-to-prevent-tragedy-column/4958478001.

64. "Building Resilience & Confronting Risk: Parents & Caregivers Guide to Online Radicalization," Polarization and Extremism Research and Innovation Lab, School of Public Affairs, American University, https://perilresearch.com/resource/building-resilience-confronting-risk-a-parents-caregivers-guide-to-online-radicalization.

65. The prevention field needs longitudinal studies that identify individuals at risk, the interventions that were used to mitigate the factors that were likely to lead those individuals down a path of radicalization, and the impact of those interventions over time. Such studies will need to be highly individualized, measuring how long various radicalization pathways take and how long interventions must be implemented to have impact. For example, if we intervene with an at-risk twenty-year-old, we need to know if they are still resisting violent extremist beliefs at age twenty-five, thirty-five, and beyond. Broadly speaking, several key questions remained unanswered: at what point in the radicalization process are intervention efforts most impactful, and what types of interventions are the most effective? These studies will need to feature dependent variables such as internet and social media activity and behaviors often associated with radicalization and extremist beliefs. Such studies would need to be longitudinal and ongoing in order to measure the efficacy of interventions modified based on the findings unearthed throughout the research process. Intervention programming needs to be more refined and prescriptive, and longer-term research is needed to achieve that goal.

CHAPTER TWELVE: HELPING THE RADICALIZED

1. For an up-to-date list, see "Extreme Risk Laws," Everytown for Gun Safety, www.everytown.org/solutions/extreme-risk-laws.

2. This list is curated from recommendations from Screenhate.org and ADL.org/conspiracy-theories.

3. Ryan Andrew Brown et al., "What Do Former Extremists and Their Families Say about Radicalization and Deradicalization in America?" RAND Corporation, 2021, https://www.rand.org/pubs/research_briefs/RBA1071-1.html.

4. Brown et al., "What Do Former Extremists and Their Families Say about Radicalization and Deradicalization in America?"

5. Brown et al., "What Do Former Extremists and Their Families Say about Radicalization and Deradicalization in America?" 4.

6. "Moonshot's Practice Standards," Moonshot, https://moonshotteam.com /resource/moonshots-practice-standards; "Formers as Peer Mentors," Life after Hate, March 2023, https://www.lifeafterhate.org/wp-content/uploads/2023/03 /Formers-as-Peer-Mentors-at-Life-After-Hate-1.pdf.

7. "The Eight Dimensions of Wellness," Substance Abuse and Mental Health Administration, July 1, 2016, https://www.youtube.com/watch?v= tDzQdRvLAfM.

CONCLUSION: SEEKING THE PEACE OF THE CITY

1. Jen Pollock Michel, *In Good Time: 8 Habits for Reimagining Productivity, Resisting Hurry, and Practicing Peace* (Grand Rapids, MI: Baker Books, 2022).

2. Mohandas Karmchand Gandhi, Mahatma Gandhi, and V. Geetha, *Soul Force: Gandhi's Writings on Peace* (N.p.: Tara Publishing, 2004), 367.

3. Juan Mascaró, trans., *The Dhammapada* (London: Penguin Books, 2015).

4. James Lankford and Tim Scott, "'People Who Are Different Are Not the Problem in America,'" *The Atlantic*, January 12, 2018, https://www.theatlantic .com/politics/archive/2018/01/mlk-today/550466.

5. Mark Sayers, *A Non-Anxious Presence: How a Changing and Complex World Will Create a Remnant of Renewed Christian Leaders* (Chicago: Moody Publishers, 2022).

6. David Brooks, "America Is Having a Moral Convulsion," *The Atlantic*, October 5, 2020, https://www.theatlantic.com/ideas/archive/2020/10/collapsing-levels -trust-are-devastating-america/616581.

APPENDIX 1: HOW TO TALK TO LOVED ONES ABOUT EXTREMISM AND WHAT TO DO IF YOU THINK A LOVED ONE IS RADICALIZING

1. Michelle Icard, *Middle School Makeover: Improving the Way You and Your Child Experience the Middle School Years* (Boston: Bibliomotion, 2014).

2. "Hate on Display Hate Symbols Database," Anti-Defamation League, https:// www.adl.org/resources/hate-symbols/search.

3. List based on my professional experience.

4. List pulled from "Building Resilience and Confronting Risk: A Parents and Caregivers Guide to Online Radicalization," SPLC and PERIL, n.d., https:// www.splcenter.org/sites/default/files/2022january31_splc_peril_parents_and _caregivers_guide_jan_2022.pdf.

5. John Woodrow Cox et al., "More Than 359,000 Students Have Experienced Gun Violence at School since Columbine," *Washington Post*, updated December 6, 2023, https://www.washingtonpost.com/education/interactive/school -shootings-database.

6. Dan Kennedy, "Richneck Elementary Isn't the First Time a 6-Year-Old Has Opened Fire at School," 13 News Now, January 11, 2023, https://www .13newsnow.com/article/news/crime/richneck-elementary-shooting-not-first

-time-6-year-old-has-opened-fire-school/291-a83717ed-92ad-4a10-988a
-eb951ff9abb4.

7. "Hate on Display Hate Symbols Database," Anti-Defamation League, https://
    www.adl.org/resources/hate-symbols/search.

8. ResilienceNet app, available at https://www.oneworldstrong.org/copy-of-how
    -we-do-it.

9. Richard Fry, "The Pace of Boomer Retirements Has Accelerated in the Past
    Year," Pew Research Center, November 9, 2020, https://www.pewresearch.org
    /fact-tank/2020/11/09/the-pace-of-boomer-retirements-has-accelerated-in-the
    -past-year.

10. Linda Searing, "More Than 1 in 6 Americans Now 65 or Older as U.S.
    Continues Graying," *Washington Post*, February 14, 2023, https://www
    .washingtonpost.com/wellness/2023/02/14/aging-boomers-more-older
    -americans; Jonathan Vespa, "The U.S. Joins Other Countries with Large
    Aging Populations," US Census Bureau, March 13, 2018, https://www.census
    .gov/library/stories/2018/03/graying-america.html.

11. Vespa, "The U.S. Joins Other Countries with Large Aging Populations."

12. National Threat Assessment Center, "Mass Attacks in Public Spaces: 2016–
    2020," United States Secret Service, January 2023, https://www.secretservice
    .gov/sites/default/files/reports/2023-01/usss-ntac-maps-2016-2020.pdf.

13. Jillian Peterson and James Densley, "Typical Mass Shooters Are in Their 20s
    and 30s—Suspects in California's Latest Killings Are Far from That Average,"
    Conversation, January 24, 2023, https://theconversation.com/typical-mass
    -shooters-are-in-their-20s-and-30s-suspects-in-californias-latest-killings-are-far
    -from-that-average-198486.

APPENDIX 2: RISK FACTORS FOR RADICALIZATION

1. Caitlin Clemmow et al., "The Whole Is Greater Than the Sum of Its Parts: Risk
    and Protective Profiles for Vulnerability to Radicalization, *Justice Quarterly*
    (2023), https://doi.org/10.1080/07418825.2023.2171902.

2. "US Violent Extremist Mobilization Indicators," FBI, NCTC, and DHS, 2021,
    https://www.dni.gov/files/NCTC/documents/news_documents/Mobilization
    _Indicators_Booklet_2021.pdf.

APPENDIX 3: INDICATORS OF MOBILIZATION TO VIOLENCE

1. "US Violent Extremist Mobilization Indicators," FBI, NCTC, and DHS, 2021,
    https://www.dni.gov/files/NCTC/documents/news_documents/Mobilization
    _Indicators_Booklet_2021.pdf.

2. "US Violent Extremist Mobilization Indicators"; indicators listed on pp. 17–20.

3. "US Violent Extremist Mobilization Indicators"; indicators listed on pp. 13–16.

4. "US Violent Extremist Mobilization Indicators"; indicators listed on pp. 6–12.

ABOUT THE AUTHOR

ELIZABETH NEUMANN served as the assistant secretary for counterterrorism and threat prevention at the US Department of Homeland Security. Neumann is an ABC News contributor and the chief strategy officer at Moonshot. She is based in the Denver, Colorado, area. To learn more, visit ElizabethNeumann.org.